FINLAND AT WAR

FINLAND AT WAR

The Winter War 1939–40

VESA NENYE

WITH PETER MUNTER AND TONI WIRTANEN

First published in Great Britain in 2015 by Osprey Publishing,
PO Box 883, Oxford, OX1 9PL, UK
PO Box 3985, New York, NY 10185-3985, USA
E-mail: info@ospreypublishing.com

Osprey Publishing, part of Bloomsbury Publishing Plc

A CIP catalogue record for this book is available from the British Library.

Vesa Nenye, Peter Munter and Toni Wirtanen have asserted their rights under the Copyright, Designs and Patents Act, 1988, to be identified as the Authors of this Work.

ISBN: 978 1 4728 0631 4
ePub ISBN: 978 1 4728 1358 9
PDF ISBN: 978 1 4728 1359 6

Index by Mark Swift
Cartography by Peter Bull Map Studio
Typeset in Trade Gothic and Adobe Garamond Pro
Originated by PDQ Media
Printed in China through Worldprint Ltd

15 16 17 18 19 10 9 8 7 6 5 4 3 2 1

Front and back cover: all images Sa-kuva

Osprey Publishing supports the Woodland Trust, the UK's leading woodland conservation charity. Between 2014 and 2018 our donations will be spent on their Centenary Woods project in the UK.

www.ospreypublishing.com

CONTENTS

PREFACE AND ACKNOWLEDGEMENTS

We entered into this project with the goal of writing the kind of book about Finland's wars that we have always wanted to read ourselves, one that describes the most important battles, accompanied by plenty of contemporary pictures and clarifying maps. In the end the project grew and grew until Osprey, our publishers, made the wise decision to split the project into two parts.

This first book describes Finland's struggles from its fledgling independence, through the Civil War and the Kinship Wars that followed. It shows how the approaching conflict with the Soviet Union was practically unavoidable, and how this small nation stood against the mightiest army in the world. The 105-day-long conflict that the world came to know as the Winter War saw Finland bravely resist, until the war-weary Soviet Union finally relented and sought peace – albeit on Stalin's non-negotiable terms. This first book finishes with the signing of the peace treaty and looks at the immediate socio-economic problems that followed.

The second volume begins with the short period known as the Interim Peace, and explores once more how conflict became inevitable. The battles of both the Continuation War and the Lapland War are examined in detail.

Most of the names in the book are given in their Finnish forms. At the end of the book the reader may find an appendix with the most common translations in English and Russian. The Soviet ranks in this volume follow the positional system in place during the Winter War era; with the start of the Continuation War, general officer ranks are once again used.

A Finnish cavalryman at Huumola on 14 December 1939. At this time, each Finnish division still fielded a separate cavalry squadron. Many of the senior officers, including Mannerheim who was a former cavalry general, seemed averse to the use of modern armoured forces. Had the Finns had even 20 or 30 tanks in their reserves on the Karelian Isthmus, things might have gone altogether differently. Even this small number would have been able to provide rapid, concentrated fire support where it was most needed. (SA-kuva)

It is worth noting that we owe a special debt to the plethora of writers who have already covered this topic. They are frequently referenced in the text. We would like to point out that much of what has been written before is conflicting or contradictory; thus in order to chart the actual course of events we have tried to use contemporary sources and unit war diaries as widely as possible. Thanks to the extensive and vigorous research of recent years, many documents in the former Soviet archives have now seen the light of day. Unfortunately, it is also clear that many of these source materials were considerably manipulated either during or after the war. For instance, accurate casualty figures or portrait photographs of disgraced Red Army front-line commanders are hard to obtain.

Ultimately, we hope we have created an accurate yet entertaining recount of those demanding times. As writers we would welcome any feedback or constructive criticism directly, and we can be reached at vnenye@hotmail.com

A project of this magnitude, covering Finland's 20th-century wars in just two books and featuring extensive illustrations and maps, would never have been possible without the help of many people.

We are especially grateful to our beloved and supportive families – Sarah & Ronja, Folke, Nora & Niklas and Jannika, who together with our hounds patiently tagged along on the many research trips, and graciously let us continue writing into the small hours of many a morning.

Marcus Cowper and Kate Moore of Osprey Publishing have been instrumental in keeping us on track and on time and getting these books published. Thanks to John Stellard of Warlord Games for his introductions and recommendations that started all of this in the first place.

Our enduring gratitude and most heartfelt thanks go to Chris Birks, who undertook the heroic task of reading through all the different versions of the manuscripts, and without whose help this book would have never been completed. Further editing and feedback were provided by Steve Morgan and Steve Yates as well as Lauri Priha, Jouni Soininen and Captain Mick Poussa.

Additional thanks must be given to the people who provided us with access and materials: Jari Saurio, the museum curator of the Armour Museum at Parola, for his encouragement and feedback throughout the editing process, and his infallible ability to recognise which tank was depicted by the smallest part jutting out in an otherwise uniformly snowy image; Engineer Major Reserves Esa Muikku, who gave us access to his valuable, previously unpublished private collections and helped to identify names and places needed for many of the image captions; Tanker Jerry Riipinen, for his photography and for all his help; the Chairman of the

Armoured Museum Trust, Jari Lemmetyinen; Armi Häkkinen, who pored over and made legible hundreds of pages of old handwritten war diaries and unit logs; and Sakari and Kirsti Nenye, who undertook the massive task of preparing all the chosen photographs (only a few more books, and then we are sure you two can actually, finally retire…).

We are grateful to a number of libraries and archives in Finland which all provided friendly and helpful aid. In particular, we would like to mention: the whole team at the Armour Museum at Parola; the Photographic Centre of the Finnish Defence Forces; the Finnish Museum of Photography; the Finnish Military Museum; the Lotta-Svärd Museum; the museum wing of the National Defence University in Tuusula; Jukka Kukkonen, for his overall, profound expertise on the historical photo archives; Colonel Pekka Järvi of the Armoured Brigade, who supported us throughout this process and helped gain access to largely unpublished material; Captain Ari Viitala, who provided us with the personal papers of his grandfather and access to the Sissi war diaries; and Senior Lieutenant Jari Markkula, also of the Armoured Brigade, for his photography and liaison work.

Further thanks are due to the following: Juhani Talvela, who gave us permission to access his grandfather's diaries stored at the National Archives; Heikki Talvela, who further enlivened the events with his stories and collections from the wars; the Sotiemme Veteraanit organisation, for the use of their images; and finally, the tank ace Reino Lehväslaiho, for his interview and inspirational repertoire of war stories and books.

Ultimately, a big thank you goes to everybody who is interested in this period and takes the time to learn more about how a few stood against the many, and about a lone fight against oppression in a darkening Europe.

DEDICATION

Sotiemme veteraaneille, jotka taistelivat meille vapaan maan. Opettakoon historia meitä.

To the veterans of our wars who fought to keep our country independent and free. May the lessons of history never be forgotten.

CHRONOLOGY

It is generally accepted that the Finnish armed forces were officially established when the country became an Autonomous Grand Duchy of the Holy Russian Empire in 1809. However, long before this, Finnish forces had distinguished themselves on the battlefields of Europe, mostly against a familiar eastern foe. The following section provides key dates from the end of the 19th century through to and including the Winter War four decades later.

1898

12 October
Governor-General Bobrikov arrives to take control of Finland, and begins by giving a speech to the Grand Duchy's governing officials. He calls Finland a 'borderland' and fails to acknowledge its special position as an autonomous state. Bobrikov declares Russia to be singular and undivided, proclaiming that love and allegiance can exist solely towards a shared Russian motherland. Bobrikov's goal of the destruction of Finnish autonomy and the Russification of its people becomes clear.

1899

15 February
Tsar Nicholas II issues the February Manifesto. It states that the Finnish Diet (assembly) has only an advisory role in making Russian imperial law, and that it cannot stop imperial laws from being enforced in Finland.

1899–1905

The Russification programme: a systematic quelling of Finnish nationalism, including language and national rights, and the disbandment of the Finnish Army (1901).

1902

New conscription for the Russian Army starts. Now, troops can be made to serve in any corner of the empire; previously, Finnish troops have only served in Finland. The Finns resist the conscription through strikes and conscientious objection. The tsar is later forced to end conscription in Finland.

1904–05

The Russo-Japanese War. Japan emerges victorious.

1904

16 June
The Finnish nationalist Eugen Schauman assassinates General-Governor Bobrikov.

1905
The Russian Revolution of 1905. A general strike begins in Finland, which leads to the creation of the November Manifesto. This document replaces the February Manifesto and removes the dictatorial rights of the governor-general.

1906

29 May
The Finnish Diet approves a new election law and the Parliament Act, replacing itself with a unicameral parliament. Tsar Nicholas II ratifies the law on 20 July. Finland becomes the third country in the world, and the first in Europe, to give women the vote as part of universal suffrage.

1907

15 March
The first parliamentary elections take place in Finland. The world's first female representatives are elected.

1908–17

A second, more intense period of Russification. All vestiges of autonomy are removed and all state matters become subject to the Russian government.

1910

The Russian State Duma takes Finnish matters under its administration.

1912

Russians receive equal rights in Finland under the Equality Act.

1914–18

World War I; martial law is declared in all of Finland.

1914

Plans for the complete Russification of Finland are cancelled due to the outbreak of World War I.

1915

The Jäger movement is founded; the first Finns make their way for Jäger training in Germany.

1917

The February Revolution in Russia ends the last of the hard-line policies towards Finland.

15 March
The last tsar of Russia, Nicholas II, is forced to abdicate.

1917

18 July
Parliament is declared the wielder of supreme state power in Finland.

7 November
The October Revolution takes place in Russia.

4 December
The Finnish Cabinet gives a notification to parliament; following its ratification, this notice is called the Declaration of Independence.

6 December
Finland declares independence.

31 December
The Russian Bolshevik government recognises Finnish independence.

1918

25 January
The Finnish Civil Guard (Suojeluskunta) is recognised as a government force.

27 January–14 May
The Finnish Civil War between the White (Civil) Guard and the Red Guard. There are over 38,000 casualties in total. Many of the defeated Reds die following capture owing to the poor conditions in the prisoner of war camps. A total of 555 Red prisoners are sentenced to death and 12,000 succumb to hunger and disease in prison camps this year.

6 March
The Finnish Air Force is founded.

21 March–2 October
The Viena Karelia (White Karelia) expedition: Finnish volunteers attempt to annex White Karelia from Russia.

Spring
First Petsamo expedition; Finnish forces attempt to take the area of Petsamo in Lapland from Russia.

18 May
Pehr Evind Svinhufvud becomes Regent of Finland.

16/17 July
Tsar Nicholas II, his family and several personal attendants are executed by the Bolsheviks in Yekaterinburg.

11 November
The first Lotta Svärd (Finnish women's volunteer movement) organisation is founded.

28 November
Estonian War of Independence begins. Finnish volunteers help drive the Bolsheviks out. The war lasts until 2 February 1920.

9 December
Prince Frederick Charles of Hesse is chosen as King of Finland, by parliamentary vote.

14 December
Frederick Charles renounces the crown of Finland following the collapse of the German Empire. Carl Gustaf Emil Mannerheim becomes Regent of Finland.

1918–20

Revolt of the Ingrian Finns.

1918–22

The Kinship Wars: armed Finnish volunteers conduct expeditions in East Karelia, Ingria and Estonia.

1919

March–June
The Aunus expedition: an attempt to annex parts of Aunus (Olonets) and parts of East Karelia.

17 July
Finland becomes a republic.

25 July
Kaarlo Juho Ståhlberg becomes the first President of Finland. He serves until 1925.

1919–1932

Prohibition in Finland. It is abolished after Finland's first national referendum in 1931.

1920

Spring
Second (unsuccessful) Petsamo expedition.

14 October
Signing of the Treaty of Tartu, between Finland and the Soviet Union. It comes into force on 31 December. Its purpose is to end the state of war caused by the 1918 Finnish Civil War, to establish borders, and to create diplomatic relations between the two countries. Petsamo is ceded to Finland while the Repola and Porajärvi areas stay with the Soviet Union. The Republic of North Ingria, which sought to be incorporated into Finland, also remains with the Soviets. The borders are an uneasy compromise for both parties, and the question of East Karelian autonomy continues to be a strain on Finnish–Soviet relations.

16 December
Finland joins the League of Nations.

1921–22

Vienan Karelians rebel against the Bolsheviks in an attempt to gain independance. Finnish volunteers fight without official backing from the Finnish government. The future Finnish generals Talvela and Pajari lead this expedition. The rebels are finally driven out in 1922.

1925–31

Lauri Kristian Relander serves as President of Finland.

1926
At the Finnish Academy for the General Staff, Talvela and Pajari write their final theses on 'The Offensive Opportunities in Ladoga Karelia'.

1929–32
The radical nationalist Lapua Movement aims to move Finnish political opinion towards the far right.

1930

7 July
The Lapua Movement organises the 12,000-strong 'Peasants' March' in Helsinki. The government yields to their demands to ban communist newspapers.

14 October
The Lapua Movement kidnaps former President Kaarlo J. Ståhlberg, transporting him from Helsinki to Joensuu. Public opinion is against this, and the movement loses support with moderate right-wingers.

1931–37

Pehr Evind Svinhufvud serves as President of Finland.

1932

21 January
Finland signs a non-aggression pact with the Soviet Union.

27 February–6 March
The Mäntsälä Rebellion: supporters of the Lapua Movement try to overthrow the government, accusing it of supporting communism. The revolt fails and the movement is disbanded. The power of the Finnish far right wanes.

1933

30 January
Adolf Hitler becomes Chancellor of Germany.

19 May
Mannerheim receives the honorific post of field marshal.

14 October
Germany leaves the League of Nations.

1934

7 April
Finland and the Soviet Union agree on extending their mutual non-aggression pact, to expire in 1945.

18 September
The Soviet Union joins the League of Nations.

1935

1 March
Saarland is reintegrated into Germany.

16 March
Germany renounces the military edicts of the Treaty of Versailles and institutes conscription.

August
Stalin's confidant Commissar Andrew Zhdanov travels along the Finnish border and begins preparations for a potential invasion.

3 October
Italy invades Abyssinia.

1936

7 March
Germany remilitarises the Rhineland.

17 July
The Spanish Civil War begins.

24 October
The Rome–Berlin Axis is formed.

25 November
Germany and Japan sign the Anti-Comintern Pact.

1937

1 March
Kyösti Kallio is elected President of Finland; he serves until 1940.

7 July
The Second Sino-Japanese War begins.

6 November
Italy joins the Anti-Comintern Pact.

11 December
Italy leaves the League of Nations.

1938

12 March
Germany occupies Austria.

29 September
The Western Powers sign the Munich Agreement, approving the integration of the Czechoslovakian Sudetenland into Germany.

1939

14 March
Slovakia declares independence.

15 March

Germany occupies the rest of Czechoslovakia.

23 March

General Franco's nationalist faction is victorious in the Spanish Civil War.

7 April

Italy occupies Albania.

17 April

Great Britain and France begin negotiations with the Soviet Union.

22 May

Germany and Italy sign a military alliance.

23 August

The Molotov–Ribbentrop Pact, a non-aggression pact between Germany and the Soviet Union, is signed. It contains a secret protocol that divides Finland, the Baltic States, Poland and Romania into German and Soviet 'spheres of influence'.

1 September

Germany invades Poland. World War II begins.

2 September

Great Britain and France present an ultimatum demanding Germany's immediate withdrawal from Poland.

3 September

Great Britain, France, Australia and New Zealand declare war on Germany after the expiration of the ultimatum.

5 September

The United States declares neutrality.

17 September

The Soviet Union begins the occupation of eastern Poland.

19 September

Finland and the other Nordic countries declare neutrality.

28 September

The Soviet Union and Estonia sign a pact of non-aggression.

5 October

The Soviet Union invites Finland to negotiate land concessions.

9 October

Juho Kusti Paasikivi departs for Moscow for negotiations.

10 October

First day of the Extraordinary Reservist Manoeuvres.

13 November

As the Moscow negotiations cease, the threat of war is imminent.

26 November

The Soviet Union blames Finland for the border incident known as the 'shelling of Mainila'.

28 November

The Soviet Union unilaterally severs ties with Finland, and renounces the non-aggression pact.

30 November

The Soviet Union invades Finland; the Winter War begins. The Leningrad Military District begins the invasion of Finland on all fronts. The Fourteenth Army advances towards Petsamo in northern Finland. The main Soviet attack, by the Seventh Army, begins on the Karelian Isthmus. The Eighth Army advances on the Ladoga Karelia front. The Ninth Army advances towards Oulu, mounting four days of unsuccessful attacks against the Finnish 15th Independent Battalion.

1 December

Prime Minister Risto Ryti's first Cabinet is appointed.

2 December

The Soviet Union signs a mutual assistance agreement with the puppet Finnish Democratic Republic (or Terijoki Government).
The Soviet Eighth Army captures the Finnish village of Suojärvi. A Finnish counter-attack the following day fails.

3 December

The Finnish 15th Independent Battalion retreats from the Soviet Ninth Army at the Purahseijoki. The Soviets do not realise they have retreated, and leave the capture of the now empty positions for another two days.

4 December

The Soviet 163rd Rifle Division reaches the Palovaara crossroads in northern Finland.

4–6 December

Soviet troops reach the Mannerheim Line on the Karelian Isthmus.

5 December

The Soviet Fourteenth Army moves towards Peranka and Suomussalmi.

6 December

Mannerheim forms Group Talvela.

The Soviet 49th and 150th Rifle divisions, part of Grendahl's Right Wing Group, attempt to cross the Taipale River on the Karelian Isthmus. They manage to obtain a small bridgehead on the north side of the river.

7 December

Finnish troops of the 24th Infantry Regiment repel the Right Wing Group's attempts to cross the Taipale in the Kiviniemi sector.

The Finnish defenders at Suomussalmi withdraw; the village is captured by the Soviet 81st Rifle Regiment.

7–8 December

Seventh Army commander Yakovlev launches bungled assaults across the Kiviniemi Rapids. He is removed from command and transferred back to Moscow for administrative duties.

8 December

Colonel Siilasvuo's 27th Infantry Regiment is transferred to the Suomussalmi area.

The Soviet Eighth Army attempts to cross the Kollaa River for the first time.

Pajari's 100-strong force raids the campsites of three Soviet battalions. Pajari suffers a mild heart attack on his return from the raid.

9 December

Soviet attacks are halted across the entire front, and Stavka takes control of operations. Seventh Army is heavily reinforced.

Soviet forces from the 122nd Rifle Division occupy Salla, in Lapland.

Tsherepanov's 56th Rifle Corps attacks the Finnish lines just north of Ladoga.

10 December

'The Sausage War' takes place near Tolvajärvi village. Ad hoc Finnish force defeats the Soviet 718th Rifle Regiment.

11 December

56th Rifle Corps reaches Kitilä, but is stopped by Colonel Hannuksela's 13th Division.

Siilasvuo commences operations to retake Suomussalmi. Finnish task forces Oinas, Jousimies and Luoti are formed north of Lake Ladoga.

12 December

Soviet troops skirting Lake Koivu are located and forced to retreat by elements of Group Talvela.

The Soviet 316th and 208th Rifle regiments capture Ruhtinaanmäki hill, and occupy the area of Lake Syskyjärvi. General Hägglund counter-attacks with groups Oinas, Jousimies and Luoti in the Ruhtinaanmäki area.

In Finland's first major victory, Colonel Talvela defeats a Soviet rifle division at the battle of Tolvajärvi.

Siilasvuo orders the attack on Suomussalmi to begin. They are unsuccessful.

13–19 December

Second Soviet offensive at Taipale. Repeated attacks by 30,000 men and 99 tanks fail to break the Finnish lines.

13–24 December

The Soviets threaten Viipuri, but are repeatedly repelled by Finnish troops.

13 December

Finnish troops begin to isolate elements of the Soviet Fourteenth Army at Suomussalmi. By 15 December, the army is completely encircled.

Major-General Wallenius receives command of Lapland Group.

14 December

The Soviet Union is expelled from the League of Nations for its aggression.

Finnish troops under command of Lieutenant-Colonel Wilhelm Teittinen manage to cross the Kollaa River, and harass the Eighth Army there.

At Kitilä, Finnish troops manage to sever the supply lines of the Soviet 18th Rifle Division.

Group Oinas fails to retake Ruhtinaanmäki hill. Red Army forces capture Syskyjärvi village and proceed to Ruokojärvi.

The Soviet high command removes Khabarov from command of Eighth Army following the defeat at Tolvajärvi. Shtern replaces him.

16 December

Talvela pursues the Soviet troops to the Äglajärvi area. Mannerheim promotes Talvela to major-general and Pajari to colonel.

16–21 December

The battle for Pelkosenniemi village. Wallenius stops the Soviet 273rd Rifle Division's offensive towards Kemijärvi.

17 December

The Soviet 122nd Rifle Division is stopped in its tracks at the Finnish Joutsijärvi strongpoint.

17–18 December

Troops from task forces Oinas, Jousimies and Luoti manage to sever Soviet supply lines, further weakening their enemy.

17–22 December

The 'Miracle of Summa': the Finns halt the Soviet advance at their most vulnerable point on the Karelian Isthmus.

17 December

The attack of the Soviet Eighth Army at Kollaa is halted.

18 December

Stavka orders Eighth Army at Kollaa to prepare defensive positions.

18–22 December

Major-General Talvela wins a significant victory at the battle of Äglajärvi. The 'Legend of Finland' gains popular international media coverage.

19 December

The Soviet 123rd Rifle Division achieves a limited breakthrough and reaches Lake Summajärvi. Mannerheim reinforces Siilasvuo's troops.

20 December

The Soviet offensive on the Karelian Isthmus is stopped. Finnish troops begin a counter-offensive at Kollaa, but are eventually forced back to their starting positions.

21 December

Stalin's 60th birthday. Adolf Hitler's congratulatory telegram to him reads: 'Best wishes for your personal well-being as well as for the prosperous future of the peoples of the friendly Soviet Union.' Stalin promptly replies with similar warmth: 'The friendship of the peoples of Germany and the Soviet Union, cemented by blood, has every reason to be lasting and firm.'

Soviet Ninth Army headquarters orders the attacking 122nd Rifle Division to dig in and prepare defensive positions in and around Joutsijärvi.

The Soviet Eighth Army is ordered to withdraw from the Äglajärvi area to the Aittojoki River.

22 December

Having retaken the village of Äglajärvi, Talvela orders his troops to follow Shtern's withdrawal. The Finns continue to advance to the Aittojoki, and dig in there.

23 December

The 'Idiot's Nudge', a costly Finnish counter-offensive, sees over 1,000 Finnish casualties suffered for little gain.

25 December

Troops and tanks of the Right Wing Group cross the frozen Vuoksi River.

26 December

Lapland Group hands over front-line responsibility to the Svenska Frivilligkåre (Swedish Volunteer Corps).

27 December

The Right Wing Group is forced to retreat after its failed attacks on Kelja.

Parts of the Finnish 36th Infantry Regiment cut the Uomaa road. The critical northern crossroads at Palovaara is retaken and occupied by Finnish troops under Siilasvuo. At the same time, the commander of the Soviet 47th Rifle Corps, Dashitsev, receives orders to withdraw from Suomussalmi. He delays.

The final attack on Suomussalmi begins. Colonel Siilasvuo's troops are victorious.

27–29 December

Further attempts to retake Ruhtinaanmäki hill by the Finnish 13th Division fail.

The Soviet attack at Kelja village is repulsed.

28 December

Tchaikovsky, Sharov and Podhumutov flee Suomussalmi. The Soviets are surrounded and 662nd Rifle Regiment is effectively destroyed by the Finns.

29 December

The last Soviet troops at Suomussalmi are defeated, and the village liberated. The Soviet 163rd Rifle Division suffers heavy losses during the operation.

30 December

Grendahl's Right Wing Group receives orders to dig in and repel any Finnish counter-attacks.

Hägglund orders the attack on Ruhtinaanmäki hill to cease. Siilasvuo receives new orders to attack and destroy the Soviet 44th Rifle Division on the Raate road.

1940

1 January

Siilasvuo makes his first concentrated attacks against the 44th Rifle Division along the Raate road. They meet strong resistance.

3 January

Finnish attempts to take Ruhtinaanmäki hill are renewed.

3–4 January

Battle of Sanginlampi. Siilasvuo is victorious, further pressuring the 44th Rifle Division. The Soviets manage to airdrop supplies onto their isolated and surrounded troops. This feat is repeated two days later.

6 January

Siilasvuo orders attacks to sever the Raate road, cutting it at several points. Vinogradov, contrary to orders, prepares his trapped troops to flee to the east.
Finnish forces attack, and force the Soviets to form *motti* at Lemetti.

7 January

The Finns win a famous victory at Raate road, capturing practically all of the 44th Rifle Division's equipment and routing this Soviet force for the remainder of the war.

8 January

Finnish Foreign Minister Väinö Tanner begins probing for peace negotiations.

9 January

Finnish troops cut the supply road to Pitkäranta, and subsequently reach Koirinoja, thus preventing the Soviet 168th Rifle Division from escaping.

12 January

The Finns divert parts of the 12th Division from Kollaa south to maintain the Uomaa *motti*.

16 January

Heavy Soviet bombardments target the Summa and Lähde sectors in Karelia. Soviet troops start to probe the defensive lines. The bombardments continue for days.

19 January

Siilasvuo's 9th Division receives new orders to proceed to the Kuhmo sector.

22 January

Finnish troops near Ruhtinaanmäki receive orders to channel all their efforts into crushing the western Lemetti *motti*.

26 January

Siilasvuo is ordered to attack the Soviet fortified positions at Kuhmo.

29 January

Soviet forces in the Kuhmo region are pushed into a *motti* by Siilasvuo's troops.

The Soviet Union agrees to negotiate with the Ryti government.

31 January

Löytövaara hill is captured by Siilasvuo's troops.

4 February

The Soviet troops in the western Lemetti *motti* surrender.

5 February

The Soviet Union rejects all offers of a peace settlement with Finland. Negotiations to allow the passage of pro-Finnish troops though Sweden also stall.

8 February

The Soviets launch renewed attacks in the Taipale sector. The front line shifts back and forth over the next few days.

11 February

A large Soviet offensive on the Karelian Isthmus begins. The Poppius bunker finally falls. The same evening, the Soviets reach the Interim Line at Lähde.
The Finns try to wipe out the northern *motti* at Saunajärvi.

12 February

Finland receives notice of Soviet peace terms.
The Red Army forms the Fifteenth Army from troops around the Pitkäranta area, near Ladoga. Its commander, Kovalyov, reports directly to Stavka. Following poor performances, he is replaced two weeks later by Kurdjumov.

13 February

Finnish troops launch an ineffectual counter-attack at Lähde. Attaching from the Merkki sector, the Soviets create a breach the Mannerheim Line several kilometres wide and deep.

15 February

Mannerheim orders Finnish forces to withdraw to the Interim Line.
Major Lovlev leads his troops out of the Uomaa *motti*, and back to friendly lines.

17 February

Colonel Autti destroys the Soviet forces escaping from the *Rykmentti motti*.
Soviet forces at Taipale are ordered to focus their attacks on the Finnish artillery.
Tactical retreat to the secondary defensive positions, the Interim Line, is completed by the Finns.

18 February

The Soviet Thirteenth Army captures Kirvesmäki and the Terenttilä sector. Instead of pushing on, they wait to consolidate their forces.

19 February

The Finns work to strengthen their Interim Line on the Karelian Isthmus.

22 February

Renewed Soviet attacks along the Interim Line; the line holds. Over the next few days, the Finns manage to retake several of the strongholds the Soviets had occupied. Lieutenant-Colonel Österman steps down as commander of the Army of the Isthmus following disagreements with Mannerheim over strategy. Erik Heinrichs takes over, while Talvela transfers to III Army Corps in the east of the isthmus (including Taipale).

23 February

Finland receives more detail about the Soviet peace terms. Near Kitelä, the Soviet troops in the *Rykmentti motti* request help and permission to withdraw; it then does so without orders, leaving the most severely wounded behind.

25 February

In the Kuhmo sector Soviets try to relieve the northern *motti* around Luelahti Bay, with little success.

26 February

Stavka prioritises taking the Kollaa region.

27 February

Finnish I and II Army Corps retreat to the Rear Line.

28 February

Soviet forces advance over the Interim Line and push towards Viipuri. Stavka orders the Red Army to break the Rear Line by 3 March.

29 February

The government of Finland decides to engage in peace talks. Grendahl's forces finally occupy the whole Interim Line. The focus switches to the Rear Line's anchor point of Äyräpää.

1 March

Finnish troops start to reinforce the Rear Line.
Soviet troops attack Äyräpää.
The Finnish defenders are forced to retreat from two peninsulae in Viipuri (Vyborg) Bay, but hold the island of Uuras.

2 March

Four divisions of the Eighth Army begin a wide-fronted attack in the Kollaa region. They make slow progress.
The Soviet 4th Rifle Division takes Äyräpää, but soon loses it again to the Finns. The Thirteenth Army commander on the Karelian Isthmus, Grendahl, is replaced by Stavka with Army Commander 2nd Class Philip A. Parusinov.
The Finnish defenders on the island of Tuppura find their situation untenable, and have to withdraw over Viipuri Bay. Soviet forces breach the Finnish 3rd Battalion positions, and advance towards Viipuri.

3 March

Wallenius orders a defensive stand on the Vilaniemi Peninsula on the western side of Viipuri Bay, but the troops withdraw prior to his orders being received. Finnish troops manage to retake the Häränpääniemi Peninsula.

4 March

The battle for Vuosalmi and bitter fighting for control of Vasikkasaari Island take place.
The last of the Finnish troops withdraw from Äyräpää. Wallenius orders the retaking of Teikarsaari Island in Viipuri Bay, but the attack is stopped by the Soviets. In return, the Soviets push across the bay towards the Vilajoki River.

5 March

The Soviet 50th Rifle Division takes Vasikkasaari Island. The Soviets also establish a foothold on the northern bank of the Vuoksi River. Catastrophic count-attack by the 'Men of Nurmo'.
Soviet forces rout the Finnish defenders on the Vilaniemi Peninsula west of Viipuri.

6 March

The Finnish 9th Infantry Regiment launches a counter-attack on the Vilaniemi Peninsula, which ultimately fails.
The Soviet 37th Motorised Division makes good progress capturing the islands on northern Lake Ladoga. The Soviets encounter fierce resistance at Maksimansaari, but eventually take the island following heavy bombardment. Over the next few days, more islands are taken, and the encircled 168th Rifle Division can finally be resupplied.
The Finnish peace delegation departs for Moscow.
The city of Viipuri is cut off from Helsinki by Soviet forces.
Simo 'White Death' Häyhä is shot and hospitalised.

7 March

General Sir Edmund Ironside informs the Finns that British troops are able to reinforce them and help.

A preliminary bombardment of the defenders of Viipuri commences.

The second wave of the Soviet attack at Kollaa. The 56th Rifle Division manages to cross the river, but is drastically weakened.

Intense battles take place for the small islands around Uuraansaari Island in Viipuri Bay.

9 March

The Soviets sever the Hamina–Viipuri road.

Meretskov orders the 34th Rifle Corps to continue its attack on Viipuri and then push on to new goals. The Soviets meet determined resistance from the city's defenders.

Öhquist seeks permission to retreat from Viipuri, but Mannerheim orders his troops to stand their ground.

The defending Finnish battalion on Uuraansaari withdraws. The islands of Ravansaari, Hapenensaari, Turkinsaari and Piispansaari are also lost.

10 March

Finnish counter-attacks at the River Kollaa are repulsed.

Lieutenant-Colonel Aaro Rautiainen and his 12th Infantry Regiment withdraw from the Majapohja sector towards the Koivuniemi Peninsula. All along the Finnish coast troops are withdrawing to their last defensive positions.

11 March

Panic spreads through the Finnish troops; they retreat from the area around Lake Patrusjärvi, and several Finnish battalions lose contact with Viipuri. The troops are rallied by Major Varko, and are formed into Group Varko, which halts the Soviet advance.

12 March

Talvela decides to withdraw to a new defensive line further west from Vasikkasaari.

Heinrichs agrees to a withdrawal from Viipuri.

The Moscow Peace Treaty is signed.

13 March

The Kollaa defensive line holds.

The ceasefire, stipulated in the Moscow Peace Treaty, comes into effect at 11:00 (Finnish time), ending the Winter War. Despite the truce, Meretskov orders the attack on Viipuri to continue until the city is in Soviet hands.

15 March

The flag of Finland is lowered at Viipuri. Troops proceed to withdraw behind the new borders agreed in the Moscow Peace Treaty.

30 March

The USSR declares any country forming or joining a Scandinavian defence union would be in direct opposition to the Soviet Union.

9 April

Germany invades Denmark and Norway.

1 May

During May, Sweden approaches Finland to discuss a military alliance.

10 May

Germany invades France and the Low Countries.

22 May

The Finland–Soviet Union Peace and Friendship Society is founded, with a secret aim of destabilising Finland's government.

10 June

Italy declares war on France and Great Britain.

14 June

The Soviets shoot down the Finnish passenger plane Kaleva over Finnish territorial waters, on its return journey from Estonia.

15–16 June

The Soviet Union demands that Lithuania, Latvia and Estonia form new governments, and grant military access to the Red Army.

17 June

Soviet forces deploy into the Baltic States.

18 June

The law for the resettlement of Karelian refugees is passed in the Finnish parliament.

22 June

France surrenders.

23 June

The Soviet Union demands mining rights for the Petsamo nickel deposits.

26 June
The Soviet Union demands the territories of Bessarabia and Northern Bukovina from Romania.

27 June
The Soviet Union demands the demilitarisation of Åland. The Soviet ultimatum to Romania is met in full.

29 June
Finland draws up a trade treaty with Germany.

8 July
Sweden agrees to allow the passage of German troops through its territory.
The Soviet Union demands the right of passage on the leased Hanko Peninsula.

10 July
The Battle of Britain begins.

21 July
The Baltic States declare themselves Soviet republics.

22 July
Generaloberst Franz Halder notes that Germany views Finland as a viable route to attack the Soviet Union.

23 July
Finland promises to sell 60 per cent of its nickel production to Germany for the year.

24 July
The Soviet Union demands the resignation of Finnish Minister of Supply Väinö Tanner.

31 July
Hitler finally decides to attack the Soviet Union.

4 August
The Finnish National Brothers in Arms Association is founded.

9 August
The law for the compensation of lost property for Finnish refugees is ratified for the benefit of those affected by the Winter War.

15 August
The Finnish Minister of Supply Tanner resigns.

17 August
Oberstleutnant Josef Veltjens approaches Mannerheim in order to request the movement of German troops and supplies through Finland.

18 August
Acting President Ryti instructs Mannerheim to verbally accept the proposed transport of German troops.

6 September
Finland signs an agreement allowing the USSR passage and access to the leased military base at Hanko.

12 September
Finland agrees to allow the passage of German troops on its territory.

26 September
Germany begins arm shipments to Finland.

27 September
Germany, Italy and Japan sign the Tripartite Pact.

7 October
Germany occupies the Romanian oilfields.

28 October
Italy invades Greece.

12 November
Molotov begins his visit to Berlin. Finland's future is discussed.

27 November
Finnish President Kyösti Kallio seeks permission to resign.

December
Hitler informs his staff and General Eduard Dietl of Operation *Silver Fox*, an attack on Murmansk from Petsamo in Finland.

16–18 December
General Talvela meets General Halder and Reichsmarschall Göring in Berlin.

18 December
Hitler approves the plans for Operation Barbarossa.

19 December
Finnish President Kallio suffers a fatal heart attack.
Risto Ryti becomes President of Finland – the country's only president not to be its commander-in-chief of the armed forces.

23 December
The Finland–Soviet Union Peace and Friendship Society is disbanded by court order in Helsinki.

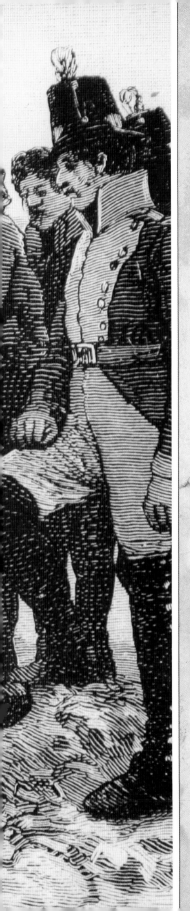

CHAPTER 1

THE RISE OF FINLAND

For centuries the lands of present day Finland had been a hotly contested prize between East and the West. Catholic, Protestant and Orthodox missionaries had all tried their best to convert Finnic pagans to Christianity. Finland was gradually annexed to the Kingdom of Sweden as a fully fledged province. Several wars against the Russians and other enemies of the king followed. In 1809, the War of Finland ended with the Treaty of Hamina. At this time Finland become an Autonomous Grand Duchy of the Holy Russian Empire.

During the early period of autonomy, Finland developed rapidly and became a model and inspiration to the rest of the Russian states. Tsar Alexander II started a wave of reforms across the empire. These had a great positive impact on the development of the Finnish economy, culture and social structure. Finnish soldiers continued

The burial of Hannu Munter, the great-great-grandfather of one of the authors of this work, Peter Munter. This ceremony took place during the War of Finland (1808–09), fought between the Kingdom of Sweden and the Russian Empire. As a result of this war, Finland became an Autonomous Grand Duchy of the Holy Russian Empire. The man holding the shovel is General Carl Johan Adlercreutz, a Finnish-born noble who went on from this defeat to lead all of Sweden's armies against Napoleon. From the book *Vänrikki Stoolin Tarinat* (1887).

to excel in the tsar's army, and eventually Alexander II restored the national armed forces, allowing annual conscription to start once again in Finland.

Darker times soon followed. First, the more conservative Alexander III slowed the modernisation programmes started by his father, and returned the control of universities, law courts and the press to Russian governance. Things degenerated further when his son Nicholas II became the Grand Duke of Finland and the Emperor and Autocrat of All the Russians. Nicholas soon realised that he would much prefer it if the Finns conformed to his autocratic rule and were not quite so independent and autonomous.

Maps showing the development of Finland's national borders

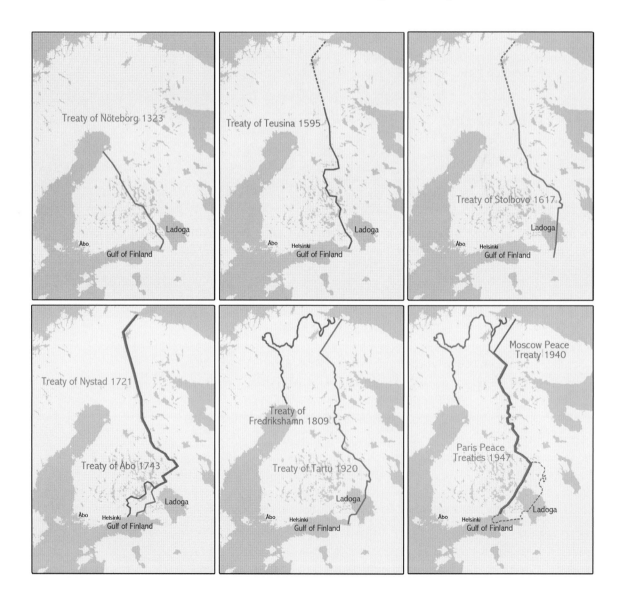

This illustration by an unknown artist shows Eugen Schauman killing Governor-General Bobrikov on the House of Senate's stairs in Helsinki. Schauman shot Bobrikov three times, and then shot himself twice.

There followed a period of Russification. This officially started when the tsar appointed Nicholas Bobrikov as a special governor-general for Finland. Bobrikov's main task was to remove any Finnish prerequisites that might facilitate autonomy or independence. This included having their own army, postal system and currency. Bobrikov was responsible for enforcing Russian laws in Finland, and in general controlling all the influential government and administrative offices. Russian was now to become an official language in the duchy. In 1904 Bobrikov was assassinated, and for a few years the practice of Russification was relaxed. However, a second more robust period of this process was not long in coming.

During the first decade of the 20th century, a growing sense of hatred of the Russians ran deep among many Finns. 'We are no longer Swedes, we will not become Russians, so let us be Finns' ran one particular slogan of the time. A Finnish nationalist movement was starting to gather momentum, and there was even talk of a rebellion. However, Tsar Nicholas II had already dismantled the Finnish Army and heavily garrisoned the country, preventing any form of coordinated unrest.

In November 1914, as the process of Russification peaked, nationalist college students met in Helsinki to plot a path to Finnish independence. Early on it became obvious that to gain its freedom Finland would again need its own army. Several countries were approached to provide military aid, but many, including Sweden, were reluctant to become involved. Finally imperial Germany agreed to support the underground freedom movement by providing secret military training for Finnish volunteers, most of whom were students, in what became known as the Jäger movement. The training provided during the Jäger movement was to play a key part in the conflicts

PAAVO TALVELA'S ROUTE TO THE JÄGER

Like many other patriots, Paavo Talvela decided to make his own way in secret to Germany for Jäger training. Talvela, who later became a general, recalled his experiences in his memoirs:

Late February 1916, I took a train north with two of my classmates. We had earlier received our secret instructions and a small travel stipend. Now we just had to make our way to the coast avoiding detection by the Russians. Upon arrival at Lapua train station, we started to ask around for the next contact point at Kosola's farm. Soon it became clear that Mr. Kosola had in fact been imprisoned earlier that very same day. Luck was with us, as a chain of local farmers passed us from house to house until finally we were close enough to our goal that one factory owner's daughter was able to take us to the coast on her sleigh. We then skied for a couple of hours along the shores avoiding all the Russian patrols until we arrived at a fisherman's sauna. Here other men like us had already been gathering. A young boy, aided by only a small pocket compass, was to be our guide for the dangerous crossing of the frozen Gulf of Bothnia [a crossing of between 60 and 80km at its narrowest point].

The early part of the trip went well. About 20 of us were on skies and we also had half-a-dozen horse-drawn sleighs with us. I remember clearly, that when we set off I saw an ice mountain on the horizon. By noon we had reached it. The shores of our homeland were now far behind us.

By the first night our situation got more depressing and during the brief stops many of us just collapsed on the snow despite the cold. This resulted in bad cold-stiffness, and many had to be placed in the sleighs to warm up. Thus our numbers kept dwindling, but we kept a close eye so that no one was left behind.

After a few more hours we came across fresh sleigh tracks on the snow. We were soon to realise that they were our own tracks and that we had been going in a circle for God knows how long. In other words our compass was broken. Therefore we decided to follow the stars and were lucky to also see the Northern Lights. Relying on these we managed to keep more or less in the correct direction.

Wintery day was again turning into night when we finally came upon a traveller on horseback. At that moment all my strength was spent and I collapsed onto the road. I had to be carried to the sleigh as my body had nothing more to give, only my will had kept me going this far. Who knows, maybe it could have carried me even further if help had not arrived.

We were now taken into a house near the town of Umeå in Sweden. There we were given food and nurtured back to life. Initially I could not eat as my tongue was very frostbitten and in general I was just too tired to chew.

It turned out that I made it through my first adventure relatively well, in the end only my fingers and toes remained a little frostbitten with no permanent damage. However, Immeli, one of my friends, was to be hospitalised for six months losing all the toes on his right foot to the cold. Even worse was the fate of one other comrade, who had to have his leg amputated from the knee down. Thus he had become an invalid even before our war had begun.

From Sweden the trip to Germany went quickly and without disturbances. And so I joined the ranks of the Jäger.

(Talvela, 1976)

of the coming years. These troops would form the backbone of Finland's officer corps; the strict discipline, theoretical training and active service provided a solid foundation for many of the country's future leaders.

In January 1915 the first 200 volunteers travelled to Germany to take part in 'scout leader training' on a four-week long *Pfadfinder* (scout) course. This training was soon extended by several weeks, and by August1915 the group had increased to the size of a full battalion. The 'scout training' ruse was gradually dropped and the troops were openly trained as fully fledged

Lockstedter Lager   Ballon-Aufnahme

Jäger, the elite troops of the German Army. As more Finnish volunteers entered, the unit was named Ausbildungsgruppe Lockstedt or Lockstedt's Practice Group.

By 1916 these men were assessed as being fully trained, and on 9 May 1916 they were entitled the 27th Royal Prussian Jäger Battalion. Shortly after, the Finnish Jäger were deployed to the Eastern Front, principally serving around Riga and Libau.

On 15 December 1917 Russia and the Central Powers agreed an armistice, later ratified with the signing of the Treaty of Brest-Litovsk in March 1918. Pressure began to grow for Finnish troops to return home. In 1918, the men received their first Finnish military ranks. These were based on their current German rank, and how well they had served so far. When the main body of the Jäger finally sailed back to Finland, Commander-in-Chief Carl Gustaf Mannerheim gave the following address: 'You will be

ABOVE
Tsar Nicholas II of Russia ruled from 1894 until his forced abdication in March 1917. During his reign, the Russification programme was launched, cancelling the special semi-autonomous rights enjoyed by the Grand Duchy of Finland. Painting by Ilja Repin.

ABOVE LEFT
An aerial photo from 1908 of Lochsted Barracks, where the Finnish Jäger were first trained. *(Vapaussodan Kuvahistoria)*

BELOW
A rare image of the 27th Royal Prussian Jäger Battalion lining up. These men were to receive their baptism of fire in the kaiser's many conflicts. *(Vapaussodan Kuvahistoria)*

Finnish Jäger in positions along the Gulf of Riga, between September and December 1916. *(Vapaussodan Kuvahistoria)*

seen as the teachers and leaders of the Finnish Army now being formed. A great and illustrious task awaits you: the creation of the army that is capable of making Finland free, great and powerful.'

INDEPENDENCE AND CIVIL WAR

On 6 December 1917, following the transfer of power to the Bolsheviks in Russia, the Senate of Finland ratified a new Finnish constitution and declared the nation independent. By the end of the year, Lenin's Soviet government had officially recognised the fledgling country. Thus reassured, other governments soon followed and acknowledged Finland's sovereignty.

This move by Lenin was not made in haste. At the time, the Bolsheviks did not necessarily have sufficient control of Russia to quell a rebellion in Finland, and Lenin also strongly believed that Finland would gladly come back to the fold of his socialist portfolio. In March 1917 Lenin, who had spent several periods as a political refugee in Finland, made the following statement: 'Let us not forget that adjoining Petrograd [soon to be named

Leningrad] we have one of the most advanced countries, a real republican country, Finland, which between 1905 [and] 1917, under the shelter of the revolutionary battles in Russia, has developed its democracy in conditions of relative peace and won the majority of its people for socialism' (Lenin, 1932). However, Lenin's high hopes for a socialist Finland were soon to be dashed by Baron Carl Gustaf Mannerheim, a stern and experienced military commander (from his time in the Imperial Russian Army), who had emerged still in his full dress uniform from the ashes of the Russian Revolution. He arrived in Helsinki by train in December 1917 accompanied by his trusted Russian servant carrying the two valises containing all his earthly possessions. Mannerheim had taken one look at the revolution and decided that it was not for him. He later wrote: 'It disgusted me to see generals carrying their own kit' (Mannerheim, 1954).

Internal tensions between the Red and White factions of the Civil Guard and the nearly 40,000 Russian soldiers still stationed in Finland made for an uneasy start. Just two weeks after approving Finland's independence, Lenin started supplying weapons to the Reds and inciting them to revolt.

In order to secure the arrival of these secret arms shipments, the Red Guard launched a surprise assault in Helsinki on 28 January 1918. They succeeded in occupying important sections of the railway line, including the main station.

ABOVE LEFT
'To the shores of raising Finland!' is a refrain from the famous *March of the Jägers* composed by Jean Sibelius. This photograph was taken from the ship *Arcturus*, which carried the Jäger back home to Finland. In the shadow of the vessel, the first welcomers can be seen on the icefields outside the town of Vaasa. *(Vapaussodan Kuvahistoria)*

ABOVE RIGHT
Väärinmaja hamlet in Ruovesi saw some of the fiercest battles of the Vilppula front during the Civil War. Pictured here are the troops of the White Guard in the Seppälä trenches. *(Vapaussodan Kuvahistoria)*

LEFT
Kauko Edvard Talvela, the elder brother of Paavo Talvela, examining a map of the front during the Civil War. Shortly after the picture was taken, Kauko was placed under house arrest by the Red Guard. Whilst vigilantes were executing other local landowners, Kauko was spared when his former tenants spoke on his behalf. They explained that he was a good man, who always gave to the poor and that no one ever had to leave his farm hungry. (Authors' collections)

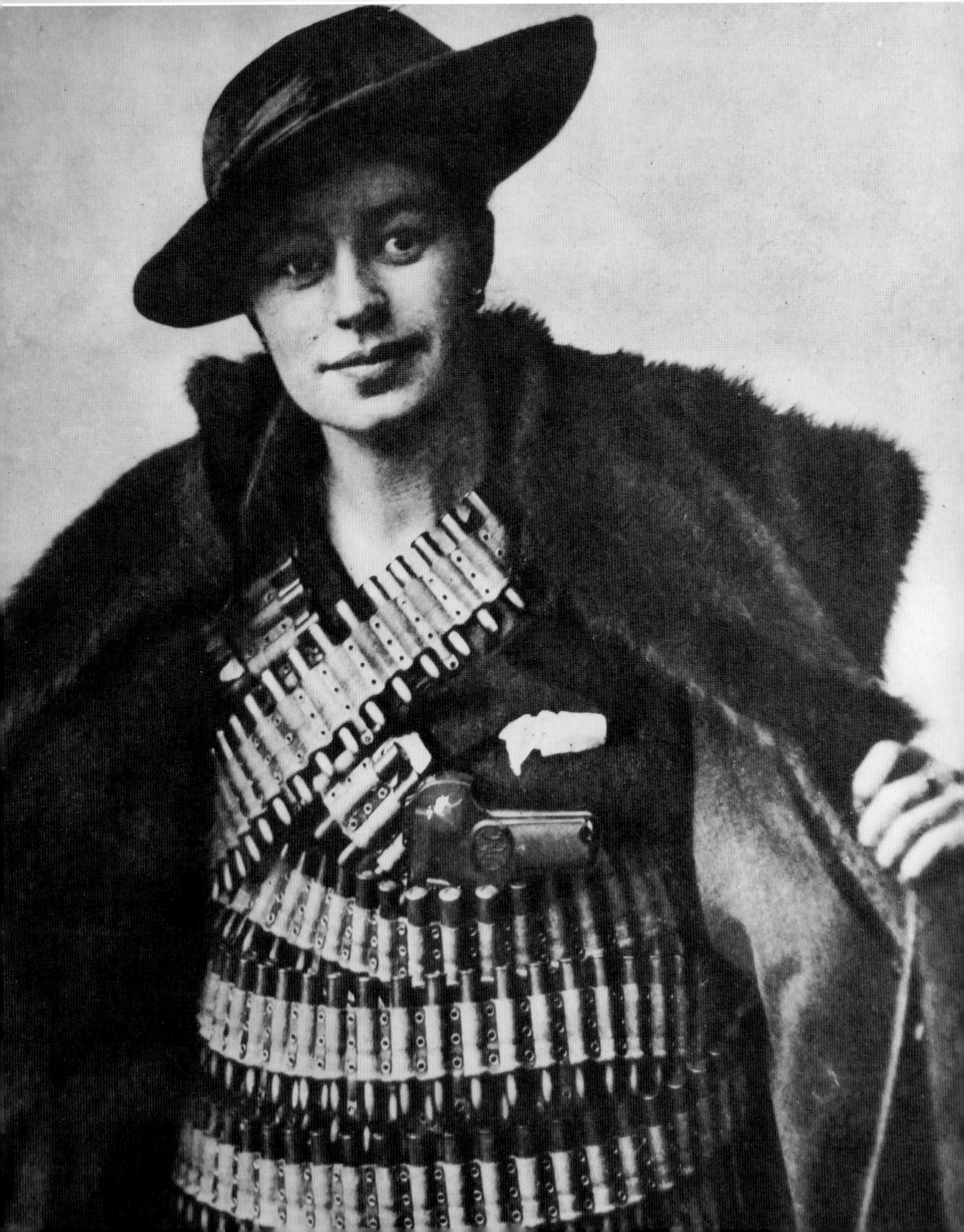

Meanwhile, the opposing White Guard, led by the recently repatriated Lieutenant-General Mannerheim, marched to take control of the central regions of Finland. Most of the Russian garrisons that Mannerheim's troops faced were so surprised that they surrendered without a fight. Once disarmed, they were sent back to their homeland on foot. Seizure of the garrisons allowed the White Guard to arm its troops with Russian weapons.

The Finnish Civil War now began in earnest. Until the end of February 1918, the war consisted mostly of isolated clashes as the small number of available troops forced both sides to congregate near roads and railways. The Whites controlled central and northern Finland while the Reds held the south. Both sides fared better when closer to their power bases. At the height of its influence the Red Guard comprised around 70,000 men. Despite these numbers the Reds lacked professional leadership and discipline, were disorganised and were poorly trained. They had also placed much faith in the support of Russian soldiers and the Bolsheviks. In the end, only 3,000–4,000 of the soldiers that had been garrisoned in Finland took part in the war.

The White faction also numbered around 70,000 men, but had one great advantage in the form of the recently returned Jäger. The latter provided leadership and military instruction to the conscripted members of the Civil Guard.

By March 1918 the tide of battle had turned in favour of the White Guard. Following fierce fighting in April, the Whites conquered Tampere, the Red's most important base. The threat of Germany sending troops to support the Whites, combined with the fall of Tampere, completely demoralised the Red faction. Their fears were not unfounded: on 14 May

Red Guard troops engaged in battle in Ruovesi. Thanks to Bolshevik support, these working-class men were well armed with machine guns and rifles. (The Finnish Museum of Photography)

During the escalation of the conflict in 1918, the men of the paramilitary White Guard received basic soldiering and weapons training. This would give them a crucial advantage, instilling the discipline needed when they were eventually placed under the command of the Jäger. This image was taken in Lavia on 14 March 1918, where these men helped to repel a Red Guard attack. *(Vapaussodan Kuvahistoria)*

Helsinki fell to a small German landing party who then proceeded to hand the capital over to the White Guard. The routed Red Guard tried to escape to Russia, but only around 10,000 ever made it across the border; the rest were captured and sent to prisoner-of-war camps. Even those who made it to Russia were not safe, as thousands were to perish during Stalin's purges in the coming decades.

Although brief, the Finnish Civil War had a high price. During the hostilities and the gruelling aftermath, over 38,000 Finns lost their lives. Most of these perished in the poor conditions of the prison camps while awaiting sentencing. An influenza epidemic reaped a heavy toll. The harsh justice of the time saw around 55,000 prisoners handed anything from one-year to life sentences. A total of 265 death penalties were carried out.

KINGDOM, KINSHIP AND KARELIA

The chaotic conditions in the wake of civil war started to swing Finnish public opinion towards the institution of a monarchy. After all, a king or a tsar had always ruled Finland in the past. The two most influential leaders in the nation, Prime Minister Juho Paasikivi and Regent of Finland Pehr

Svinhufvud, supported this move in the senate. The still incomplete senate rushed through a motion to turn Finland into a constitutional monarchy, voting 58 for and 44 against. As a show of gratitude for Germany's help during the Civil War, Prince Frederick Charles of Hesse was chosen as the first King of Finland. It was to be a very short-lived period of sovereignty. While en route to his new kingdom, the repercussions of the collapse of the German Empire in the aftermath of World War I forced Prince Friedrich to abdicate on 14 December 1918. After this fiasco the Finns decided against the monarchy and opted for a presidential republic instead, which they have maintained ever since. After the fall of the German Empire, Finland sought out closer relationships and alliances with Sweden, Great Britain and France.

◇◇◇

Finnish nationalists had always dreamed of unifying and liberating the whole Finnic race spread throughout the neighbouring lands. After the declaration of independence, this movement started to gain political backing and approval. It would develop into what became known in Finland as the Kinship Wars (1918–22).

In February 1918 Carl Gustaf Mannerheim, the leader of the White Guard, made his famous 'Sword Scabbard Declaration':

Antrea
February 23, 1918
To all Karelians of Finland and Viena [White Sea] Karelia.
Upon my arrival at the Karelian front I hail all those heroic Karelians who have so valiantly fought against Lenin's scoundrels and their wretched henchmen, against those men who, bearing the mark of Cain on their foreheads, are now attacking their own brothers.

Lenin's government, which on one hand promised independence to Finland, has with the other hand dispatched its armies and hooligans, as he himself has declared: to reconquer Finland and with the assistance of our domestic Red Guard militants to drown our newfound liberty in blood.

Now when he starts to see our growing strength he seeks to deceive our people in a similarly treacherous and dastardly manner. He tries to buy our people, bargaining with the rebels in Finland, promising them Viena Karelia, which even now is being plundered and destroyed by his Red Army.

We know the value of his promises, and we are strong enough to preserve our freedom and defend our brothers in Viena Karelia. We do not need the charitable donation of a land which already by the virtue of blood-ties

belongs to us, and I swear in the name of the Finnish peasant army, whose commander-in-chief I have the honour to be, that I will not sheath my sword before law and order reigns in the land. Not before all the fortresses are in our hands, not before Lenin's last soldier and hooligan is driven not only from Finland but also from Viena Karelia as well.

Believing in our just and noble cause, confident in the heroism of our men and the sacrifices of our womenfolk we shall now create a mighty and great Finland.

Mannerheim[1]

Men of the White Guard assembling in Helsinki. (The Finnish Museum of Photography)

The foreign powers strongly objected to Finnish nationalist plans for expansion and the conquest of Karelia. From Germany's point of view, it was important that their peace with Russia would endure. For the British and Americans it was key that Finland, which they still considered to be closely linked to the Kaiser's Germany, should not gain greater access to the Arctic seas. Eventually this 'threat' may have contributed to Britain's decision to deploy its own forces in the Arctic in an attempt to secure Murmansk and the Kola Peninsula for itself.

Despite the top Finnish military leadership opposing the eastern operation, three expeditions manned by volunteers invaded Karelia in the spring of 1918. They ended up fighting mainly against the Bolsheviks and the escaped former members of the Finnish Red Guard, with very modest successes. By autumn of the same year, the invading Finns had retreated across almost all fronts.

Further Finnish military operations took place during this period in Estonia. In November 1918 units of the Russian Red Army invaded the newly recognised and independent Estonia. Its government asked the people of Finland for military assistance to help in the fight against these Bolshevik forces. With the permission of the Finnish government, 3,700 volunteers participated in the Estonian Liberation War. These volunteers greatly improved the morale of the Estonians, and in January 1919 the Finns participated in the decisive counter-offensive that drove the Bolsheviks out.

The 10,000-strong German Baltic Sea Division, led by General Rüdiger Graf von der Goltz, landing in Hanko on 3 April 1918. From there these soldiers launched a rapid attack towards the capital, Helsinki. *(Vapaussodan Kuvahistoria)*

---

1 Twenty-three years later, in July 1941, when the Karelian Isthmus was finally liberated, Mannerheim would refer back to this promise.

After the fall of Helsinki, the main body of the German troops advanced northwards. Here they are seen approaching the town of Hämeenlinna in an armoured train. Hämeenlinna was captured on 26 April 1918. *(Vapaussodan Kuvahistoria)*

OPPOSITE
Both sides committed atrocities during the Civil War. Most common were the White Guard's summary executions of suspected rebel leaders or the Red Guard's killing of local landowners. Often personal vendettas were carried out in the name of a greater good. After the war, 265 Red Guard activists were sentenced to death and shot by firing squad. (The Finnish Museum of Photography)

Emboldened by the success of these volunteers in Estonia, plans were made for the liberation of Aunus (Olonets), the largest town in Karelia. Secretly supported by the government, around 1,000 volunteers crossed the borders at the end of March 1919. Despite the early victories they achieved, by June the expedition was forced to retreat to Finland.

After the Aunus expedition, Jäger officer Paavo Talvela was promoted to lead the next operation into Karelia. In his preliminary recommendation to the government, he strongly advocated an assault during the winter months as well as joining forces with the British troops in the Murmansk area. This would then place further strains on the German–Russian peace treaty. The Finnish government refused to ratify the expedition's expenses, or give other visible aid to these troops and the planned winter attack did not materialise. Meanwhile, a new opportunity caused this next planned expedition to be postponed for a couple of years.

At this stage, Mannerheim saw a brilliant opportunity to occupy (or liberate, as he saw it) the Russian capital of St Petersburg. It looked to be an easy and very achievable target due to the ongoing conflict between the White

and Bolshevik revolutionary forces within Russia. However, in the end the government of Finland could not agree on the objectives for such a mission. Most were not sure they wanted to help return the tsarist monarchy to power. Moreover, France and Great Britain refused to directly support the invasion. The plan was voted down by the narrowest of margins, and cancelled.

ABOVE
At the town of Lahti, the Red Guard's advance was finally halted. Following this defeat, 20,000 men, women and children who supported the rebellion were imprisoned in the fields of Snellman. *(Vapaussodan Kuvahistoria)*

ABOVE LEFT
On 16 May 1918, the victorious White Guard celebrated with a parade through Helsinki. Here Carl Mannerheim is greeted by the mayor of the capital. *(Vapaussodan Kuvahistoria)*

ABOVE RIGHT
The wounded war veteran and general Frederick Charles, Prince of Hesse, was to become Finland's first monarch. However, the prince never made it to his kingdom. While en route to Finland, the German Empire collapsed, forcing him to stand aside before even taking the throne.

Finland's military commanders subsequently criticised the government for failing to seize such opportunities. They believed that with the help of Great Britain and its allies, a greater Finland would have been formed. The internal turmoil in Russia and its inability to send military support to the regions in question would have made a Finnish victory likely.

Finland and Soviet Russia finally signed the Treaty of Tartu on 14 October 1920, defining the border between the two countries[2]; the Estonian–Russian border had already been settled with a previous treaty signed in February 1920. With this peace, Finland regained the contested Petsamo region and parts of the Rybachi Peninsula with an important access to the Arctic Sea, but had to give up both the Repola and Porajärvi areas in turn. Many Finnish nationals saw this accord as a humiliating defeat, as not all of the Finnic peoples in Karelia gained their independence as well. What they failed to take into account was that Russia remained a world power while Finland was a small, newly formed nation.

2 See the map on page 24.

In October 1921, a new opportunity for Finnish nationalist ambitions arose when a rebellion broke out against the Bolshevik government in Karelia. The rebels publicly requested aid from the Finns. Officially, the Finnish government refused to support them, but in secret material support was provided and recruitment to the rebel cause was permitted in Finland. Around 500 volunteer soldiers under the command of Paavo Talvela – and even a large group of schoolchildren – travelled to help the people of Viena Karelia organise local guerrilla forces. According to Paavo Talvela's memoirs, his goal was twofold: first and foremost, to destroy the Murmansk Railway, the backbone of Russian control of the region and a vital asset for any future operations; and secondly, to clear the area of Bolshevik influence, in order to foster a Finnic independence movement. On 22 November 1921 Talvela wrote: 'As their own blood flows, so will their desire for independence grow stronger. This way we will make the insurgency easier to palate internationally and it can be seen as the Karelian's own initiative.' By December 1921, Talvela's guerrillas had repatriated the Repola and Porajärvi areas lost in the Tartu Treaty.

Eventually, in 1922, the concentrated efforts of the government of the newly formed Union of the Soviet Socialist Republics (USSR) and its decision to transfer over 13,000 reinforcements to the region succeeded in forcing the last of Talvela's guerrilla fighters over the border and back into Finland.

When hostilities ended, around 15,000 refugees left Soviet territory and settled permanently in Finland. Public opinion urged the Finnish foreign office to put forward the case for Karelia's independence in international forums. At the time, Paavo Talvela publicly prophesied: 'Without a free Karelia Finland will never be great and powerful. Without an independent Karelia [as a buffer between Finland and the USSR], Finland cannot even defend its current borders. This is what every Finn has to keep in mind when thinking of Karelia.'

Without official government support and the cooperation of foreign powers, these expeditions were doomed to fail. Despite the small number of volunteers, these Finnish nationalist forces still managed to hold back large Russian formations in lands that would see plenty of fighting in the years to come. Ultimately these expeditions were not wasted efforts. Estonia managed to retain its independence until the Soviet Union's occupation

The crown of the 'King of Finland and Karelia, Duke of Åland, Grand Prince of Lapland, Lord of Kalevala and the North', recreated in the 1990s by the goldsmith Teuvo Ypyä from the original drawings. This crown can be seen today at Kemi Museum.

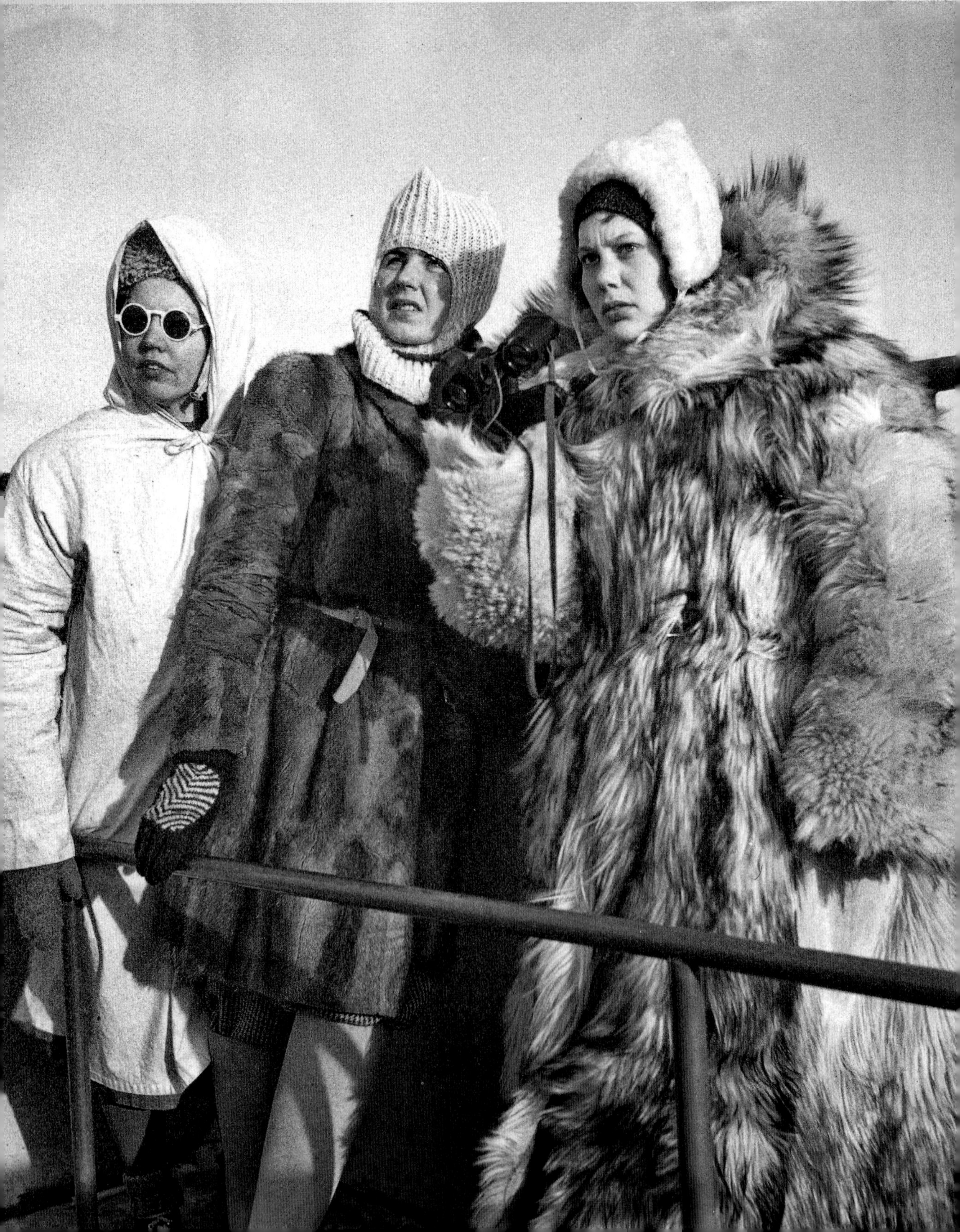

in 1940, and the operations provided valuable experience for many future senior Finnish officers.

Following the 1920 Treaty of Tartu, Finno-Russian relations remained cool. In the following decades Finland put its faith in the League of Nations and its ability to protect smaller nations. The League even made a decision favourable to Finland when it granted it sovereignty over the Åland archipelago. By the mid-1930s, however, public faith in the League was rapidly diminishing. In 1935 Finland declared that it would uphold the Scandinavian principles of non-aggression and peace.

Regardless, it was deemed important that the Finnish Army should be able to stand on its own two feet. In accordance, the training regime for the officer core was formalised, and by 1935 mandatory refresher training was set for all reservist troops. By the autumn of 1939 an estimated 7,200 officers and 172,000 non-commissioned officers and soldiers had completed this programme.

In 1927 the Civil Guard's position was legalised as a volunteer organisation with direct government support. Its principal duties were to help to defend the country and uphold civil peace. By 1930 its membership had already exceeded 120,000 men. In 1918 a women's volunteer organisation, Lotta Svärd, had been formed. This became an important channel in harnessing all of the nation's defence resources, and at its height membership rose to around 240,000. Both organisations were critical to the upcoming war efforts.

Members of Lotta Svärd engaged in aerial observation work during the Winter War. Lotta Svärd was a female volunteer organisation officially established in 1921. During the wars of the 1940s, these women provided invaluable support by carrying out observation, medical, supply and communication duties. By 1944, Lotta Svärd had grown to include around 240,000 women, making it the largest voluntary auxiliary organisation in the world. After the Continuation War, the Soviet Union demanded that Lotta Svärd be disbanded. (SA-kuva)

CHAPTER 2
THE ROAD TO WAR

Lenin had been unconvinced by Finland's ability, and indeed desire, to repel any future attacks towards the USSR proceeding across its sovereign territory. Especially alarming was the prospect that Finland might one day ally itself with Germany. These views were certainly upheld by his successor Joseph Stalin, who had risen to become the leader of the Soviet Union by the end of the 1920s. During his tenure of power it seemed to outsiders that the great Soviet project might be working. The USSR had become an economic giant, while the Workers' and Peasants' Red Army was widely considered to be a strong fighting force. Internally, however, living conditions for most of the population did not hold up to scrutiny.

In Finland, Mannerheim spent much of the 1930s arguing with the politicians who were making further cuts in military spending.

A French-made Renault F.T. Modèle 1917, with a 37mm Puteaux SA 18 gun. Before the war, the Finnish armoured forces had been largely neglected and only on the eve of the conflict had interest in this field been rekindled. They took part in only one battle, near the city of Viipuri. This ended in a resounding defeat. Despite the lacklustre performance of their own tanks, the Finns were to receive ample evidence of their usefulness when fielded by the Soviets. (SA-kuva)

THE FINNISH DEFENCE CORPS

Known in Finnish as *Suojeluskuntajärjestö*, with other names commonly used Protection Corps and Civil Guards or the White Guards, was a voluntary militia organisation aimed at defending the nation. The White Guards were originally formed as independent national organisations from autumn of 1917 onwards. In early 1918, the returning Jäger's then set up a officer's school for the Guards and the whole organisation was nationalised. Led by Carl Gustaf Emil Mannerheim the White Guards then played a critical role in upholding the democratic government against the Soviet supported Red Guards during the Finnish Civil War.

In 1927, the Finland passed a law stabilising the status of the Suojeluskunta. During the 30's the still volunteer organisation was heavily developed into a regional and local arm of the National Armed Forces. Its main task in the case of war would be responsible for the mobilisation of the nation. At the same time the Corp's independent organisation structures were amalgamated with the regular army. The organisation continued to have important role in upholding reservist training during the times of peace.

Throughout the wars most of the Defence Corps members served at the front lines, only the oldest and youngest members remained in the rear in guard and anti-aircraft duties.

At its height the organisation had 127.000 members

The Corps was outlawed and disbanded as a fascistic organisation by the Allied Control Commission following the interim peace with Soviet Union in 1944.

He soon realised that the country could not be defended by the few, isolated army concentrations that could be afforded. These would be too easy to bypass or to overcome with superior forces. Instead, he recommended spreading the Finnish Army out so thinly that observers could not identify its location. In accordance he counselled for an increased reliance on the Defence Corps (the Civil Guard system), noting that an aggressor would find the going immensely slow if every hamlet and every village was a strongpoint, defended by armed and trained men with intimate knowledge of the local terrain (Clemens, 2012).

In the mid-1930s Stalin made a decision that would fundamentally change the face of the Red Army. In his great purge of the Communist Party, not only party members but also undesirable military officers were expelled and sometimes imprisoned or even executed. Mannerheim later estimated that three-quarters of the officers had been culled, and those who survived were not the most capable. As the historian Roy Medvedev later put it, 'Never, has the officer corps of any army suffered such losses in any war, as the Soviet Army suffered in this time of peace' (Amis, 2013).

Reputedly, as early as August 1935 Leningrad's commissar Andrei Zhdanov had travelled along the Murmansk Railway, running parallel to the Finnish border. He had also gone to the effort of travelling by car, horse or foot as close to different parts of the Finnish border as he could. Based on his observations, the Soviets then started to build railway spur tracks leading west towards the Finnish wilderness. Key sections were aimed at the Kuusamo, Suomussalmi, Kuhmo and Lieksa areas. The Soviets were quite clearly preparing to invade; these tracks could have served no other purpose than to transport troops and materiel, since little trade passed through these sparsely populated hinterlands (Eagle and Paananen, 1973).

In 1938 Soviet consulate staff approached the Finnish authorities and expressed their fears that Germany planned to attack the Soviet Union

ABOVE
'We do not want a single foot of
foreign territory; but of our territory
we shall not surrender a single inch
to anyone' – Joseph Stalin's comment
recorded in the Political Report of the
Central Committee to the XVI Party
Congress (29 June 1930). (SA-kuva)

LEFT
Juho Kusti Paasikivi and Väinö Tanner
about to board the train to Moscow
for the negotiations on 31 October
1939. Behind them a dense crowd of
well-wishers looks on. Stalin's dire
warning to Finland rang: 'I can well
understand that the people of Finland
wish to remain neutral, but I can
assure you that this is not possible.
The great powers simply will not allow
it.' (SA-kuva)

through Finland. They wanted Finland to agree to repel any German
attack and to accept direct Soviet military intervention whilst doing so.
No agreement was reached, but Finland promised to protect its sovereign
territory and repel any foreign troops trying to enter the country.

The Soviets were to reissue these demands twice more in 1939.
Eventually their offer turned into a suggestion of trading the Repola
and Porajärvi areas lost in the Tartu Treaty of 1920 for the strategically
important outer islands on the Gulf of Finland. These included the large
Suursaari (Gogland), Lavansaari, Tytärsaari and Seiskari. The Soviets also
demanded that the border on the Karelian Isthmus be straightened all the
way to the Koivisto Islands on the west, the Finns were prepared for far
smaller adjustments. Mannerheim himself found the terms favourable,
especially as he could not see how Finland would have been able to defend
the isles, and supported this exchange. However the Finnish government
wanted to make it absolutely clear that Finland was not for sale and
would continue to remain independent and impartial, and so the offer
was declined. The Swedish Prime Minister, Per Albin Hansson, replied
to a final plea for Sweden's help from the Finnish Finance Minister Väinö
Tanner, who was a personal friend: 'You must not in your calculations
count on Swedish intervention, for it would split the Cabinet. Personally I
would like to do much more, but I have to deal with a nation that is selfish
about peace' (Eagle and Paananen, 1973).

By 1939 the USSR was also embroiled in a border conflict with the
Empire of Japan. Despite the victory that the Soviet General Georgy Zhukov

 CARL GUSTAF EMIL MANNERHEIM
COMMANDER-IN-CHIEF, FIELD MARSHAL

(1867–1951)

Mannerheim was born on 4 June 1867 to an aristocratic Swedish-German family. Having attended cadet school in Hamina, Finland, in 1887 he enrolled in the Nikolajevski Cavalry Academy, Russia. Following graduation, Mannerheim served in Grand Duke Nikolai's 15th Alexandrian Cavalry Regiment until he received the honour of joining the tsar's Chevalier guard.

Mannerheim saw action on the front line during the Russo-Japanese War of 1904–05. In 1911, he received the command of the Ulan regiment of the tsar's personal guard, and in 1913 was appointed a commander of a cavalry brigade. During World War I, Mannerheim served as commander of the elite Guards Cavalry Brigade on the Romanian and Austro-Hungarian fronts. In 1915, he was handed command of the 12th Cavalry Division. By April 1917, however, Mannerheim, now a lieutenant-general, found himself out of favour with the post-revolution Bolshevik government in Russia. He was relieved of duty that autumn, and retired from service that winter.

After Finland declared its independence, Mannerheim returned home in January 1918, and soon became involved in the conflict between White and Red. Mannerheim was appointed to lead the White Guard nationalist troops, which he did to victory.

After the war, he briefly acted as regent, travelling abroad to gain international support for the newly independent country. In July 1919, he stood as a candidate for the first presidential election, but failed to win, and withdrew from political life.

Mannerheim headed the Finnish Red Cross from 1919 to 1951, and sat on its international board. He founded the Mannerheim League for Child Welfare, and was chairman of the Bank of Helsinki until 1934. He was also a member of the board of the Nokia Corporation.

When President Pehr Evind Svinhufvud was elected in 1931, he appointed Mannerheim to Finland's Defence Council. In 1933, Mannerheim was granted the rank of field marshal.

When the Soviet Union invaded Finland in 1939, Mannerheim was appointed the commander-in-chief of the Finnish Army, a position which he came to hold for the duration of World War II.

achieved at the decisive engagement of Khalkhin Gol in late August, Stalin was worried about the state of Soviet forces. He realised that more time was needed to reorganise the decimated officer corps, while avoiding at all costs the increasing threat of German invasion and the possibility of bifrontal war. As a result, Stalin's emissaries began seeking allies in the West. By the summer it had become clear that, despite the long negotiations, no common goals could be agreed with the British or the French. Therefore, while the negotiations were still underway, Stalin decided to turn to Hitler, whom he considered a man capable of swift and decisive action. Neither of these dictators was hindered by the need to heed governmental consensus or popular opinion.

In the East, Stalin was also observing matters closely and correctly calculated that he could incite Hitler into attacking Poland and thus start a war in the West, buying him the time he needed to reorganise the Red Army. This led to the creation of the Molotov–Ribbentrop Pact, named after the Soviet and German foreign ministers. Officially this was a non-aggression pact between Germany and the USSR. However, in its secret protocol all of Eastern Europe was to be divided between the two. The USSR was to gain Finland, Estonia and Latvia whereas Germany would take Lithuania and Western Poland. Eastern Poland and Bessarabia, part of Romania, would also fall under the Soviet sphere of influence. When Hitler occupied the last parts of Czechoslovakia in March 1939, Mannerheim made

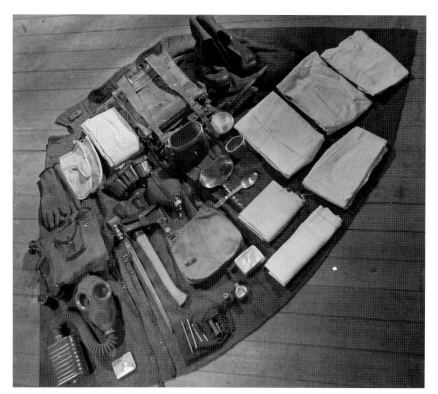

LEFT
Around one-third of the Finnish soldiers began the war with practically no issued equipment. Their meagre gear, consisting of rifle, belt and national cockade, was dubbed 'model Cajander' after the prime minister whose government had failed to invest in the armed forces before the war. Officially, the equipment was supposed to contain a rifle, knife, woollen military coat, winter overalls, and the following items shown here on top of the uniform: gloves, mittens, footwraps (used instead of socks), rucksack, leather boots, shoe polish and brush, gasmask and protective bag, bullet clips for belts, bayonet, hand-axe, flask, messenger-style 'bread' bag and carry straps, rifle cleaning kit, mess kit with spork, a change of clothes and handkerchiefs. Underwear, and a warmer winter coat, were in most cases brought by the men from home. (SA-kuva)

BELOW
A standard Finnish Army pack. (SA-kuva)

the following comment: 'It seems, quite simply to be his aim to change the people of Europe into white Negroes in the service of the Third Reich' (Screen, 2014).

By now, the movements in Europe and Germany's annexation of Austria were causing alarm bells to ring in Finland. The threat of war loomed ever closer. The Finns put their last hopes for peace into the formation of a mutual Scandinavian alliance and in particular into the promise of help from the sizeable Swedish Army. Such hopes were dashed, however, when the Swedes caved in to German and Soviet pressure on the question of mutually fortifying the island of Åland. By the autumn of 1939, Sweden had made it clear that in future conflicts its troops would remain inside its own borders. Still, many Finnish government ministers did not believe that war would come, trusting in the peace treaties signed with the United States and Great Britain. Moreover, the non-aggression pact signed with the Soviets in 1934 still had nearly five years left to run.

While Stalin and Hitler proceeded to re-arm, the Finns concentrated on preparing for the XII Olympic Games, which were to be held in Helsinki in 1940. Ironically, it was the Soviet–Japanese conflict that had helped Finland win the hosting of the Olympiad from Tokyo (which had originally been granted the event). Stalin's ensuing act of aggression would result in the event being cancelled completely until the 1948 London games.

∞∞

On 1 September 1939 the German Army crossed into Polish territory from the west and from East Prussia in the north. Early that morning, the first bombers struck Warsaw, beginning a conflict that was to engulf the whole world.

Hitler was confident that Great Britain and France would not interfere and go to war over Poland. On 3 September he was proven wrong, as both nations proceeded to declare war on Germany. Hitler knew that his armies were not ready to fight against all the Western powers, but he had expected the British and French governments to see the wisdom of fighting the greater Bolshevist enemy in the East. In mid-September the Soviet Union invaded eastern Poland and the whole country vanished from the map. This prompted Mannerheim to make his prophetic statement in a letter to his sister: 'And whose turn is next, when the appetite of these two gentlemen has managed to grow?' (Screen, 2014).

Once Stalin had gained a foothold in eastern Poland, he started to apply pressure in the rest of the territories specified by the Molotov–Ribbentrop pact. To begin with, he demanded concessions and unhindered military access from Estonia, Latvia and Lithuania. This development alarmed the Finns further, so hundreds of volunteers began digging fresh fortifications on the eastern border. By the end of November scores of anti-tank barricades, sleeping quarters and over 150 concrete bunkers had been

(1878–1953)

JOSEPH STALIN
GENERALISSIMUS OF THE SOVIET UNION

Joseph Vissarionovich Stalin was born in Georgia on 21 December 1879. He began studying to become a priest in 1894, but was expelled in May 1899. From 1917 to 1922 Stalin was the People's Commissar for National Matters, earning himself a reputation for ruthlessness within Lenin's government.

In 1922 Lenin made him the General Secretary of the Central Committee of the Communist Party, a position Stalin was to hold until his death.

In 1938 Stalin became a member of Stavka, the Soviet Union's leading military council. In May 1941 he was also elected as Chairman of the Council of Ministers. When Operation *Barbarossa*, the German invasion, began in June 1941, Stalin made himself the People's Commissar of Defence and Supreme Commander of the Armed Forces.

In 1945 Stalin was made a Hero of the Soviet Union.

constructed along key sections of this main defensive 'Mannerheim Line'.

On 5 October 1939 a Finnish delegation was suddenly summoned to Moscow to negotiate similar land concessions and a mutual peace agreement, as had been done with the Baltic States. The basis of the negotiations was still mainly land trade and rental agreements where Finland would give control of strategically important locations to the Soviet Union. They were also once again asked to provide direct support to the USSR in the event of war. Mannerheim later recalled Stalin's words to him: 'I well understand you wish to remain neutral, but I can assure you that it is not at all possible. The Great Powers will simply not allow it' (Mannerheim, 1954).

At this point Hermann Göring approached the Finnish government and encouraged them to hand over the naval bases demanded by the Soviets, or no further support would be forthcoming from the Germans. Most

CYRIL MERETSKOV
ARMY COMMANDER
2ND CLASS, SEVENTH ARMY

Cyril Afanasjevtsh Meretskov began his career in the Red Army in 1918. He rose to become commander of the Leningrad Military District in 1939, and thus the whole invasion of Finland during the Winter War.

(1897–1968)

Due to the shocking start to the offensive, which failed to meet any of the strategic objectives for the campaign, Meretskov was demoted on 9 December 1939 to command of the Seventh Army on the Karelian Isthmus. The overall command of the war was now left directly in the hands of Stavka.

In 1940, Meretskov was made chief of general staff. A year later he was named as Deputy People's Commissar.

For the first part of the Great Patriotic War of 1941–45, Meretskov served as an army and front commander. On 22 February 1944, Meretskov, who well knew the strength of the Finnish fighting spirit, was given command of the Karelian Front. In October 1944, his army managed to capture Petsamo from the Germans. Elsewhere the Finnish lines held.

On 26 October 1944, Meretskov was appointed marshal of the Soviet Union. In the spring of 1945, he was transferred to command the front in the Far East, taking part in the war against Japan in Manchuria and North Korea.

Several senior military district commands followed, until he was given the role of inspecting general in 1964. Meretskov died in service on 30 December 1968.

of the Finnish population was strongly against any form of compromise to its territorial integrity and did not want to see any part of the nation ceded to foreign powers. On 3 November, by which point the latest round of negotiations had stagnated, Molotov commented: 'Now the civilian officials have tried to solve this matter and failed. Therefore, it is time to hand the matter over to the military' (Siilasvuo et al., 1989).

Despite his belligerent rhetoric, Stalin was surprised that Finland did not accede to the Soviet demands like the neighbouring Baltic countries had done previously. Nevertheless, he had already decided to take the territory in question by force if necessary. Negotiations finally broke down on 13 November. Finland had only managed to gain a small respite and now had very little time left to prepare its defences. In Moscow, Soviet politicians started to assemble their own new 'national government' for Finland.

DAVID VERSUS GOLIATH

The Winter War has often been described as a battle between David and Goliath, based on the disparity in numbers and levels of armament.

The Finnish divisions could only field one artillery regiment composed of three understrength batteries using mostly obsolete tsarist-era howitzers and light 3in cannons. In addition to riflemen, each division also had a light detachment of roughly 500 men and included a 180-strong cavalry unit, a bicycle company and a separate machine-gun squadron. At the outbreak of hostilities, the Finnish artillery had enough ammunition to last for roughly one week of fighting.

In comparison, each of the Soviet divisions had their own heavy howitzer and cannon regiments as well as an anti-tank company equipped with 12 45mm anti-tank guns. In addition to the divisional batteries, each regiment had its own tactical anti-tank battery and four regimental cannons. Thus the Soviet artillery within each division already outshot the Finns by more than two to one. Each Soviet unit also contained its own armoured battalion, with 10–40 tanks, as well as a reconnaissance battalion.

The Finnish heavy artillery units comprised four separate artillery batteries whereas the Red Army had whole artillery regiments. Thirty-two Vickers and a handful of obsolete Renaults were the only tanks the Finns possessed. The Soviet forces had at their disposal several armoured brigades containing hundreds of tanks.

In November 1939 a prophetic conversation took place in the Kremlin. The Commander of the Leningrad Military District, Cyril Meretskov, was chairing the discussion about the 'liberation plan' for Finland; also present were the jubilant Deputy People's Commissars for Defence, Gregory I. Kulik and Lev Z. Mekhlis, and the somewhat less enthusiastic Chief Marshal of Artillery Nicholas N. Voronov. What happened next is described in Voronov's memoirs. Kulik said:

'You have come in at a good time, do you know of the dangerous situation arising from Finland?'

Voronov nodded his acknowledgement. Kulik and Mekhlis then proceeded to ask how much ammunition Voronov needed for the forthcoming campaign.

'That depends,' replied Voronov. 'Are you planning to attack or defend? … With which forces and on which sectors? … And by the way, how much time is allotted for the operation?'

The reply to the last point came quickly:

'Between 10 and 12 days.'

Eyeing the map of Finland hanging on the wall, Voronov replied:

'I will be happy if everything can be resolved within two to three months.'

Everybody laughed derisively.

'Marshal Voronov,' Kulik replied sternly. 'You are ordered to base all your estimates on the assumption that the operation will last a maximum of 12 days' (Voronov, 1963).

The Soviet Union had been planning and preparing an invasion of Finland since spring 1936, but it appears that the final decision to launch the attack was not made before the end of October 1939. Stalin's general staff had originally prepared a realistic and comprehensive plan for occupying Finland. This proposal took into account the true strengths of the defending forces, the terrain and other logistical considerations. The conservative pace of this plan did not please Stalin, who wanted a quick and decisive victory. Therefore, instead of utilising all of the Red Army's resources that the original plan had called for, the operational responsibility for an invasion

Soviet infantry (Rifle) division (c.17,000 men)	Finnish infantry division (c.14,200 men)
3 x rifle regiments of 4,000 men	3 x infantry regiments of 3,000 men
3 x infantry battalions	3 x infantry battalions
Reconnaissance company	–
Artillery battery (4 x 76mm cannons)	Artillery company (4 x 37mm anti-tank or field cannons)
Anti-tank battery (6 x 45mm anti-tank guns)	–
Four mortar squads (8 x 82mm mortars)	Mortar company (6 x 81mm mortars)
Howitzer regiment (1,300 men) 36 x howitzers	Artillery regiment (2,400 men) 12 x 122mm howitzers and 24 x 76mm cannons
Artillery regiment (1,900 men) 36 x cannons or howitzers	–
Separate tank battalion	Cavalry squadron (180 men)
T-32/T-28 tank company (10–40 tanks)	–
T-26 tank company (10–40 tanks)	–
Chemical-tank company (not always present)	–
Separate anti-tank battery (18 x 45mm AT cannons)	Machine-gun detachment
Separate anti-aircraft battery	–
Separate reconnaissance battalion (328 men)	Light detachment (500 men)
Motorcycle company	Bicycle company (190 men)
Armoured car company	–
Tank company	–
Separate communications company	Separate communications company
Separate pioneer company	Two separate pioneer companies

of Finland was handed over solely to the Leningrad Military District. Army Commander 2nd Class Cyril A. Meretskov, who was the senior officer in charge, had to quickly devise new plans for the attack. The key deadline for Finland's capitulation was to be Stalin's 60th birthday on 21 December. This left Meretskov with little room for error, and perhaps consequently his plan ended up being conservative and unimaginative. Convinced of its forthcoming success, Andrew Zhdanov the Chairman of the highest legislative body in the Soviet Union, commissioned a celebratory piece of music by Shostakovich to be played by the Red Army marching band in the streets of Helsinki.[3]

---

3   Shostakovich's Suite on Finnish Themes would soon be forgotten. The suite was eventually premiered in September 2001 in Finland. 'Party Piece Uncovered', The Telegraph (6 September 2001).

Finnish soldiers during the Extraordinary Autumn Manoeuvres of 1939. These military exercises gave the Finns time to accustom their troops to wartime responsibilities and contexts. A few months later, war came to this part of the Karelian Isthmus. (The Finnish Museum of Photography)

While the Finnish delegation was still negotiating in Moscow, the Soviets started to assemble troops along the border. Stalin also ordered the propaganda war to start, and youths from all over the Leningrad district were being press-ganged into service. 'Visit Finland before Finland visits you' ran one propaganda slogan (Edwards, 2006).

Meanwhile, growing political pressure and the alarming developments in Poland and the Baltic States drove the Finns to commence their own deployment. During October all Finnish reservists were called up to take part in a joint operation and refresher training. The pretext of these additional military manoeuvres justified the mobilisation of the whole of the armed forces, allowing troops to move peacefully into their new wartime deployment zones and familiarise themselves with their assigned responsibilities and equipment.

By mid-November the general consensus in Finland was that tension had been diffused and war seemed less likely. Schools were being reopened on the border zones and many of the people who had been encouraged to leave the area were starting to trickle back home. The government was just

In the period of increased tension during the autumn of 1939, the Finns started to clear the border zone of civilians and their most valuable possessions. When the threat of war diminished, these peoples started to trickle back home. (The Finnish Museum of Photography)

about to give orders to send the reservist troops back home when the Soviet propaganda machine produced a blatant lie about a transgression.

On 26 November, following direct orders from Leningrad, one battery from the Soviet 221st Artillery Regiment fired a salvo at their own comrades located in the village of Mainila in Russia. As this artillery battery was located north of the small Russian village, it appeared that the shells had come from Finland. This gave the Soviet Union an excuse to cut diplomatic relationships with Finland and to cast aside the mutual peace agreement. It was the *casus belli* Stalin had needed.

The Soviets quickly tried to escalate the conflict further. In the Murmansk area they kidnapped a couple of Finnish soldiers, and all along the border they attempted to provoke the Finns by launching feints. However, Finnish troops were under strict orders not to return fire until Soviet troops had actually crossed the national border. This would not be long in coming.

OPPOSING PLANS

Soviet plans for the invasion were hurriedly pulled together during the first weeks of November. In accordance with Stalin's wishes, the conquest of Finland was still a local operation for the Leningrad Military District. Meretskov's plan was simply to destroy the Finnish forces at the border and then use the existing road networks to quickly advance deep inland.

Soviet assumptions about the poor quality of their opponents' equipment proved to be correct. The supply situation was so dire that some of the recently recalled Finnish reservists were given only a rifle, a national cockade, a soldier's cap and a belt. For many, personal clothing and the uniforms kept from their time in the Civil Guard provided better protection from the cold than the available German-style uniforms.

In contrast, Meretskov had at his disposal four well equipped complete armies. They were to execute his plans on a front spreading from the Gulf of Finland all the way to the Barents Sea.

The main push was to be conducted by the Seventh Army on the Karelian Isthmus. There, Army Commander 2nd Class Vsevolod F. Yakovlev had at his disposal nine full infantry divisions and four armoured brigades. Yakovlev could also call on further reinforcements of several artillery regiments and three armoured brigades. Seventh Army's mission was to quickly overrun the Finnish defences on the Karelian Isthmus and conquer Finland's second city, Viipuri. From there Seventh Army was to continue north towards the

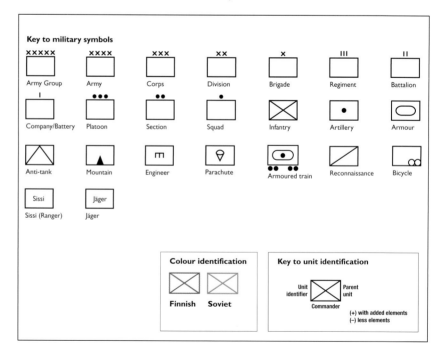

Finland in 1939: initial attacks of the Winter War and Soviet objectives

IVAN KHABAROV
DIVISION COMMANDER, EIGHTH ARMY

Due to the poor performance of his troops during the opening phases of the Winter War, Khabarov was removed from the command of Eighth Army on 13 December 1939. He continued to serve in several administrative roles for the duration of the conflict.

During the Continuation War, Khabarov held several positions as second-in-command of several armies, but did not manage to receive further promotion. He retired from active service due to poor health on 26 May 1950.

(1888–1960)

town of Lappeenranta, then turn west towards the city of Lahti, before the final push to the capital Helsinki.

The Soviets lacked detailed information on the Finnish fortifications. Based on their findings, Seventh Army was expected to complete the operation in a maximum of three weeks. In hindsight, this was overly optimistic. Even without opposition, reaching the stated objectives within the allotted timescale would have required the infantry units to advance without pause at a pace close to their maximum peacetime marching speed.

The Soviet Eighth Army was led by Division Commander Ivan N. Khabarov. His force consisted of five infantry divisions and one light armoured brigade. Its task was to attack to the north of Lake Ladoga, in the region known as Ladoga Karelia. Khabarov was then expected to continue the drive deep into western Finland. A breakthrough on this front would also give Soviet forces an option to swing back towards the rear of the defenders on the Karelian Isthmus, should such a manoeuvre be required.

Corps Commander Michael P. Duhanov led the Soviet Ninth Army, with four infantry divisions. At the outbreak of hostilities, one of these, the 44th Rifle Division was still on its way to the front. Duhanov's mission was to march to the town of Kajaani and then proceed to the city of Oulu on the west coast. This would effectively cut Finland in two at its narrowest point.

In the far north, Corps Commander Valerian A. Frolov's Fourteenth Army consisted of two regular infantry divisions and one mountain division. Together with the Northern Fleet, they were to seize control of the Petsamo region and prevent any foreign intervention through Norway or the Barents Sea. Most of Fourteenth Army's troops arrived late at the front.

Despite the hastily drawn up plans, the soldiers of the Red Army were in confident mood. They had recently defeated the Japanese in Mongolia and had annexed Eastern Poland, Western Ukraine and Belarus. Their

equipment was modern, and for the duration of the 1930s the army had remained undefeated.

Finnish tactics were limited by the availability of equipment and ammunition. This meant avoiding fighting in open terrain where inferior Finnish firepower would likely spell disaster. Conversely, the Soviets had the opposite in mind as their inflexible doctrine was designed for all-out frontal assaults supported by massed artillery and armour. This tactical rigidity meant that the Red Army would often repeat the same failed attack with the same formations again and again. As the Finns became aware of this, they attempted to strike deep into enemy lines using the cover of terrain to their advantage.

To the Red Army's great advantage, these large-scale guerrilla tactics could not be employed on the Karelian Isthmus. There, a much more conventional war would have to be fought, with far superior Soviet forces attempting to weaken heavily fortified Finnish lines. Any Finnish successes would depend on the quality of their leaders, their military skills and discipline and above all their *sisu* (a simple term that has become a byword for the endurance, grit and 'never give up' attitude demonstrated by the Finns).

The Karelian Isthmus had always been the weak point in the Finnish defences, and conversely one of the biggest threats to the USSR, as enemy forces could easily threaten Leningrad through this corridor. In order to plug this gap in their defences, the Finns had fortified defensive positions across the isthmus on a main line – the so-called Mannerheim Line. The total length of the line was around 150km. There were virtually no defences at all along the remaining 1,300km-long border with Russia.

ABOVE RIGHT
The Finns did their best to use natural features to their fullest effect. It was clear from the outset that the frozen lakes and rivers would provide the Red Army with unparalleled open space in which to bring their armoured columns to bear. To counter this threat, the Finns would plant lines of explosives under the ice. In this image, two soldiers float a string of explosive bottles under the ice during the Continuation War. Deploying a line under the ice is an old fisherman's trick, which is still used today when laying nets during the winter months. (SA-kuva)

ABOVE LEFT
A Finnish soldier digging a hole for an anti-tank mine on the frozen Summa road, 14 December 1939. Earlier in the war the Finns had planted strings of mines across frozen lakes. When detonated, they broke the ice under the advancing Soviets; the tactic forced them to stick to the narrow roads. This was just what the Finns had counted on, as now the enemy would advance in a far more predictable manner. (SA-kuva)

MOTTI TACTICS AND SOVIET DOCTRINE

During the Winter War the world's press adopted a new word: *motti*. It relates to a specific tactic that the Finns developed when dealing with the much larger Soviet formations. The exact origin of the term is still debated in Finland and certainly some earlier military writings used different words to describe similar manoeuvres. Nevertheless, this tactic, which contributed so greatly to the Soviet losses, is still taught in military academies around the world. According to the Finns, a classic *motti* operation can be split into three parts:

1. Reconnoitring the enemy positions and ensuring that the operation begins when they are suitably constrained by the terrain. For instance, on isthmuses or on narrow roads that force troops into long columns or to bunch up together.
2. Fast, strong and concentrated attacks where the enemy forces are pinned down. These attacks should be aimed at the most vulnerable points of the enemy formations. The goal is to cause the enemy forces to lose cohesion and isolate them into smaller, more manageable pockets. Each pocket should be completely surrounded to prevent the enemy from escaping.
3. Destroying the pockets one at a time, starting with the weakest. Winter conditions and hunger would meanwhile weaken enemy resistance in the larger *motti*.

The extent to which the *motti* tactic was officially taught to officers in pre-war Finland remains unclear. Certainly the skills that were needed for this kind of action were the cornerstones of basic soldier training. Each man was able to ski for many miles and most were considered crack shots.

Perhaps most importantly, the Finns had a comprehensive understanding of the enemy forces and their capabilities. Mannerheim and many of his senior officers had served in the tsarist army and therefore knew Russian (and thus Soviet) battle doctrine intimately. They also believed that Stalin's purges had culled the best two-thirds of the Red Army's officer cadre. This further enabled the Finns to make some very accurate predictions regarding their Soviet counterparts' mindsets and actions. They believed that due to the rapid promotion of second-rate officers, little creativity or initiative could be expected when it came to reacting on the battlefield.

The Soviet war doctrine of the time remained rigid, regardless of the front on which its troops were fighting. The officers tried to focus on retaining control and discipline, while trying not to get shot in the process. The problem was that Finnish terrain distinctly lacked the roads, junctions, railways and villages that were the norm in much of the rest of Europe. Therefore retaining this kind of order, and bringing massed artillery and armour to bear, became very difficult. In the Finnish wilderness, the only way these doctrines could be followed was by sticking closely to the few available roads. Unfortunately, these roads most often happened to be single-track paths more suitable for a cart than a whole motorised division.

The *motti* tactic, in contrast, suited these conditions perfectly. Finnish ski troops were highly mobile and were able to attack the Soviet columns from unexpected directions. Due to their skills in using the terrain to their advantage, relatively few men were able to prevent much larger, encircled Soviet forces from escaping.

The main problem the Finns faced was that often the *motti* created were simply too large for them to destroy. With more artillery and better heavy weapons, or simply with more time and men, this could have been accomplished with greater frequency. As it happened, some of the biggest pockets were never cleared during the war.

When the fighting started, not all sections of the main defensive line were heavily fortified and most of the strongholds were already obsolete against modern artillery. Contrary to the propaganda that both the Finns and Soviets published, none of the defences bore much comparison with the famous Maginot Line in France. According to a contemporary source, unknown to Cyril Meretskov, Soviet intelligence had already been passed a detailed map of the main Finnish defences as early as September 1939 by General Arniké, who had served as the Wehrmacht's military attaché in Helsinki. For some reason, however, the map was never used. Arniké's breach of etiquette was coldly received by his colleagues: upon his return to Germany, he was wordlessly offered a loaded pistol by his fellow officers. Arniké did not complain and without further ado used it upon himself. This event highlights what many in the German officer corps thought of the pact Hitler had made with the Soviet Union (Elliston, 1940).

The strongest points of the defences of the Mannerheim Line were located at its two ends: on the Gulf of Finland in the west, and on Lake Ladoga in the east. In these locations coastal artillery could be used to break up any massed enemy formations. The weakest point was near the village of Summa towards the western end of the line, where water could not be integrated as a natural defensive element and where the open terrain was ideally suited to Soviet tanks.

The approaches to the Mannerheim Line were protected by vast areas of barbed-wire entanglements, tank barricades and minefields. In places where the banks of the Vuoksi River did not offer any natural obstacles, a steep-sided anti-tank ditch had been excavated just in front of the Finnish dugouts. The major weakness of the defensive lines lay in the number of bunkers and emplacements, which were too few and far between to give mutual fire support to each other. By systematically destroying the outlying positions, Soviet forces would be able to start rolling up the line one sector at a time. An even greater concern was the lack of artillery; the forward bunkers often only boasted Maxim machine guns, and there was a huge shortage of heavy artillery behind the front line.

At the beginning of the conflict, there were deep concerns about the reliability and trustworthiness of Finland's own troops. Memories of the recent Civil War against the Soviet-supported Red Guard were still fresh in everyone's mind. However, continuous military practice and the effects of several years of Western propaganda had helped unify the armed forces.

THE FINNISH DEMOCRATIC REPUBLIC

In 1939 Terijoki (now called Zelenogorsk) was a small holiday village; it lay on the Finnish–Soviet border, not far from the city of Leningrad (St Petersburg). It also had the misfortune of being the first city to be 'liberated' by Soviet forces.

It was here that Stalin created the Finnish Democratic Republic, informally also known as the Terijoki Government. Its president was Otto Wille Kuusinen, a former leader of the Red Guard who had fled Finland in the aftermath of the 1918 Civil War. Kuusinen's overnight rise to high office was followed by a grandiose treaty-signing ceremony, at which were present Kuusinen himself, Stalin, Molotov, Zhdanov and Clement Voroshilov.

The opening words of the treaty included the following: 'Since the Finnish people [only four of which were present] have now created their own democratic government, which derives its support entirely from the people, the time has come to establish good relations between our countries and, with united forces, to protect the security and inviolability of our nations.'

Now that the newly elected president of the Finnish Democratic Republic had officially asked for the help of the Red Army in removing any opposition in Helsinki, Stalin could do little but respond to this plea for assistance. Stalin then formed the Finnish National Army from Red Guard veterans and Eastern Karelians. Little is known about this force and its role in the fighting that followed, although film evidence does exist of its troops on parade (Trotter, 1991).

Ever since Mannerheim had received his honorific post of field marshal in 1933, he had been trying to heal the wounds between the Reds and Whites. One example of the conciliatory way forward that he sought, taken from one of his speeches, is provided here:

> Where war is waged, life is trodden down and property devastated. The all-destroying strength of modern weapons confers on modern war its ghastly grandeur … Where chivalry and magnanimity are lacking and Hatred commands the sword, there is no room for a lasting peace. But we live in a troubled and threatening time … let us extend an open hand to everyone who wants to work and do his duty in this country. A patriotic spirit, expressed in the will to defend the country and to stand in the ranks like a man if some day it has to be defended, is all we ask. We do not need to ask any longer what position a man took fifteen years ago [during the Civil War]. (Jagerskiold, 1987)

The Soviet Union's alliance with Nazi Germany and the subsequent grab for European land helped create a wider consensus of nationalist opinion. The last vestiges of widespread pro-communist sympathies were finally shred immediately after the invasion began when the Soviets established the puppet Finnish Democratic Republic (or Terijoki Government). Even the most ardent Soviet sympathisers were forced to reconsider their allegiances. However, from the outset it seemed to be a given that Finland would be overrun by Soviet Russia; the question was only how many hours, or perhaps days, it would take.

At the beginning of the Winter War, Stalin set up his own puppet government for Finland, the Finnish Democratic Republic (or Terijoki Government). As his first act of office, the 'elected' President Otto Wille Kuusinen (standing, far right) agreed to all the Soviet demands on Finland, and then proceeded to seek Soviet military help in clearing the country of 'White' elements. Also witnessing Molotov signing the treaty are (from left) Zhdanov, Voroshilov and Stalin. Kuusinen died of cancer in 1964. He is the only Finn ever to have been buried inside the Kremlin Wall. (Wikipedia)

CHAPTER 3
THE KARELIAN ISTHMUS, DECEMBER 1939

The Soviet military leaders thought that a decisive strike across the Karelian Isthmus would be the key to a swift victory. This task fell to the Soviet Seventh Army, which had amassed roughly 120,000 infantry supported by 1,500 artillery pieces, 1,400 tanks and roughly 1,000 aeroplanes. The original plan was to support the land-based assaults with strike forces from the First Ladokan and the Baltic fleets. These naval operations were soon abandoned due to the worsening weather conditions. The Finnish forces facing them amounted to 26,000 infantry armed with a mere 71 artillery pieces and 29 anti-tank guns.

The defence of this critical sector was the responsibility of Lieutenant-General Hugo Österman's Army of the Isthmus. During peace time Österman had been the Finnish supreme military commander, a position that from

Upon the outbreak of the Winter War, barbed wire was collected from all the farms and fields in Finland. Most of this was to be deployed on the Karelian Isthmus. The Finns realised quickly that the danger to their homeland increased with every kilometre from north to south. Losing Petsamo in the Arctic would affect morale and cut off Finland's access to the northern supply routes by sea, but this was nothing compared to the potential losses further south, where the battle was about the survival of the nation. The Karelian Isthmus and the lands just north of Lake Ladoga would thus form the critical sector. (SA-kuva)

now on would rest with Mannerheim. Österman's defending forces were further split between II Army Corps, led by Lieutenant-General Harald Öhquist on the west side of the isthmus, and III Army Corps, positioned on the east side and under the command of Major-General Erik Heinrichs. At the start of hostilities troops had been stationed in the vicinity of the border in the so-called delay-positions. These positions were meant only to hinder and weaken the enemy while the Finns slowly performed a fighting retreat towards the well-fortified lines.

On Thursday 30 November 1939, just after the fighting had started at the fronts, those on their way to work in the capital Helsinki also got a taste of things to come. The air-raid sirens shrieked, and dozens of Soviet aircraft dropped leaflets over the city, stating, 'You know we have bread – don't starve. Soviet Russia will not harm the Finnish people. Their disaster is due to the wrong leadership. Mannerheim and Cajander must go. After this peace will come!' On the very same afternoon, bombing took place. Over the first two days of air raids, 91 people perished in the fires and collapsed buildings. From that point on, it was clear that Soviets dealt in death and not in provisions, and thus the Soviet aircraft were ironically known as 'Molotov's breadbaskets'. (The Finnish Museum of Photography)

Finally, on the morning of 30 November 1939, without waiting for a declaration of war, Soviet troops crossed over into Finland. Immediately, the massed Soviet artillery opened up and the first red-starred bombers appeared over Finnish cities. For many Finnish soldiers this was their first experience of combat. Several recounted afterwards that at first it felt strange aiming and firing their weapons against other human beings. After a couple of hours all such sentiments had been shaken off; there was no shortage of Soviet troops to shoot at. As one Finnish soldier astutely summarised the situation on the eve of the war: 'We are so few and they are so many. Where will we find the room to bury them all?' (Warner, 1967).

The first line of defence had been left to the elements of the small peace time army forces and reservists called in from the Isthmus itself. On the Ladogan side III Army Corps commanded Task Force Rautu and the 11 Division guided Task Force Lipola (both named after local villages). These formations managed to greatly slow down the Soviet attack, and despite some conflicting commands that caused part of the men to retreat early they were not forced to withdraw to the main defensive positions before 4 December. Quite a feat considering that the distance to the Soviet border had been a mere 12km at its shortest. The initial focus of the Soviet invasion was the city of Viipuri on the western shores of the Karelian Isthmus. There, the fighting retreat was executed by Task Force Uusikirkko and Task Force Muolaa. While the Soviet forces attempted to encircle their foes, they did so very cautiously and the Finns were able to evade the advancing enemy.

In the end Task Forces U and M stalled the invasion until 6 December. This week-long delaying action had been fought by around 28,000 Finns versus the 200,000 men of the Red Army. Considering this, the Finnish casualties of 133 deceased, 79 missing and 188 wounded were extremely light. Eventually, the Soviet 24th Rifle Division was the first to reach the Finnish main defensive lines. However, the division's initial attempts at achieving a breakthrough were all summarily repelled. In some places the attacking regiments failed even to clear the Finnish forward outposts and picket lines, losing several tanks in the process.

By delaying the Soviet advance all along the border, the Finns had won precious time to complete civilian evacuations and to finalise camouflaging their fortifications. Considering that the Finns had no tanks of their own and that the Soviets had to advance a distance of no more than 50km at the widest point of the isthmus, it was a significant achievement. In his book *Talvisota 1939–1940*, Wolf H. Halsti remembered the following words from one company commander after the delay phase of the operation had finished:

> The Russian infantry always fire over our heads, I think they must be lying prone behind the stumps and tufts of grass while shooting at the skies. If our positions were not surrounded on every occasion due to the lack of troops, we would still be there. Also the Russians did not seem willing to advance. We did not have to worry a lot about artillery. Anti-tank rounds penetrate the Russian tanks like butter. However, with their massed numbers the Russians poured through and around the gaps in our lines. Therefore, when we left, we did it because we were forced to leave, rather than waiting for any orders from behind. This will go well for us yet. (Halsti, 1957)

THE TAIPALE AND KIVINIEMI SECTORS

In the east of the Karelian Isthmus, on the shores of Lake Ladoga, the Finnish defenders proved to be less tenacious and the Soviet assault somewhat more effective. Based on the progress of his troops in this sector, Yakovlev soon focused the main efforts of his Seventh Army on the lakeside village of Taipale. With effect from 3 December, he tasked Corps Commander Vladimir D. Grendahl and the newly formed Right Wing Group with securing a desperately needed breakthrough. Although less of a priority for the time being, the push towards Viipuri in the west of the isthmus was left in the hands of two whole rifle corps: Division Commander Philip Gorelenko's 50th Rifle Corps advanced along the Viipuri road, while Division Commander Theodore Starikov's 19th Rifle Corps was to follow a parallel route along the railway line.

Karelian Isthmus: stopping the advance, December 1939

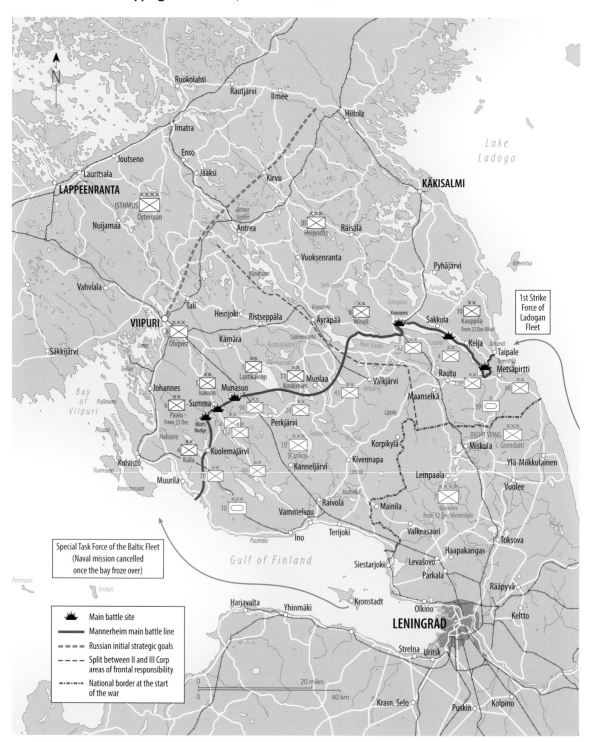

Legend:
- ✹ Main battle site
- ━━━ Mannerheim main battle line
- ┅┅┅ Russian initial strategic goals
- ╌╌╌ Split between II and III Corp areas of frontal responsibility
- ╌·╌·╌ National border at the start of the war

Scale:
0 — 20 miles
0 — 40 km

Special Task Force of the Baltic Fleet
(Naval mission cancelled
once the bay froze over)

1st Strike
Force of
Ladogan
Fleet

N

Place names (north to south, selected):
Ruokolahti, Rautjärvi, Ilmee, Hiitola, Imatra, Enso, Joutseno, Jääksi, Kirvu, Lauritsala, LAPPEENRANTA, ISTHMUS Österman, Antrea Station, Antrea, Heinrichs, Räisälä, KÄKISALMI, Nuijamaa, Vuoksenranta, Pyhäjärvi, Konevitsa, Lake Ladoga, Vahviala, Tali, Heinjoki, Ristseppälä, Äyräpää, Winell, Kiviniemi, Sakkola, Kauppila From 22 Dec Blick, VIIPURI, Öhquist, Kämärä, Laatikainen, Muolaa, Koskimies, Valkjärvi, Kelja, Taipale, Terenttilä, Metsäpirtti, Rautu, Säkkijärvi, Johannes, Isakson, Munasuo, Maanselkä, Summa, Paalu From 23 Dec, Idiot's Nudge, Perkjärvi, Lipola, Korpikylä, RIGHT WING, Miskula, Grendahl, Kuolemajärvi, Starikov, Kivennapa, Ylä-Miikkulainen, Koivisto, Kaila, Kanneljärvi, Lintula, Lempaala, Vuolee, Muurila, Raivola, Mainila, Valkeasaari, Toksova, Vammelsuu, Terijoki, Haapakangas, Yakovlev from 12 Dec Meretskov, Ino, Siestarjoki, Levašovo, Parkala, Rääpyvä, Puumala, Gulf of Finland, Harjavalta, Yhinmäki, Kronstadt, Olkino, Keltto, Peninsaari, Seiskari, Strelna, Uritsk, LENINGRAD, Krasn. Selo, Puskin, Kolpino

On Finnish Independence Day, 6 December, the 49th and 150th Rifle divisions of Grendahl's Right Wing Group attempted a crossing of the fast-flowing Taipale River. Despite the current, it appeared an easier option than the 200m-wide Vuoksi River to the west. Here the outlying Finnish pickets quickly retreated to the safety of the main defensive line.

In anticipation, Colonel Viljo A. Kauppila's 10th Division, responsible for this stretch of terrain, had already zeroed in their artillery. Now they proceeded to shell the advancing Soviets with devastating effect. Their fire proved so accurate that the Kaarnajoki Battery became known by the Finns as the 'Angel of Taipale'.

The Soviet plan was to cross the Taipale River at three locations, but the south bank and the surrounding areas comprised flat farming fields offering no cover to the advancing pioneers and pontoon battalions. Despite

(1884–1940)

VLADIMIR GRENDAHL
ARMY CORPS COMMANDER, RIGHT WING GROUP

Vladimir Davidovich Grendahl (at the time Gröndahl, before his name was Russified) was born on 3 April 1884 in the Grand Duchy of Finland. He followed in his father's footsteps and joined the military, rising to the rank of general in the tsar's army.

By the time of the Russian Civil War, Grendahl had reached the rank of colonel. He joined the Revolutionary Red Army in 1917, and now that the hostilities had broken out, he could not desert his post and return to his wife and children, who were living in Estonia at the time. Grendahl's family ended up relocating to Helsinki, and during the Winter War father and son faced each other on the Karelian Isthmus in opposing armies.

At the outbreak of the Winter War, Grendahl was the highest-ranking artillery officer on the Karelian front. He was soon made the commander of the Right Wing Group, whose focus was the Taipale sector. Later, this command morphed into Thirteenth Army, still headed by Grendahl.

Ten days before the end of the Winter War, Grendahl was removed from front-line command and demoted to the role of commander of artillery of the south-east front. This transfer may have resulted from his sudden diagnosis with lung cancer.

On 4 June 1940, Grendahl was made colonel-general. He finally lost his last battle against cancer on 16 November 1940, and was buried with full military honours.

Evacuees fleeing their homes. (SA-kuva)

A soldier taking up position on the
Karelian Isthmus prior to the arrival
of the war and the first snow, in
November 1939. (SA-kuva)

VILJO KAUPPILA
COLONEL, 10TH DIVISION

(1892–1973)

Viljo Antero Kauppila studied at the Kazan Military School in Russia from 1914 to 1915. When he heard of the Jäger movement, he immediately escaped back to Finland and from there to Germany. Kauppila saw combat first at Misse River and then at the Bay of Riga and the Aa River. During the Finnish Civil War, Kauppila served as a squad leader, and was lightly wounded at the battle of Viipuri.

After the Civil War, Kauppila worked his way up to command of a regiment (1933–38), and then to lead the entire Middle Finland Military District (1938–39). He had passed the Senior Military Academy Commanders' Course in 1928, with general staff officers' studies completed by 1932.

From the outset of the Winter War, Kauppila led the 10th Division at Taipale River. However, he was relieved from command at his own request on 21 December 1939. He was replaced temporarily by Colonel Aarne Blick, who held the post until 9 January. At that time, in order to deceive Soviet intelligence, the whole unit was renamed the 7th Division, with command passed to Colonel Einar Vihma.

After leaving the front line, Kauppila continued to serve as Director of the Reserve Officers School until his retirement in 1946. From 1946 to 1958 he worked as a bank branch manager in the town of Kuusankoski.

heavy losses, the Soviet troops were still so numerous that they managed to gain a small bridgehead. Over the next few days the Finns repelled several assaults, destroying many enemy formations. The Soviet 19th Rifle Regiment, for example, lost practically all of its senior officers and so many men that it had to be withdrawn from the front.

In the end, the Finnish counter-attacks and efforts to hold the Koukkuniemi Peninsula just forward of the main defensive lines around Taipale were not enough. Soviet forces took the area, thus securing a staging zone for further attacks towards Taipale and for the 39th Armoured Brigade, which was now on its way to the front.

Over the following days the bridgehead was slowly enlarged. The use of heavy artillery and tanks enabled the Soviets to capture southern parts of the defensive lines. Here the Finnish tactic of launching immediate counter-attacks to regain lost positions failed, and by 12 December Red Army forces were in a good position to launch an attack across the whole Taipale sector.

Evacuations on the Karelian Isthmus at the beginning of the war. As the Finnish soldiers went around encouraging and helping people to leave their houses, they came across a grumbling old peasant. He had previously refused to leave, but was now finally convinced that the war would reach his home before nightfall. When he did depart, the little cottage was put to the torch. Later the next morning, when the soldiers again passed by the area, they saw the same old man poking at the ashes of his dwelling with a long stick. When they asked why had he returned, with a grim smile he retorted: 'This farm was already burned down twice on the account of the damned Russians – once by my grandfather and once by my father. I don't reckon it will kill me to do it either, but I'll be damned if I could drive away without first making sure that you'd done a proper job of it.' (Trotter, 1991; photo SA-kuva)

Meanwhile, the area around the town of Kiviniemi, 30km to the west of Taipale, was defended by the 24th Infantry Regiment from Colonel Bertel Winell's 8th Division. Kiviniemi formed the second natural crossing point over the Taipale River. The retreating Finns had already completely destroyed the road bridge here and had also managed to partially demolish the railway bridge across the river.

The 24th Infantry Regiment had regrouped into the main defensive positions built just behind the Kiviniemi Rapids. Here the Soviets were, for the first time, to meet tenacious resistance from these men; so far the regiment had been under orders only to conduct a fighting retreat and not to risk its meagre forces in the open. The firestorm that met the advancing Red Army troops took them completely by surprise and the leading regiment attempting to cross the river was routed.

Soviet Seventh Army commander Yakovlev was now under pressure from his superiors to produce results. The Chief of the General Staff Boris Shaposhnikov reprimanded him for failing to keep Moscow informed of events on the ground, ending with the words: 'This is the last time I warn Commander Yakovlev about the purposeful negligence of his staff concerning the actions of his own troops' (Van Dyke, 1997).

Shaposhnikov's threat soon led to the fateful decision to try to rush the attack across the river. The pontoon battalions which had been delayed en route made it just in time for the scheduled start of the crossing. There was

ABOVE LEFT
Keeping the dugouts clear of snow gave the men plenty of exercise, helping them to keep warm. This might be done several times a day if there was heavy snowfall. (SA-kuva)

ABOVE RIGHT
Dugouts in the Terenttilä sector at Taipale. Rifleman Vesteri Lepistö recalled this period: 'Our squads had eight men. Soon the pressure from lack of sleep and rest was so overwhelming that the only thought was to get out, do our jobs, and get back in the dugouts as soon as possible. We were always short of ammunition; our hand grenades, which had been produced in seven different countries, were really dangerous. Every time you used them your life was at stake. Our most aggravating work was to get out there in forty below zero, and then work right in front of the enemy lines setting up barbed-wire barricades. We had to work without gloves and we dared not make any noise. Everything was done at night … we were always hungry. We could not even get water out of the snow because it has been contaminated by so many explosions and would cause painful stomach problems.' (SA-kuva)

LEFT
Headquarters of the 24th Infantry Regiment at Kiviniemi. The dense forests protected and hid the Finns from the superior Soviet air force. (SA-kuva)

RIGHT
The partially destroyed railway bridge at Kiviniemi. On 7 December, a small Soviet detachment managed to cross the Taipale River, scaling these ruins. Once they realised that they were stranded across the river, they first hid and then later surrendered. (SA-kuva)

no opportunity to perform any forward scouting whatsoever. Most of the supporting artillery at Seventh Army's disposal was still stuck in traffic well behind the front lines and only half of the required shells had so far arrived.

In the pitch-black night of 7 December, the Soviets launched their attack. The infantry crossing via the pontoons was supported by amphibious T-38 tanks and the little artillery that they had been able to deploy in time. As the troops reached the midway point of the crossing, the strong current started to drag them downstream away from their intended landing zones. At this moment, the Finns switched on their searchlights and opened fire from the opposite bank. Out of the nine pontoons spanning the river only four survived, while most of the troops manning these vessels had already been wounded or killed. The few Soviet tanks that had made it to the other side of the river failed to advance any further due the steep and stony riverbanks. The force of the water soon dragged them down into the rapids. Around 30 soldiers managed to cross the river using the remains of the railway bridge. When these men realised that they were now completely cut off from their comrades, they went to ground. They were all eventually captured by the Finns.

Despite this night time fiasco, Yakovlev reported to his superiors that he had managed to secure a bridgehead with two battalions. He ordered further attacks to start immediately, but his troops refused to attempt what they considered to be a suicidal crossing before the promised artillery had arrived. At this stage Yakovlev recommended to Meretskov that the main

At Kiviniemi, on 17 December 1939, two soldiers are shown bringing back captured Soviet rifles. Repatriated equipment and ammunition were of great importance for maintaining and building up Finland's arsenal during the war. Bicycles were used on the roads, but everywhere else the snow was so deep that only skis or sleighs worked. (SA-kuva)

focus should be moved back to the drive on Viipuri since the Finns in this sector were determined and well dug in.

On 8 December, before Meretskov could respond to Yakovlev's recommendation, all attacks across the whole Karelian Isthmus were temporarily halted by Stavka, the Soviet high command. The next day control of the war against Finland was taken over by Stavka.[4] Meretskov, who had originally been responsible for leading the whole operation against Finland, was immediately demoted to leadership of the Seventh Army only, while the incompetent Yakovlev was transferred to Moscow for administrative duties. Stavka planned to nearly double the forces at the disposal of Seventh Army prior to a new offensive, and reinforcements slowly began to arrive. Combat troops were to increase to over 250,000 men and another

BORIS SHAPOSHNIKOV
CHIEF OF THE GENERAL STAFF

(1882–1945)

Boris Mikhailovitch Shaposhnikov graduated from the Military Academy as a general staff officer in 1910. By October 1917, he had reached the rank of colonel and in December accepted his first divisional command.

From 1921 to 1925, Shaposhnikov was employed as the deputy chief of staff for the Red Army. Subsequently, he commanded first the Leningrad and then the Moscow military districts. Several senior postings followed, and in 1935 Shaposhnikov became a professor. He is best known for his work *Mozg Armii*, or 'The Brain of the Army'.

In 1937 Shaposhnikov became chief of the general staff for the Red Army. Following the Winter War, he was promoted to the rank marshal of the Soviet Union.

Shaposhnikov resigned from the post of chief of the general staff in April 1942 due to poor health, but continued to serve as People's Commissar for Defence until June 1943. Shaposhnikov's last position before his untimely death was as head of the Academy for General Staff. Shaposhnikov's body was interred in the Kremlin Wall.

4   Stavka was chaired by Voroshilov; other key members of the high command included Stalin and Shaposhnikov.

KLIMENT VOROSHILOV
COMMANDER-IN-CHIEF OF THE RED ARMY

(1881–1969)

Kliment Yefremovich Voroshilov was a founding member of the first Lugansk Bolshevik Committee in 1904. As a result of his involvement with the underground movement from 1908 to 1917, he was first imprisoned and then exiled. During the Russian Civil War, Voroshilov commanded the Tenth and Fourteenth armies, as well as the Ukrainian Front army. He was made a full member of the Politburo in 1926.

In November 1934, Voroshilov was appointed People's Commissar for Defence, in effect the commander-in-chief of the Red Army. He received the rank of marshal of the Soviet Union in 1935.

On 7 May 1940, due to the Red Army's failures during the Winter War, Voroshilov was replaced by Marshal Simon Timoshenko in the top military post. However, Stalin still had faith in his trusted comrade, and Voroshilov was given a role in Stavka just before the German onslaught began in June 1941. Voroshilov was soon made the commander of the North-Western Front. Despite personally leading an attack armed only with his service pistol, he could not prevent the Germans from surrounding Leningrad.

Post-war, Voroshilov served as Chairman of the Allied Control Commission in Vienna until 1947. This posting was followed by a pivotal political career in the highest echelons of the Soviet government. Voroshilov was buried in front of the Kremlin Wall.

300 artillery pieces were to be added. More tanks and air support were also made available.

Now that Stavka was in direct command, Voroshilov decided to follow Yakovlev's prior recommendation and move the focus back to the western part of the isthmus. This resulted in chaos as troops, artillery and armour tried to traverse the isthmus using just two small roads. This brief lull in the Soviet attacks gave the Finns time to fortify and regroup. Troop reserves were quickly moved into those sectors most in need. The success of the Finns in the Taipale sector prompted Mannerheim to muse: 'I did not think that my men were so good, or that the Russians could be so bad' (Citrine, 1940).

By 13 December the Soviet 150th Rifle Division had managed to establish a strong bridgehead on the Finnish side of the peninsula at the Taipale River. The freshly demoted Meretskov ordered a new offensive using the full

An M1910 Maxim-Sokolov machine gun with Winter War-era ski-mounts. (SA-kuva)

Messenger dogs and their handlers in the Summa sector during December 1939. (SA-kuva)

might of his Right Wing Group. In addition to the 30,000 men of the 49th and 150th Rifle divisions, he had at his disposal heavy artillery as well as the 69 regular and 30 flamethrower T-26 tanks from the 39th Armoured Brigade. On the western side of the isthmus Meretskov's Left Wing Group was to initiate a simultaneous attack towards Viipuri.

Unfortunately for the attackers, once again the Finnish positions had been expertly camouflaged, with machine-gun emplacements dug in to provide crossfire over the open fields. This meant that the Soviet artillery was largely firing blindly into a large wooded area in the hope of hitting something. Even after 3 hours of extensive preliminary bombardment, very little actual damage had been caused. The troops leading the assault would not have known this; to them it might have seemed impossible for anyone to have survived the firestorm their comrades had unleashed.

Then the Finns struck back at the advancing infantry and tanks with all their firepower. This quickly caused the two attacking elements to become separated. Eventually the tanks had to halt their advance and instead had to start driving back and forth in order to maintain contact with the ponderously advancing infantry. All this had to be done while under highly accurate fire from hidden anti-tank guns. After each shot the Finnish crews would drag their gun back and move from one prepared position to the next. This denied the Soviets a clear point for their spearhead to focus on. In the end, in most of the sectors the Red Army managed to advance only a few hundred metres, up to the Finnish anti-tank ditches.

A captured Soviet T-28 tank in the Summa sector. Soon this weapon would be sent to the rear to be repaired and added to the Finnish Army's growing arsenal. (SA-kuva)

Over the next few days Soviet forces relaunched their offensive several times. At each stage the Finns managed to repel these efforts, and by using effective localised counter-attacks they inflicted massive losses on the Red Army.

On 19 December, having lost most of their tanks and a great number of troops, the Right Wing Group was finally granted a small respite. By now the troops at the bridgehead were badly demoralised due to so many failed attacks. On Christmas Eve, these exhausted men attempted one more push against the Finnish lines; their only reward was to be repelled once more.

Meanwhile, the Soviet troops had fared a little better near the small neighbouring village of Kelja, lying on the shores of the wide and slow-moving Vuoksi River, roughly halfway between Kiviniemi and Taipale. Early on Christmas Day the Soviets began to cross the frozen Vuoksi in four places. The timing of the attack surprised the Finns, and they did not immediately react to the intelligence reports clearly stating that large Soviet formations were approaching. A limited counter-attack was launched, but this turned out to be very weak, as reports of the enemy forces were grossly underestimated. The poor coordination of Finnish forces meant that they did not manage to remove the foothold that Soviet troops had gained quickly enough. Once the situation became clear, more troops were committed and eventually only a small bridgehead at Kelja remained. Here the Finnish artillery was poorly positioned and was thus unable to offer proper support for any counter-attacks. However, it proved very capable of preventing the Red Army from reinforcing their positions. On 27 December, the newly arrived 6th Independent Battalion and the 3rd Battalion from the 29th Infantry Regiment led repeated attacks against the Soviets at Kelja. Their second push caused the enemy to retreat onto the ice, making them easy targets for the massed Finnish guns. By evening, the north side of the river was once again completely in Finnish hands. The Soviet high command was greatly disappointed that so much time (not to mention lives and equipment) had been wasted in this effort and that the main body of the army was not immediately brought over the lake in time to take advantage of the opportunity.

By the end of December it was clear that Grendahl's Right Wing Group had failed in all its efforts stretching from Kiviniemi to the shores of Lake Ladoga. For now these troops were ordered to dig in and to repel any possible Finnish counter-attacks.

THE WESTERN KARELIAN ISTHMUS

On the western side of the Karelian Isthmus the initial Soviet attempts at achieving a breakthrough had been beaten back by the 1st, 4th, 5th and 11th divisions of the Finnish II Army Corps. However, the Finns were woefully short on reinforcements. The southern end of the Mannerheim Line was held by Colonel Kaila's 4th Division. At Summa, the focus of the Soviet hammer blow was to fall on Colonel Selim E. Isakson's 5th Division. Just east of Isakson's men stood Laatikainen's 1st Division and further towards Lake Muolaanjärvi was Colonel Koskimies' 11th Division.

Finnish tank destroyer tactics involved a soldier digging a small man-sized hole and waiting for his prey to roll over the top. Sitting tight hugging several kilos of satchel charge was a true test of a person's *sisu* (grit). Despite a near 70 per cent mortality rate among such troops, there was no end of volunteers to carry out these missions. This photo was taken in the Summa sector on 14 December 1939. (SA-kuva)

On 5 December, II Army Corps' headquarters gave out the following orders:

> When this first decisive battle draws near, each division commander must make it clear to all their subordinates, all the way down to individual rank and file, that we are to engage in defensive battle to halt the enemy. The enemy assault must break against our determined resistance. Therefore, there is no other choice but to stand our ground and to fight to the very last man even if the enemy manages to reach our dug outs. In addition, if the enemy tanks at times manage to break through our lines, our troops must hold their ground and calmly destroy the infantry following in the wake of their armour.

A key initial Soviet objective was to break through the 12km section of front between Summa village and Lake Muolaanjärvi. Where the attacks failed to achieve this, the Soviets left the 24th Rifle Division in place as the vanguard of the 19th Rifle Corps, on the shores of the lake. Its attacks would continue until the end of December, resulting in the loss of more tanks and even more men; the Finns would keep hold of their positions.

On the 24th Rifle Division's left flank, the 90th Rifle Division finally arrived in place. It was to begin a two-pronged attack on 17 December. To the west, the Soviet 50th Rifle Corps was to perform a simultaneous assault using two divisions of its own to overcome the fortified positions at Summa.

As the 90th Rifle Division's attack finally got underway on the 17th, the temperature was just below freezing and the deep snow banks prevented the division's T-26 tanks from moving forward. After a relatively brief preliminary bombardment, the Soviet artillery was ordered to provide direct-fire support. The 1st and 2nd battalions of the 588th Rifle Regiment moved

During the Winter War the Finns found that most of their anti-tank obstacles to be woefully inadequate. A skilled driver could drive straight over the granite boulders, as is clearly shown in this demonstration using a captured T-34 during the Continuation War. Following such studies Finnish defensive fortifications were modified to have a more pronounce effect on enemy armour. (SA-kuva)

The following bizarre incident occurred in the Summa sector during the coldest days of February 1940. Through the smoke caused by heavy Soviet shelling, a Finnish officer on duty saw a man staggering towards him from no-man's land. Recognising the remnants of white camouflage on top of a thick sheep-wool coat, he ordered his men not to shoot. Just when he was about to reach the Finnish lines a burst of Soviet bullets hit the man in the back. Finnish soldiers dragged the corpse to the rear, and the dead soldier was taken to the makeshift morgue-tent, where corpses were stored until medics could organise their shipment away from the front line. Upon inspection, the Finns saw six bloodless holes in the dead man's chest. Later during the night, the clerk on duty heard a croaky voice saying, 'Hey, give me a cigarette.' The dumbfounded clerk gave him a cigarette, and the talking corpse told the astonished onlookers: 'Looks like my legs are working fine.' It turned out that the soldier had been stunned by a grenade, and left to lie in the snow. The fierce cold had prevented him from bleeding to death. As he made his way back to the Finnish dugouts, his thick sheep's wool coat had saved him from further harm. (SA-kuva)

towards the Finnish barbed-wire defences. Each time they tried to reach the Finnish positions, more officers and men fell. The attacks continued, with an equal lack of success, the following day. By this point the 1st Battalion alone had lost 375 men.

The second spearhead of the 90th Rifle Division's attack towards a nearby hill, carried out by the 173rd Rifle Regiment, also failed. Of the six Soviet tanks involved in the assault, four were destroyed before they reached Finnish lines, and the two that did manage to cross the trenches were later blown up behind them. The regiment lost practically all of its company commanders as well as some of its senior officers.

To the left of the 173rd, the 286th Rifle Regiment fared no better. In its sector, the bog-like terrain prevented the use of horses and tractors, so troops had to drag the heavy artillery pieces into emplacements themselves. Some of these men positioned themselves too close to the Finnish lines and were subsequently wiped out.

By 20 December, the 173rd Regiment was withdrawn from the lines while the 286th Regiment continued to haemorrhage casualties. By 22 December, only around 500 effective men were left of the leading battalion of the 588th Regiment. Despite these incredible losses they were ordered to execute yet another push. The supporting artillery and the T-26 tanks managed to destroy a Finnish machine-gun emplacement and scored five hits against another bunker. Regardless of this small success, the Finnish fire grid was still functioning well and the battalion had to dig in to positions in front of the defensive lines at the Mustaoja stream. The demoralised and decimated troops now refused to carry out another assault.

During the defensive battles, Mannerheim had given permission for a counter-attack proposed by General Österman, commander of the Army of the Isthmus. The purpose of the counter-attack was to surround and destroy the opposing forces near Summa village. To achieve this, Lieutenant-General Öhquist's II Army Corps was reinforced with the 6th Independent Division, which had so far been left as a reserve under direct command of the Finnish headquarters. On the morning of 23 December the Finns attacked without any preparatory bombardment. A total of five divisions lent troops for the operation but due to poor communication and the tight assembly schedule, not all the forces joined the attack from the start. By mid-afternoon the failed attack had been recalled. Finnish losses had already risen to 360 dead, over 777 wounded and more than 191 men missing. This badly coordinated and poorly communicated attack was aptly named the 'Idiot's Nudge' by the troops.

However, the attack had caught the Soviets off guard. Stavka originally dismissed it as atypical Finnish reconnaissance in force. It then proceeded to criticise the actions of the 90th Rifle Division: the latter had only managed to grind forward at a rate of few hundred metres a day, and then during the course of a single afternoon it had given up over 3km of front.

The 90th Rifle Division tried to act more cohesively, and made three more assaults against the Finnish lines. However, poor coordination between artillery, armour and infantry led to failure on each occasion. The division all but lost its ability to fight as a result; its three leading Rifle Regiments had suffered 484 dead, 1,938 wounded and 249 missing in action, in addition to 925 men suffering from severe frostbite. On 30 December the unit received reinforcements; however, it turned out that many of the new arrivals entirely lacked military training. Going forward sector saw less fighting as the 90th Rifle Division attempted to integrate these new troops into its cadre.

Meanwhile in the Summa sector, between 14 and 16 December the Soviets engaged in aggressive reconnaissance trying to gain more accurate knowledge of the Finnish lines and making small inroads into the barbed-wire defences. On 17 December a major push began with a preliminary bombardment, shelling both the front lines (manned by the Finnish 13th and 15th regiments) and rear areas. However, around only one-third of the available Soviet artillery pieces were in place and operational for this bombardment.

(1893–1941)

FILIP ALJABUSHEV
BRIGADE COMMANDER, 1ST ARMY CORPS

Filip Fjodorovitsh Aljabushev joined the Red Army as an infantryman in May 1919. The following year he had already completed leadership training. Several company and senior divisional commands followed. Between 1938 and 1939 Aljabushev was in charge of the 24th Rifle Division.

During the Winter War, Aljabushev was given command of the 123rd Rifle Division on the Viipuri front. This post was to last until 25 February 1940, when upon receiving the coveted Order of Lenin Aljabushev was transferred to another front.

During the Great Patriotic War, Aljabushev, now a major-general, led the 87th Rifle Division on the Ukrainian South-Western Front. He was killed only three days after the start of Operation *Barbarossa*, personally leading a bayonet charge against the encircling German forces.

At Munasuo the 255th Rifle Regiment, accompanied by strong tank formations, spearheaded the 123rd Rifle Division's assault. Many of the tanks passed through the stone anti-tank defences and drove deep into the rear of the surprised Finns; although the Soviets managed to penetrate around 500m into the lines, they failed to destroy any of the bunkers and emplacements. The Finns fought back from the protection of the Poppius and Miljoonalinnake bunkers. By nightfall a breakdown in communication and the heavy losses suffered by the 255th Rifle Regiment caused the attack to be halted. The Finns now had a chance to regroup, and prepared for their counter-attack. When the Soviet infantry failed to arrive to defend the armoured forces behind the Finnish lines, the Finns managed to destroy 23 out of the 35 tanks that had crossed the lines earlier that day. Despite these successes, the Soviets still managed to keep hold of parts of the Finnish lines and had the Poppius bunker surrounded.

On 18 December the remaining troops of the 123rd Rifle Division recommenced their attack supported by 68 tanks. However, Finnish artillery quickly exploited the poor deployment of the tanks in their staging area, leaving 12 tanks destroyed 1.6km south of the Finnish defensive lines. Conversely, the Soviet artillery spent most of the day waiting for munitions and only at nightfall were its batteries able to begin their own fire missions.

The 138th Rifle Division's attack towards Summa village was slightly more successful. The 768th Rifle Regiment managed to clear a path through the anti-tank obstacles, but their advance was halted by combined fire from four artillery batteries. The 650th Rifle Regiment achieved a notable success by reaching the anti-tank ditch near the centre of the village.

The high point of the Soviet offensive so far came on 19 December. After several hours of fierce preliminary bombardment, the attack started across the whole front. Despite the devastating crossfire dished out by Finnish artillery and the interlacing machine-gun emplacements and bunkers, some elements of Brigade Commander Philip Aljabushev's 123rd Rifle Division made good progress. By evening the neighbouring 138th Rifle Division to

The Finnish trenches at Summa. Contemporary reports suggested that the Soviets were driving Polish prisoners of war, dressed in Red Army uniforms, at gunpoint in front of the main body of their troops. The Poles were allegedly being used to detonate mines in the path of advance. *(Naiskohtaloita sotakuvien takana)*

their left had also done well, reaching the forests around Lake Summajärvi.

The supporting 20th Armoured Brigade spent the day exchanging fire with the Mannerheim Line bunkers. Eight of the Soviet tanks made it through to the forests at Summa. The Finns retaliated with a counter-attack, retaking some sections of their defensive lines. They were denied complete success by the Soviet tanks enfilading them at close range along the length of the trenches. Meanwhile, the 10th Tank Corps was kept further back in reserve in order to exploit any breach made by the infantry. Finnish artillery managed to immobilise 13 of their tanks in corps' staging area.

The following day, 20 December, the final Soviet attempts to take the Summa sector ended in a Finnish defensive victory. Meretskov telegrammed Stavka to state that he was planning on temporarily halting the assault. It had become clear that the only way to breach the Finnish lines was through destroying the fortifications and bunkers one at a time. This would take much longer to achieve and required greater preparation. Nevertheless, new plans for an attack against the city of Viipuri were already being drawn up.

Meanwhile, the Finns launched counter-attacks to try to regain the lost stretch of main defensive line at Munasuo, to the east of Lake Summa. Many of the Finnish defenders had retreated into the Poppius bunker and faced a dire situation, with Soviet troops controlling sections of trench on two sides of them.

Damage caused by artillery shells whilst trying to hit the firing slits of a Finnish bunker in the Summa sector, in an image taken after the war. One Finnish lieutenant recalled such fortifications: 'Black concrete bunkers stood in sparse forests without any communication cables or trenches. They were an intolerable place to be in combat, one had to always be ready to bail out immediately. Despite their high cost, they were hopeless rat holes and I am wondering why the enemy did not fry them all. If these bunkers were equipped with anti-tank weapons, one could defend oneself against tanks. In reality, all we could do was sit inside the bunker and wait for a tank to drive up and do what he pleased.' (SA-kuva)

On 22 December, following five days of fighting at Munasuo, the Soviet 255th Rifle Regiment was finally forced to retreat from the Finnish lines. Its troops had fought hard when repelling the Finnish attacks with their machine guns; only a lack of grenades had prevented the Finns from succeeding earlier. When finally pushed back, the 255th lost almost all its ability to fight. An estimated 300 Soviet soldiers died in the fighting around the Poppius bunker and another 35 were taken prisoner; Finnish fatalities were high at 90, but they had succeeded in regaining their main defensive line.

On 23 December, a Finnish counter-attack towards the Soviet lines at Munasuo was forced to retreat under heavy fire. This action, however, revealed that the Soviets had audaciously positioned their rear-guard troops at a depth of only 10m from the Finnish lines.

Throughout the rest of December, Finnish troops managed to thwart all

Members of the 'Company of Death' (4th Light Detachment) at Summa on 20 December 1940. At front right is Randall Nybom. He was wounded twice during the Winter War and later became one of the founding members of the Mannerheim Heritage Society. (SA-kuva)

of the Red Army's efforts to eliminate the Poppius bunker, refusing to grant the Soviet infantry any further footholds in their lines in this sector. By this stage, the lack of Soviet military success across the whole Karelian Isthmus had demonstrated to the members of Stavka that the lightning war they had envisioned would never be. It would take much longer to tame the unruly Finns, and neither side could predict with any degree of confidence what the New Year might bring. In an effort to make certain that 1940 would go their way, the Red Army was to adopt a defensive posture while a month-long process of reinforcement and attack preparation took place.

Semyonov, the Brigade Commissar of the 50th Rifle Corps, informed Voroshilov in his April debrief: 'It has been said here that we studied Finland insufficiently in peacetime, we did not study it properly. In our war games, it was very simple. We reached Viipuri in a jiffy, with a break for lunch' (Kulkov, Rzheshevskii and Shukman, 2002).

CHAPTER 4
LADOGA KARELIA, DECEMBER 1939

At the time war broke out, the region of Ladoga Karelia, comprising the lands to the north of Lake Ladoga, was defended by Major-General Juho H. Heiskanen's IV Army Corps. The core of this force was the 12th and 13th infantry divisions. Their orders were to use the natural obstacles of lakes and rivers as main anchor points for their line of defence, there was neither the time nor the resource available to prepare fortified positions.

The Finnish forces in Karelia faced the Soviet Eighth Army, under the command of Ivan Khabarov. Along this 350km-long front Khabarov spread out his 1st and 56th Rifle corps. The two corps totalled six infantry divisions altogether, consisting of 75,000 men, over 150 tanks and 500 artillery pieces. More than 100 planes provided air cover, all but overwhelming the sole Finnish fighter squadron available for the defence.

An image taken at Suojärvi at the beginning of December 1939. Private Juha Aho, facing the camera, was part of the 6th Company of the 34th Infantry Regiment attempting to stop the overwhelming enemy forces in this direction. (SA-kuva)

Front-line troops resting at the Kollaa River in December 1939. According to the Finns, the best thing about the daily propaganda speeches the Soviets broadcast along the front was that during these the shelling always stopped. It was without doubt the safest time to change the guard or to attend to ablutions. (SA-kuva)

ROMAN PANIN
BRIGADE COMMANDER, 1ST RIFLE CORPS

Panin began his military career as an ensign in the Imperial army. In 1921 he took part in quelling the Kronstadt Rebellion as a company commander.

By the onset of the Winter War, Panin had risen through the ranks to command the 1st Rifle Corps. On 13 December, Panin was

(1897–1949)

demoted and after Brigade Commander Stepanov was wounded at Äglägärvi, he was transferred to lead the 75th Rifle Division. Despite his disgrace and the force's poor performance, Panin was promoted to the rank of major-general on 4 June 1940.

In June 1941, Panin was handed command of the 42nd Rifle Corps. In September that year, when Lieutenant-General Frolov was promoted to lead the Karelian Front army group, Panin inherited Frolov's old post at the head of Fourteenth Army.

Panin was relieved from front-line command due to health reasons in 1942. In June 1943, however, he did return to command the 7th Rifle Corps, and a year later completed two short tours as acting commander for the 123rd Rifle Corps and 90th Rifle Corps. Towards the end of the war, Panin took over the duties of the acting commander for the Fifth Army of the Belarus Front group. Post-war, Panin received a post in the Soviet Military Academy. He died in service in 1949.

Eighth Army's operational goal was to advance eastwards into Finland and occupy a 90km front between the towns of Joensuu and Sortavala. The expected timescale to accomplish this was within ten days, after which its forces were to swing south around Lake Ladoga and attack the rear of the Finnish defences on the Karelian Isthmus.

Soviet Division Commander Ivan N. Tsherepanov led 56th Rifle Corps, comprising three front-line divisions. The 18th and 168th Rifle divisions were to conduct a three-pronged attack between lakes Ladoga and Jänis; the 56th Rifle Division was to attack directly east towards the Loimola crossroads. The 75th Rifle Division was held back as the corps reserve.

Further to the north, the 1st Rifle Corps, under Brigade Commander Roman I. Panin, would attack towards the villages of Ilomantsi and Korpiselkä with its two divisions.

SUOJÄRVI AND THE KOLLAA RIVER

The Soviets attacked north of Lake Ladoga both quickly and decisively. The strong attack by Panin's 1st Rifle Corps forced Lieutenant-Colonel Veikko Räsänen's 4,000-strong Task Force Räsänen to withdraw from the border. The village of Suojärvi – a strategically important road and rail crossing – fell to the Soviets already by 2 December.

The following day the Finnish 12th Division, led by Colonel Lauri Tiainen, made an unsuccessful attempt to retake Suojärvi. This counter-attack went so badly that some of the troops panicked and fled past their assembly area, abandoning the planned defensive positions. Erkki Palolampi was an eyewitness to the incident:

> **LAURI TIAINEN**
> **COLONEL, 12TH DIVISION**
>
> **(1890–1958)**
>
> Lauri Taavetti Tiainen volunteered as a Jäger and attended the 1915 *Pfadfinder* course. During the Finnish Civil War, he organised several arms shipments and set up new units and training for the White Guard. Towards the end of the conflict, Tiainen led the vanguard for the capture of Oulu city. At the battle of Tampere, he commanded two separate battalions.
>
> In 1933, Tiainen was made commander of the Karelian Military District. At the start of the Winter War, he took over the 12th Division on the Kollaa front. On 31 January 1940, he was compelled to resign this post due to a heart condition. Tiainen continued to work at the headquarters of the Defence Corps until his resignation in 1945.

Tanks rattled onwards on the roads and also tried entering into the forest … Firing is intense and then somebody starts to shout that the tanks are now attacking from behind: 'They have breached through!' The man's eyes are round with fear, another man sees his terror and the shout spreads from soldier to soldier. Nothing can stop it now: 'Tanks are coming, tanks have breached through…' Men start to run without hearing the commands and curses of their officers. Panic spreads … fear grips more and more of the companies … everybody has only one thought, to escape the terrible tanks. A young man tries to jump into a passing sleigh shouting: 'Now the men of Finland are no match for the Russkies, tanks have broken through and troops are routed. Tanks will kill us all!' … Even two or three days later, there were still scared men wandering around the Loimola area looking for their companies. (Palolampi, 1940)

Mannerheim held Major-General Juho Heiskanen accountable for the loss of the Suojärvi area, and had him replaced as the IV Army Corps commander on 4 December by Major-General Hägglund. Over the next few days, having abandoned their prepared positions, many Finnish soldiers fled all the way back to the Kollaa River and dug in. This new defensive feature would

AARNE JUUTILAINEN
CAPTAIN, 6TH COMPANY OF
THE 34TH REGIMENT

(1904–76)

Aarne Edward Juutilainen attended the Reserve Officer School in 1925 and continued his education at the Cadet School during 1926 and 1927. His lifestyle was considered unbefitting to an officer, and he left the army in 1928.

In June 1930, Juutilainen joined the French Foreign Legion, in which he served for the next five years. A bold and distinctive Legion veteran, known as the 'Terror of Morocco', Juutilainen led the 6th Company of the 34th Infantry Regiment during the Winter War. Finland's most famous sniper, Simo Häyhä, fought in Juutilainen's unit and was based in his command tent in Kollaanjoki.

Teittinen, his regimental commander, held Juutilainen in high regard. He especially valued Juutilainen's cold-headedness and the way he inspired courage with his example and fighting spirit.

In the Continuation War, Juutilainen ended up serving as the commander of the 31st Prisoner of War Company from May 1944 onwards. According to 7th Division's records, his transfer resulted from 'continuous drunkenness and the battery of a subordinate in April 1944'. During the summer of 1944, Juutilainen once again served as a company commander on the direction of Loimola.

Juutilainen's battalion, from which the reservists had already been discharged, followed the retreating Germans to Kaaresuvanto and Lätäseno in the Lapland War. There, Juutilainen received word that he would have to formally request to resign from the army.

Aarne Juutilainen was the brother of the double Mannerheim Cross recipient, fighter ace Ilmari Juutilainen.

have appeared less than imposing to the Soviet troops; the meandering Kollaa was barely 2m wide in places. Assessing the predicament of his new command, General Hägglund posed the question: 'Will Kollaa hold?' The resounding reply came from Lieutenant Aarne Juutilainen: 'Kollaa will hold, unless we are told to run!'[5]

On 5 December, Mannerheim attempted to relieve the pressure on this sector by creating a new corps-sized force called Group Talvela, under the command of Colonel Paavo Talvela. Mannerheim ordered Group Talvela to recapture Suojärvi. This would relieve pressure on the Finnish 12th Division, diverting Soviet attention and helping the men at Kollaa to regain their fighting spirit.

Given that the Soviet attack towards Kollaa was of secondary significance compared to the main push in the south towards Kitilä village on the shores of Lake Ladoga, the Finnish 12th Division took a calculated risk by only defending the main approaches to the Kollaa River and leaving the vast areas of difficult terrain to the south largely unguarded. As the situation became more serious for the defenders, further troops had to be assigned to block the Soviet advances in the area. The Finnish contingency plan was that, in case the positions at the Kollaa River could not be held, the troops were to withdraw to prepared defences at Loimola village. If this key crossroads were lost, there would be no stopping the Red Army.

The Finnish 34th Infantry Regiment, under the command of Lieutenant-Colonel Wilhelm Teittinen, had fought at Suojärvi, but once the village had been lost to the Soviets, its troops were sent to rest at the rear. Colonel Tiainen

5 Map on p.219

decided to let Teittinen's regiment redeem 12th Division's honour by preparing to receive the spearhead of the Soviet attack at Kollaa. Teittinen was to arrange his men into defensive positions along the river, securing the train tracks and the road running in a westerly direction. Teittinen's command was further strengthened by an armoured train and one battery from the 12th Field Artillery Regiment.

From 8 December onwards, the Soviet infantry and armour attempted breakthroughs daily along both the road and the railway line. The Finns were faced with a difficult task of balancing their meagre resources between halting these attacks and forming reserves against the enemy's limited attempts at encirclement. Despite the shortage of men, the Finnish lines continued to hold while Soviet losses mounted, particularly in numbers of tanks, which suffered at the hands of accurate Finnish artillery fire.

(1893–1963)

WOLDEMAR HÄGGLUND
MAJOR-GENERAL, IV ARMY CORPS

Johan Woldemar Hägglund started his military career as a Jäger on the German *Pfadfinder* course of March 1915. After the Finnish Civil War, he served first as the commander of the Helsinki Civil Guard District, and then in the role of an operational commander of the general staff. From 1931 to 1932, Hägglund furthered his education at the Swedish Military Academy. In August 1934, he was given command of the peacetime 2nd Division.

During the Extraordinary Autumn Manoeuvres of 1939, Hägglund did not immediately receive a front-line command. The situation was rectified when he took over IV Army Corps, the leadership of which he was to hold for the rest of the Winter War.

When Finland remobilised in 1941, Hägglund led the newly formed VII Army Corps until its disbandment in June 1943. Following this, he continued to report directly to Mannerheim as inspector general. In the autumn of 1944, Hägglund was appointed chairman of the Fortifications Committee.

After the hostilities with the USSR ended, Hägglund transferred to become Chief of the Military Camp Research Centre. He resigned from this position in January 1945.

Sortovala station on 1 January 1940. The Finnish Army had two armoured trains during the Winter War. The 1st Armoured Train served in the Kollaa sector. Both trains featured a mix of artillery and machine-gun carriages. (SA-kuva)

A Soviet T-26 tank advances on 12 December 1939, firing rapidly, near the Kollaa River. (SA-kuva)

 GREGORY SHTERN
ARMY COMMANDER
2ND CLASS, EIGHTH ARMY

Despite his Jewish background, Shtern managed to hold several senior positions in the Soviet army. Shtern's early posts included commissariats at division and army corps level. He graduated from the Military Academy in 1929 and in 1934 he became People's Commissar for Defence. He also took part in the Spanish Civil War between 1937 and 1938 as a military advisor. Shtern was made a Hero of the Soviet Union in 1939, and on 13 December Stavka made him the commander of the Eighth Army. After the Winter War he was promoted to the rank of colonel-general.

(1900–41)

From 22 June 1940, Shtern served as the commander of the Far Eastern Front. After this posting, he was appointed the head of Anti-Aircraft Command. Shtern was unexpectedly arrested on 8 June 1941. During his imprisonment, he seems to have been tortured, and confessed to being a German spy. He also confessed to several other traitorous actions. Shtern was executed on 28 October 1941.

Shtern was posthumously rehabilitated in 1954; an investigation found that he and many others had been falsely accused in 1941.

On 12 December, two Soviet rifle battalions were observed disengaging from the battle and skiing westwards around Lake Koivu. The Finns surmised, correctly, that that was an attempt to encircle their positions from the south. Immediately, two infantry companies were sent to intercept the Soviets. During the following day, these companies made contact with the tails of the two Soviet columns and engaged them in light skirmishing. The Soviet columns were forced to withdraw from the southern flank of the Finnish defences a few days later.

On 14 December, the morale of Teittinen's 34th Infantry Regiment received a major boost when one of its companies managed to launch a successful counter-attack across the Kollaa River. They proceeded to destroy five enemy tanks and capture

Defenders armed with a light Lahti-Saloranta M/26 machine gun on the Kollaa front line in December 1939. (SA-kuva)

valuable equipment, including two anti-tank guns and three machine guns. That same day, Army Commander 2nd Class Gregory M. Shtern took over command of the Soviet Eighth Army from Khabarov.

Later that day, reports came in that Soviet forces were attempting another encirclement, this time to the north. Once again, troops were stripped from the Finnish front-line positions, and sent to counter this threat. By 17 December the assault had been halted, and the Soviet forces had begun to retreat. The pressure now began to ease on the Kollaa front. At noon on 18 December, Stavka gave orders for Eighth Army to cease all offensive actions and move to the defensive.

The Finns launched a counter-offensive on 20 December, as temperatures plummeted to -25°C. Elements from the Finnish battalions were sent to encircle the Soviet positions. After an aborted first attempt to take the railway line at Näätäoja, three days later 12th Division commander Tiainen ordered the attack to be reattempted. This time the tired men managed to capture the

(1893–1940)

WILHELM TEITTINEN
LIEUTENANT-COLONEL, 34TH REGIMENT

'War-Ville' Teittinen was involved with the Civil Guard and fought in the Finnish Civil War with the White forces. During one battle he lost most of the hearing in his left ear when a grenade detonated nearby.

In the Winter War, Teittinen served as the commander of 34th Infantry Regiment on the Kollaa front. Strained by battle, Teittinen fell ill in February 1940; he died in the 19th War Hospital in Sortavala soon after the end of the war. Teittinen is buried in Hietaniemi Cemetery in Helsinki.

SIMO HÄYHÄ
THE WHITE DEATH

(1905–2002)

Corporal Simo 'Simuna' Häyhä, who served with the 6th Company, 34th Infantry Regiment, can lay claim to being the most lethal sniper ever to have lived.

Häyhä was the second youngest child of eight. Born on 17 December 1905 in the village of Kiiskisenkylä, he attended grammar school and helped run the family farm. His hobbies included skiing, shooting and hunting as well as Pesäpallo, the Finnish form of baseball.

At the age of 17, Häyhä joined the Civil Guard. He was already an expert marksman, winning competitions by hitting a small target at 150m range six times within one minute. From 1925 to 1927, he completed his national service in a bicycle battalion. Häyhä gained the rank of corporal upon completion of an NCO training course. In 1927, he underwent specialist sniper training.

On the Kollaa front, he applied his craft using his old Civil Guard service rifle that he had brought with him to war. Although Häyhä did not keep track of his own achievements, his comrades did. Early in December, he managed to kill 51 enemy soldiers in just three days. Initially, even his closest superiors did not believe these numbers.

As this relentless kill rate continued, Lieutenant-Colonel Teittinen ordered an official observer to follow him. When Häyhä was close to his 200th kill and had just returned from dispatching a particularly troublesome enemy sniper, his promotion to the rank of junior sergeant was suggested.

The troops nicknamed Häyhä 'the White Death'. As news of his deeds spread beyond Finland, a Swedish businessman, Eugen Johansson, gave a special rifle to him as a gift.

Häyhä preferred to use only the basic rifle sights as they would neither frost over, nor reflect sunlight like optic scopes would do. It also allowed him to lie flatter, thus offering a smaller target.

On 6 March 1940, while adopting a high-knee shooting position, Häyhä was shot in the face with an explosive bullet. The round that entered the top of his lip and pierced his left cheek was prohibited by international convention. Although the newspapers proclaimed 'Simo is dead!', Häyhä managed to recover, with the help of ten operations. He was prohibited from returning to front-line service and instead served his country by procuring horses for the military.

In an interview with *Helsingin Sanomat* magazine in 2001, Häyhä was asked how he felt about his role during the war: 'I did what I was told to do, as well as I could. There would be no Finland if others would not have acted likewise.'

Häyhä's tally of 542 confirmed kills had been achieved in a space of just 100 days. After the war, he returned to a life of farming and hunting. Häyhä passed away on 1 April 2002.

railway line but were unsuccessful in severing the parallel road; eventually, the Finns were forced back to their starting positions.

Following these forays by the Finns, the Soviet infantry counter-attacked with tank support over the Christmas period. This push also failed, and the Finns took the opportunity to expand and strengthen their defensive positions along the Kollaa River.

Brigade Commander M. S. Yevstigneyev's 56th Rifle Division had been the strongest Soviet formation in the sector, fielding a total 15,876 men and over 100 tanks. By the end of the year, it had suffered 678 killed, 2,086 wounded and 58 missing in action. In addition to these losses, 1,417 men were incapacitated by frostbite. On 23 December, the commander of the 1st Rifle Corps, Roman Panin, was replaced by Division Commander Dmitry T. Kozlov.

ABOVE LEFT
Soviet dum-dum rounds. This expanding bullet ammunition was forbidden by international conventions. Even a relatively poor hit by such a bullet could cause horrendous damage. Simo Häyhä, the legendary sniper, was hit in his cheek by one of these rounds. He survived but never served in the front line again. (SA-kuva)

ABOVE RIGHT
Simo Häyhä giving a guided tour of his old sector during a visit to the Winter War battlegrounds near the Kollaa River in 1942. (SA-kuva)

North-east of Lake Ladoga, Colonel Svensson presents Simo Häyhä with a sniper rifle and certificate donated by a Swedish businessman, Eugen Johansson, on 20 February 1940. This gift created a great opportunity for the whole regiment to celebrate Häyhä's achievement and thus boost the morale of the men. (SA-kuva)

SOUTHERN LADOGA KARELIA: KITILÄ

The main attack by Soviet Division Commander Ivan N. Tsherepanov's 56th Rifle Corps was to hit the Finnish lines just north of Lake Ladoga. The 168th Rifle Division, led by Colonel Andrew Bondarev, was to advance north along the coastal railway, while Brigade Commander George Kondrashev's 18th Rifle Division followed the road west towards Lemetti. The combined strength of these two divisions was 29,521 men, 119 artillery pieces and 46 tanks. These forces were further strengthened by the corps-level artillery and armoured assets.

The Finnish line in this sector was defended by Colonel Hannu Hannuksela's 13th Division. His first task was to delay the Soviet advance as long as possible. Having witnessed the divisions' defensive positions being overrun at Käsnäselkä junction, he gave the order to retreat, via the village of Uomaa, to the prepared defences at Kitilä.

Sergei Ivanovich Kovalev, the Divisional Chief of Operations for the 18th Rifle Division, summarised the events for the 208th Rifle Regiment, around Uomaa on 5 December:

> The 208th Rifle Regiment encountered strong fortified positions. In front of Uomaa they were faced with barbed-wire obstacles, behind these was a minefield, and on the edge of the village there were dugouts for forward observers. Brigade Commander Kondrashev gave orders for a series of direct attacks, but they all failed. Two of our tanks hit mines and were destroyed. Machine-gun fire mauled the soldiers, who once or twice dared to rise up for an attack. At noon we dragged over our heavy howitzers; they struck the machine-gun dugouts with direct fire. By the evening we had nearly surrounded the village. The Finns started to burn down the houses and then headed into the woods. (Gordijenko, 2002)

(1893–1942)

HANNU HANNUKSELA
COLONEL, 13TH DIVISION

Like so many of his contemporary high-ranking Finnish officers, Hannu Esa Hannuksela was an ex-Jäger. During and after the Civil War, Hannuksela served in the artillery. In 1934 he became commander of the Savo Military District, a position which he held until the start of the Winter War. At that time, Hannuksela was appointed to command the 13th Division on the Ladoga Karelia front.

During the short Interim Peace, Hannuksela served as an inspector of artillery, and commander of the Southern Pohjanmaa Military District.

At the beginning of the Continuation War, Hannuksela led the 19th Division, again on the Ladoga Karelia front. He was promoted major-general on New Year's Eve 1941, and soon took command of the 2nd Division. Hannuksela died of a heart attack at his headquarters in May 1942.

The Soviet divisions capitalised on Hannuksela's retreat by pushing ahead so rapidly that they had already reached Kitilä by 11 December. Here Hannuksela dug in with the five battalions under his command, finally halting the Soviet advance on a line from Kitilä to Lake Syskyjärvi. The coastal defence troops stationed on the islands of Valamo and Salmi village

A messenger relaying commands. During the Winter War, radio equipment was often unreliable or of limited availability. The most effective way of sending a message to the front was to make a dash for it. (SA-kuva)

A shortened 76mm Soviet cannon, manufactured in 1913, in its firing position. Many of the Finnish artillery pieces were obsolete at the start of the Winter War. The desperate need for guns and howitzers, combined with the severe lack of ammunition, forced the Finns to utilise all available weapon. Captured Soviet equipment boosted the Finnish armoury considerably. (SA-kuva)

sector in Lake Ladoga helped to hold back a Soviet breakthrough, and sniped at the enemy's rear.

At Kitilä, both the attacking Soviet divisions converged. Bondarev's 168th Rifle Division was ordered to turn due west continuing its offensive against Kitilä village, whilst Kondrashev's 18th Rifle Division split its attack in two. The 208th Rifle Regiment veered north towards Lake Syskyjärvi, while the 316th Rifle Regiment made for Lake Ruokojärvi. On 12 December, after a brief fight, these troops occupied Ruhtinaanmäki hill and hamlet. By noon the following day, the Soviets had also secured the area around Lake Syskyjärvi to the north. This would mark the furthest advance for Kondrashev's 18th Rifle Division.

A wounded Soviet soldier later recalled the capture of Ylä-Uuksu village as the division advanced towards Pitkäranta:

Our mission was to capture the church. I used my binoculars and could not believe what I saw. A soldier and a girl pushing a heavy machine gun up the hill. The girl was clad completely in black, maybe she was

Finnish 13th Division's first counterattack, 12–14 December 1939

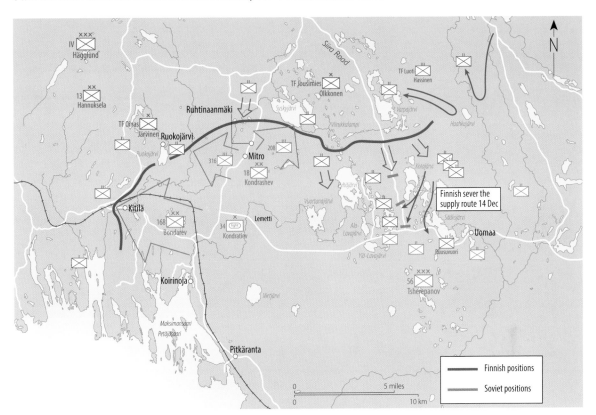

a nun or something, tall and strong nevertheless. We started shooting at the pair. Our bullets did not hit them. They pushed the heavy machine gun into the church and then manhandled it into the tower. The Finns also have Maxims [machine guns]. Then they began to dish out such a beating, that God spare us! One could not even lift one's head up. If you did, you got [a bullet] immediately. There was nothing for it, we had to swallow our pride and ask for the artillery's help ... Their third round felled the Finns. Naturally the church tower went with them. (Gordijenko, 2002)

(1896–1967)

 DMITRY KOZLOV
DIVISION COMMANDER,
1ST ARMY CORPS

Dimitry Timofeyevich Kozlov began his military career in the tsar's army as an ensign. In 1918, he volunteered to join the Red Army and went on to serve as a battalion and regimental commander during the Russian Civil War. From 1938 to 1939 he held the position of tactical lecturer at the Soviet Military Academy.

On 23 December 1939, Kozlov was made commander of the 1st Rifle Corps, Eighth Army, positioned against the Finns in northern Karelia. He managed to hold this position until the end of the war.

Afterwards, Kozlov spent several years in senior army positions and fought against Nazi Germany in the Great Patriotic War. He was promoted lieutenant-general on 19 January 1943. Kozlov resigned from active service due to poor health in 1954.

The tent of a Finnish squad in the forest near Lake Syskyjärvi. The clever positioning of the chimney, in the branches of the snow-laden fir tree, helped to almost completely disperse the tell-tale smoke. (SA-kuva)

The fighting retreat of the Finns had cost the Soviets dearly. They had worn down the assaulting troops, with both regiments in the vanguard reduced to fewer than 500 active men. The Soviets' situation was further exasperated by the difficult supply conditions, as they could only rely on one road to the rear. To guard this obvious vulnerability in their defences, many of the tanks were held in reserve. Despite these precautions, the Finns did manage to temporarily sever the Soviet supply route east of Lake Ylä-Lavajärvi as early as 14 December. In light of this, Colonel Hannuksela's earlier decision to fall back as far as Kitilä had proved to be a wise move, as it stretched the Soviet supply lines significantly.

Major-General Hägglund, commander of IV Army Corps, decided to gamble his northern Kollaa River front by stripping away some of the defenders to strengthen the 13th Division. This enabled him to free more troops for a counter-offensive he had ordered starting on 12 December. The plan was to destroy the Soviet forces advancing along the Lemetti road, and to push back the formations of the 168th Rifle Division coming from the south.

To accomplish this, Colonel Hannu Hannuksela, commander of the 13th Division, divided his troops into three battle groups. Lieutenant-Colonel Eino Järvinen was to lead Task Force Oinas ('Ram') comprising five infantry battalions and two artillery batteries. His task was to tie down enemy formations from the defensive positions in the Kitilä area. Colonel Matti Olkkonen led Task Force Jousimies ('Archer') consisting of six infantry battalions and two artillery batteries. Their attack was to start from further east in the area of Lake Varpajärvi proceeding directly south towards the Lemetti road. Task Force Luoti ('Bullet') was to outflank the enemy attacking the same road even further east on the other side of Uomaa village. Two battalions were combined under the command of Major Toimi B. J. Hassinen for this mission. The rest of the Finnish forces in the area stood as divisional reserves.

The offensive began as planned, before dawn on 12 December. Fearing Soviet armour, the Finnish troops avoided movement by road and advanced cross-country. From the outset, the terrain proved challenging for the two attacking formations. It took Task Force Jousimies most of the day to advance the relatively short distance of 5km to their designated jumping-off point at Lake Kotajärvi. These men were then ordered to proceed towards the road objective a further 5km distant. By the evening, they were utterly exhausted and the whole task force had to retreat to the vicinity of Lake Kotajärvi. Only one battalion, under Major Armas A. Ruusuvuori, managed to push on and capture a section of the road west of Lake Sääksjärvi. There his men occupied the area near an old tar factory until nightfall. Meanwhile, a Soviet counter-offensive dispersed other Finnish troops advancing south along the Siira road.

North-east of Task Force Jousimies, the original plan had called for the two battalions of Task Force Luoti to perform a two-pronged attack towards Lake Haahkajärvi. Both units met enemy forces long before they were able to unite, and after a skirmish, were forced to retreat north.

On 13 December, Major-General Hägglund decided to interrupt the offensive and withdrew his men back into positions along lakes Syskyjärvi and Varpajärvi. Meanwhile, the defensively oriented Task Force Oinas withstood all the Soviet attacks thrown against its positions. The situation had looked critical for a while, as the enemy managed a minor breakthrough around Kitilä Station. However, a reserve battalion commanded by Captain Onni A. G. Karhama managed to push the Soviets back and plug the gap in the defences.

In light of what this Finnish counter-attack had achieved, 18th Rifle Division's commander Kondrashev now moved one of his regiments away from the front line in order to better guard the supply lines. Despite the heavy losses and its now diminished striking capacity, he still wanted his division to continue to attack. Regardless of the critical importance of maintaining continuous pressure against the Finns, Kondrashev's men were now so fatigued that he was forced to beg for a minimum two-day respite in his latest report to Eighth Army command.

Unsurprisingly, the Soviet formations managed to hold their ground all along the Lemetti road, where their artillery and tanks could best be deployed. Any Finnish success against these positions was likely to come from attacking through the woods, where mobility and loose formations would be an advantage.

To this effect, 13th Division's commander Colonel Hannuksela decided to try to liberate the crossroads at Ruhtinaanmäki. This small hamlet lay on a hillock just in front of the defensive positions of Task Force Oinas. On 14 December, the Finns launched a two-pronged attack against this position. Both attempts were unsuccessful, and the men had retreated by nightfall.

When this first effort failed, Hägglund immediately gave orders for another attack. Before this action could start, the Soviets launched their own assaults towards the villages of Syskyjärvi and Ruokojärvi. At the end of the day, the Red Army managed to capture Ruokojärvi and challenged the Finns for possession of the positions along the Syskyjärvi River.

On the night of 15 December, whilst the Soviets were pushing north and west against the Finnish defenders, a second Finnish counter-attack was launched. All attempts at capturing Ruhtinaanmäki were again repelled.

So far, all the Finnish operations had failed at least partially due to the circuitous approach marches the troops had to complete before committing to the assault. Over the following days, the Finns were to change tactics to a more straightforward rushing of the Soviet lines on a narrower front. However, this in turn enabled the Soviet reserves and artillery to be concentrated on the narrower area, making such forays both suicidal and ineffective.

Nevertheless, these fierce encircling attacks forced the Chief of Staff of the 18th Division, Major Zinovi N. Alexejev, to request help from his superiors at the 56th Rifle Corps general staff. Too many of his men had suffered frostbite, and as a result, most of the divisions' supply personnel had been forced to serve in the front lines. In addition, his attention was divided between the assaults at Ruhtinaanmäki and protecting the rear of his line.

As the Soviets focused on preserving their hold on the vital supply route, the Finns managed to regain total control of the Syskyjärvi area. At Ruokojärvi village, the three attacking Soviet battalions of the 316th Rifle Regiment had by now shrunk to fewer than 100 fighting men each. Partially surrounded, they were soon forced to retreat back to the fold of the division, thus leaving Ruokojärvi to the Finns.

By lunchtime on 17 December, the supply situation was becoming desperate for all of the Soviet forces. This included machine-gun coolant, the lack of which caused many of the weapons to overheat and malfunction. Newly arrived reinforcements of 130 men were completely inadequate as

A Finnish ski patrol passing a captured Soviet OT-130 flamethrower tank at Ruhtinaanmäki on 21 January 1940. (SA-kuva)

by now the three battalions of the 208th Rifle Regiment engaged at Lake Syskyjärvi had also been reduced to quarter-strength.

By 18 December, the Finns had again managed to cut off the division's supply road. Connections were restored the following day, but by this time the Eighth Army commander had already given orders to cease all assaults. Instead, the Soviets were to dig in and hold their current positions until considerable reinforcements had arrived. When these fresh troops had been added, the 18th and 168th Rifle divisions were to continue with a forceful attack west.

On 27 December, two battalions from the Finnish 36th Infantry Regiment began fresh attacks on the Soviet supply columns. Despite their initial success in capturing a section of the road, the Soviet 18th Rifle Division was galvanised into action and somehow managed to throw the Finns back. Nevertheless, Finnish attacks recommenced the following day, and the Finns finally managed to cut the Uomaa road. The blockade was quickly reinforced, and from that point on, no further supplies were to reach the besieged Soviets.

Over the next two days, several Finnish battalions again attempted to retake the Ruhtinaanmäki area. The Soviets managed to hold this position, repelling all of the 13th Division's attacks. On 30 December, Major-General Hägglund ordered all the attacks towards Ruhtinaanmäki to stop for a couple of days.

A Soviet OT-130 flamethrower tank that fell victim to the anti-tank ditch on the Syskyjärvi front. The snow helped hide such traps by softening the outlines and contours. The drivers had very little time to react before disaster struck. (SA-kuva)

Politruk (political commissar) Nikolai I. Klimov's diary entry from 28 December tells how his friend Toivo (a Karelian Finnish speaker fighting in the Red Army) decided to retaliate personally for the nightly Finnish raids aimed at capturing prisoners:

> I asked to be given the identity details of a fallen Finn. I dressed up warmly and then during the night I snuck towards their trenches. At a pre-agreed signal, my comrades opened fire. Soon I started shouting in my fluent Finnish, 'Guys, help me! I'm wounded! My name is Pekka Perttinen from Major Valkama's battalion. My legs have been hit! Help me! Save me, I'm freezing to death! Help me for Christ's sake…' I had to shout for more than half an hour, before two crawling figures finally approached me. I let them get a bit closer before I said: 'Have a grenade, guys!' Afterwards, only a wet stain remained. I then repeated the same feat on the left flank. This time I took a partner and together we silenced two would be rescuers with our knives, while the third we took prisoner. At first he refused to speak, but I soon taught him. My fists still ache. (Gordijenko, 2002)

At Ruhtinaanmäki, the Soviet 208th Rifle Regiment and the supporting tank battalion continued to fight valiantly, holding their ground until the beginning of January. By then, the supply situation was getting worse by the day. On 3 January, the Finns started to prepare another major offensive aimed at finally driving the enemy back or destroying them where they stood.

Men from the 1st Company of the 8th Independent Battalion on 13 December 1939 at Lake Ruokojärvi. Many of the recalled reservists were given only a hat, cockade and rifle before taking up their wartime positions. Luckily, the Finns were used to the cold climate and had bought their own warm clothing. The frostbite statistics tell us that the same could not be said for the Soviet troops in the area. (SA-kuva)

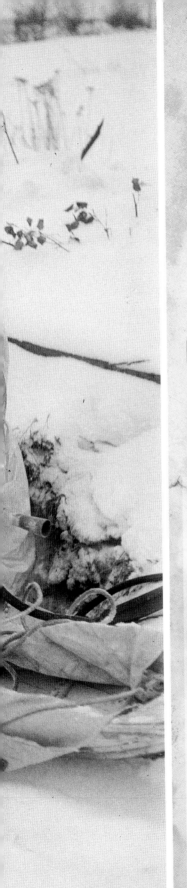

CHAPTER 5
GROUP TALVELA

Having taken the important road junction of Suojärvi on 2 December, Panin of the 1st Rifle Corps split his forces and began an effective two-pronged attack. He ordered Brigade Commander Peter Alexandrov's 155th Rifle Division to attack in the direction of the town of Ilomantsi. For this mission, Alexandrov had at his disposal 14,128 men, 22 tanks and over 100 artillery pieces. The 139th Rifle Division performed the second thrust from Suojärvi. These troops, under Brigade Commander Nicholas I. Beljalev, were to proceed first to Tolvajärvi and from there further inland towards Korpiselkä. Beljalev's force consisted of 15,362 men, 20 tanks and 90 artillery pieces.

When the Finns launched their first counter-attacks, additional reinforcements were sent to these Soviet formations. However, few of these troops arrived in time to have much of an impact

Finnish troops were able to move quickly and quietly even when deploying their heavy weapons. Here officer cadets practise using a Maxim machine gun mounted on a sleigh. (SA-kuva)

NICHOLAS BELJALEV
BRIGADE COMMANDER,
139TH RIFLE DIVISION

Nicholas Ivanovitch Beljajev took part in the Russian Civil War between 1918 and 1921. In November 1939, he was promoted to brigade commander and put in charge of the 139th Rifle Division.

Unfortunately, Beljalev's unit did not fare well against Group Talvela's men. By 13 December, Beljalev's superior Gregory Kulik had already decided to relieve him. He was replaced by Brigade Commander Paul G. Ponedelin, who led the 139th Rifle Division until the end of the war.

(1897–1976)

When the former system of general ranks was reinstated in the Soviet Union in 1940, Beljalev was made a major-general. Out of favour, he continued to work as a commissar for several different units until 1945. Beljalev was subsequently demoted to the rank of major and retired from service early.

on events. The designated 75th Rifle Division, from Eighth Army's reserves, was delayed en route, and arrived after the battle at Tolvajärvi had already been decided. The 34th Light Tank Brigade did not take part in the battle as it received new orders while en route, being redirected south to help the 56th Rifle Corps near Lemetti village.

Colonel Paavo Talvela had been recalled to the colours on the eve of the Winter War, during the Extraordinary Reservist Manoeuvres of 1939. He initially served in the Ministry of Defence on the Chief of Operations Staff for the Army Supply Committee. This was to prove a very short assignment, but one that brought Talvela once again into the inner circle of Mannerheim's wartime councils.

From the outbreak of hostilities, Talvela had kept a close eye on the region north of Lake Ladoga. He felt a close affinity to this area, as he had previously fought in the region as commander of the 1919 Aunus expedition during Finland's Kinship Wars. At the Finnish Academy for the General Staff, he had led several war games focusing on this theatre and in 1926, together with the then Major Aaro Pajari, he wrote his final thesis on 'the offensive opportunities in Ladoga Karelia'.

When, on 2 December, Talvela received alarming news of the rapidly deteriorating situation stemming from the loss of Suojärvi, he immediately approached Mannerheim with his concerns and recommendations. Suojärvi was a village that he had long considered the key for holding all of northern Karelia. From there a network of roads opened south towards Pitkäranta and west towards Värtsilä. By this point the Red Army had already advanced more than half way towards the Värtsilä railway junction. The danger was that if these crossroads were also lost, then the whole front could collapse, as Soviet forces would continue to pour into the rear of the Mannerheim Line on the Karelian Isthmus.

According to Talvela's own memoirs and diary from the time, during this first meeting with Mannerheim he refused command of a division in the area in favour of a more senior officer. Instead, he requested the command of just a single brigade. Mannerheim rejected this idea, considering it too junior a position for an officer such as Talvela. One direct benefit of the meeting was that Talvela managed to convince Mannerheim to immediately send the 16th Regiment, led by Lieutenant-Colonel Aaro Pajari, to reinforce the beleaguered defenders in the area. The situation continued to worsen by the hour as the Red Army continued its relentless advance.

On Finnish Independence Day, 6 December, Mannerheim again spent the whole day with Talvela. The commander-in-chief expressed his frustration over the fact that his army was not fighting back and mapped out the lines to which he expected the army would have to retreat. According to Talvela's personal diary, Mannerheim seemed depressed by the failure of the army to fight back and that his officers were too readily giving land rather than contesting every step. Elements of the Finnish IV Army Corps had performed especially poorly, which prompted Mannerheim to order the formation of a new corps-sized force, Group Talvela. After the War Mannerheim explained why he had chosen to place most of his remaining reserves and hopes in Talvela: 'A fearless and strong-willed commander, who possessed that degree of ruthlessness required in an offensive against a greatly superior adversary' (Mannerheim, 1954).

(1893–1950)

PAUL PONEDELIN
BRIGADE COMMANDER, 139TH RIFLE DIVISION

Paul Grigorejevitch Ponedelin joined the Imperial Russian Army in 1914. In the Russian Civil War he was first a regimental and then a brigade commander, until he was wounded. Ponedelin was awarded two orders of the Red Banner for his efforts on the Polish front. He graduated from the Frunze Military Academy in 1926, and took up a position as a tactics instructor.

During the Winter War, Ponedelin was first the chief of staff for the 1st Rifle Corps, but was then demoted to lead the 139th Rifle Division on 13 December 1939. Ponedelin remained in this post until the end of the war.

He was made major-general in 1940 and promoted to the role of chief of staff of the Leningrad Military District.

In August 1941 whilst directing the Twelfth Army, Ponedelin was captured, together with Major-General H. K. Kirillov, by the Germans. Following this, they were forced to pose for propaganda photos.

Ponedelin was tried in absentia by the Military Collegium of the Supreme Court and sentenced to death in 1941. His wife Nina and father Gregory were also arrested as members of a traitor's family.

Ponedelin remained in a German prisoner-of-war camp until 1945, when he was released by American troops and handed back over to Soviet authorities. Subsequently, he was imprisoned by his own countrymen. During the following years, Ponedelin tried in vain to get his case re-examined. Eventually, he was executed on 25 August 1950 for having collaborated with the Germans. He was posthumously rehabilitated, on 13 March 1956.

(1897–1973)

PAAVO TALVELA
COLONEL. GROUP TALVELA

After the Finnish Civil War, Jäger-trained Paavo Talvela was promoted to the rank of major – the youngest in Finland. In order to pursue his nationalistic passions, Talvela temporarily resigned from the army to act as a leading figurehead for the Finnish volunteers during the Kinship Wars of the 1920s.

In 1923, Talvela graduated from the Coastal Artillery School's Battery Commander Course in Great Britain. He graduated from the Finnish Academy for General Staff in 1926. In 1930, Talvela again resigned from the army, this time as a political gesture and in order to focus on his business career.

During the Winter War, Talvela commanded the corps-sized Group Talvela. His audacious victory over the Soviets at Tolvajärvi buoyed the Finnish defenders on all fronts. A few weeks before the end of the war, Talvela took command of III Army Corps on the Karelian Isthmus.

During the Interim Peace, Talvela was granted near dictatorial rights in setting up vast foreign shipments and trade operations through Petsamo, Finland's only port on the Arctic Sea. At Mannerheim's behest, he also frequently travelled abroad, especially to Germany, lobbying for support.

At the outbreak of the Continuation War, Talvela's VI Army Corps was the first formation to reach their objectives, for which he was rewarded with Finland's highest military honour, becoming the second Knight of the Mannerheim Cross. Talvela ended up spending most of World War II as Mannerheim's military liaison at the German High Command (OKW). In 1944, he returned to lead the Finnish forces in eastern Karelia against the Soviet onslaught.

In the post-war years, Talvela held numerous senior business positions. On 6 December 1966, he was promoted to the rank of infantry general.

Group Talvela was to stand outside the normal army hierarchy and report directly to Mannerheim. Talvela's mission was to halt the Soviet I Rifle Corps's advance and regain the areas lost by the rapid withdrawal of IV Army Corps in the pivotal Suojärvi area.

When Talvela took command at the end of the first week of the war, the Finns had already withdrawn some 60km. At this rate, the Red Army would be able to attack the rear of the main defensive lines on the Karelian Isthmus within a matter of weeks. If this happened, all of Finland would fall by the end of the year.

Thanks to Talvela and Mannerheim's rapid intervention, the forces in the area, namely Task Force R, led by Lieutenant-Colonel Räsänen, had already been reinforced by two more battalions from IV Army Corps. Then, on 7 December, as one of his first orders, Talvela transferred overall command of Räsänen's forces to the recently arrived Lieutenant-Colonel Pajari.

These two gentlemen had already worked together during the 1919 Aunus expedition; in the Kinship Wars, Pajari had served under Talvela as his Northern Commander. Talvela considered him one of the most effective front-line commanders in the whole army, and had personally recommended Pajari for this post. This faith was quickly rewarded, as Pajari regrouped the nearly routed Finnish defenders, finally stopping the Soviet tide at the Kivisalmi narrows between lakes Taivaljärvi and Tolvajärvi.

Upon their first inspection of the front, both Pajari and Talvela were mortified to see the demoralised state of the men. They heard of many instances where sheer panic had infected both veterans and new conscripts,

Group Talvela Tolvajärvi and Äglajärvi

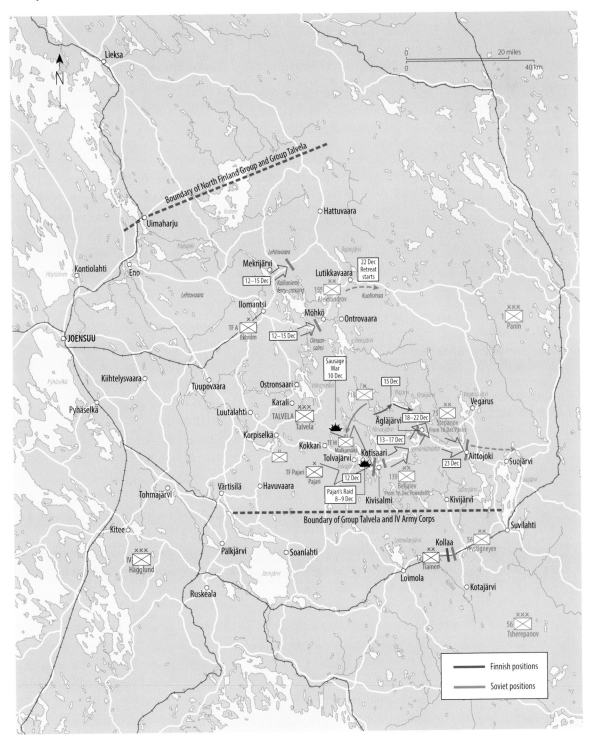

Lieksa

N

0 20 miles
0 40 km

Boundary of North Finland Group and Group Talvela

Uimaharju

Koitere

Hattuvaara

Kontiolahti   Eno   Höytiäinen   Koitajoki

Mekrijärvi   Lehtovaara   Ilajanjärvi   22 Dec
12–15 Dec   Kallioniemi   Lutikkavaara   Retreat
ferry-crossing   starts
Lehtovaara   155   Kuolismaa
Ilomantsi   Aleksandrov
Möhkö   1
TF A   12–15 Dec   Ontrovaara   Panin
JOENSUU   Ekholm   Oinaan-   Vieksjärvi
salmi
Sausage
War
10 Dec
Kiihtelysvaara   Ostronsaari   Viiksinselkä   15 Dec
Karali   718   Ylijärvi   Keskijärvi   Vegarus
Pyhäselkä   Luutalahti   TALVELA   Äglajärvi   18–22 Dec   7   Stepanov
Korpiselkä   Talvela   Hirvasjärvi   From 16 Dec Panin
Pyhäselkä   TF M   13–17 Dec   Aittojoki
Malkamäki   Kotisaari   23 Dec   Suojärvi
Kokkari   Tolvajärvi   Tolvajärvi   139
TF Pajari   Beljalev   From 16 Dec Ponedelin
Tohmajärvi   Pajari   12 Dec   Kivijärvi
Värtisilä   Havuvaara   Pajari's Raid   Kivisalmi   Salonjärvi   Suvilahti
8–9 Dec
Kitee   Boundary of Group Talvela and IV Army Corps
Loimolanjärvi   56   Yevstigneyev
IV   Pälkjärvi   Soanlahti   Kollaa
Hägglund   Jänisjärvi   12   Tiainen
Loimola   Kotajärvi
Ruskeala   56
Tsherepanov

Finnish positions
Soviet positions

 ## AARO PAJARI
LIEUTENANT-COLONEL, 16TH REGIMENT

(1897–1949)

Aaro Pajari graduated from college in 1916, and joined the Civil Guard the following year. During the Finnish Civil War, he rose to lead an infantry company, and was wounded twice, in the battles for Oulu and for Heinola. Pajari took part in the Aunus expedition, reporting to Talvela as Northern Commander.

During the Winter War, Lieutenant-Colonel Pajari commanded the 16th Infantry Regiment, leading it to the first major Finnish victory in the Tolvajärvi area. He was promoted to colonel on 18 December 1939. When Talvela transferred to the Karelian Isthmus, Pajari took over command of the whole of Group Talvela. Upon his departure, Talvela sent Mannerheim a glowing recommendation of Pajari as a front-line commander, despite his apparent heart condition.

At the beginning of the Continuation War, Pajari's 18th Division achieved a breakthrough on the Karelian Isthmus. This feat gained Pajari his first Mannerheim Cross on 3 October 1941. In 1942, the now Major-General Pajari was given overall responsibility for the audacious winter operation to capture Suursaari Island in the Gulf of Finland. In October 1943, Pajari took command of the 3rd Division at Uhtua, and then fought in the decisive battles on the Karelian Isthmus.

Pajari's landing in Tornio was to kick-start the actual fighting during the Lapland War. For his success in that war, Pajari was made a Knight of the 2nd Class Mannerheim Cross for a second time on 16 October 1944. He was one of the only four people ever to receive Finland's highest military honour twice.

In 1949, Pajari's heart condition finally took its toll, and he died following a cardiac arrest on his way to work.

spreading like a virus. On 8 December, as Baljalev's 139th Rifle Division continued its attack at the Kivisalmi rapids, they witnessed for themselves defenders running away in terror. This in turn prompted Pajari to utter his dire warning to his battalion: 'You can run, but you will only die tired!'

By now, the Red Army had reached the edges of lakes Tolvajärvi and Hirvasjärvi. This forced the Finns to regroup and throw every man they could muster into saving Tolvajärvi village on the western shore. Following the desperate struggles of the last few days, Talvela realised that they needed some kind of victory in order to curb the panic, regain the initiative and show the men that the Soviets were not invincible. As he had earlier reasoned to Mannerheim: 'In situations like this, as in all confused and hopeless situations, an energetic attack against the nearest enemy was and is the only way to improve the spirits of the men and to regain control of the situation' (Tuompo and Karikoski, 1942).

Accordingly, Talvela then devised a plan proposing a daring counter-attack to the rear of the enemy positions. However, his men talked him out of personally leading the attack, and the honour fell to Pajari instead.

It was agreed that Pajari would gather volunteers for his raid, while Talvela would oversee the defence of the Tolvajärvi front line. The raid was scheduled for the night of 8/9 December. This was to be the first time during the Winter War that the Finnish forces had gone on the offensive.

One company was to conduct a feint before the planned flanking raid. The men who had been set this task soon retreated in haste. Their frontal assault had met with heavy fire from the Soviets, causing the troops to lose their company commander for the second time within a week.

Men fastening captured Soviet weapons onto a sleigh, near Lake Patomäki, on 17 December 1939. (SA-kuva)

Meanwhile, Pajari's two raiding parties traversed the frozen Lake Tolvajärvi, bypassing the Soviet positions on Kotisaari Island. Soon after the crossing, the second party became separated. Upon encountering some open water and finding no way to cross, these men were forced to turn back.

Only the soldiers under Pajari's personal command fared somewhat better. After soundlessly dispatching a small enemy patrol with their puukko knives, they set eyes on their objective for the first time. In a valley near the Kivisalmi Bridge, a Soviet battalion had bedded down for the night. Further off they were also able to spot two more battalions resting by their huge campfires. Pajari now endeavoured to engage the entire enemy regiment.

Under cover of the pitch-black night, his men fanned out along the ridgeline. When they opened fire, the surprise was so complete that not a single shot came back towards their positions. Pajari then had his men repeat the process by moving and opening fire against the second encampment. In the confusion, the enemy battalions started firing on each other; the exchange of fire was still fierce when Pajari's men passed out of earshot a few hours later. When skiing back, Pajari collapsed – the only Finnish casualty of the night – and had to be carried back by his men. The 42-year-old lieutenant-colonel had hidden his heart condition now had suffered a mild heart attack.

A captured OT-26 flamethrower tank on a ridge overlooking Lake Tolvajärvi. When Talvela and Pajari arrived at the front, they were told of men whose fighting ability had been broken by enemy armour. These men were so shocked that when they heard the sound of tanks advancing towards them, they would immediately desert their positions. (SA-kuva)

By the second week of the war, the Soviet troops were almost completely spent. The fast advance had stretched their supply lines, as well as exhausting the men physically. The fear of further Finnish attacks on their camps made for many more sleepless nights. The badly gridlocked single supply road added to their woes, as this meant that most had not had a warm meal for days. Many of the senior officers had fallen, forcing the promotion of junior lieutenants to lead full companies. All these concerns prompted Brigade Commander Baljalev to ask his superiors for a few days' respite while his men prepared for the next stage of the assault. However, Eighth Army headquarters did not believe his claims that Finnish reinforcements had arrived in the area, and so they ordered him to attack again on the following day.

The short lull in hostilities that Baljalev's request created enabled the men on both sides to gain vital rest and regroup. The day's respite was especially beneficial to the Finns. Due to a communications error, one of their front-line battalions had abandoned their positions for a few hours, leaving them completely unguarded. If Baljalev had been following the original plans instead of requesting rest, this section of the lines would certainly have been breached without resistance.

After the armistice of 13 March 1940, Colonel Pajari (on the right) describes to reporters the fierce battles fought at the Tolvajärvi crossroads. (SA-kuva)

Meanwhile to the north, the attack of the Soviet 155th Rifle Division towards Ilomantsi had ground to a halt. There a Task Force A, commanded by Colonel Per O. Ekholm, had stopped the onslaught just to the west of Möhkö village. The following weeks of counter-attacks by the Finns proved ineffectual, and as both armies concentrated on other fronts, the lines around Ilomantsi stabilised for the remainder of the war.

As the Finns were preparing their next counter-attack on the evening of Sunday 10 December, news of a threat to their rear reached Talvela. After a long march, the Soviet 718th Rifle Regiment had finally arrived in the area. Instead of settling down to rest, these troops had immediately pressed on. Swinging west around the side of Tolvajärvi village, they were now about to encircle the Finns, threatening the undefended artillery and supply columns. Despite their initial success in overcoming the surprised defenders, the Soviet attack halted as soon as the Finnish soup kitchens had been secured. After their five-day forced march, the men of the 718th Rifle Regiment were so hungry and tired that they now forgot all about fighting and proceeded to gorge on hot sausage stew.

As luck would have it, Pajari also happened to be in the area. The unwitting Soviets had given the Finns the respite needed to organise their defences by pausing their attack. Now, with his usual alacrity, Pajari formed up a couple of ragtag companies from cooks, clerks and other rear-echelon staff who had been previously scattered by the Soviet assault. In the dead of night, the Finns began their counter-attack; this soon turned into fierce hand-to-hand combat.

In the cold light of dawn, it came apparent that the supply troops had emphatically blocked this Soviet pincer movement. During the fighting, the Finns had lost 20 dead and 55 wounded, but left over 100 dead Red Army troops on the field. Pieces of sausages were recovered from the freezing bodies of the fallen foes; the surprise had been so complete that some had even died with food still in their mouths. This episode became known as the 'Sausage War'.

While the Finns were still taking stock after the night's fighting, the listening posts at Tolvajärvi issued warnings of a wide-fronted assault over the frozen lake. This advance notice gave the Finns time to set up an effective ambush. When the first machine-gun volleys hit home, the enemy had nowhere to hide on the frozen vastness, and they were forced to flee in disarray. Some 200 Soviet troops died on the ice, while the rest made their escape in the morning's gloom.

Talvela and Pajari must have been pleased with the victories in these past few days and the rapid improvement this had on morale. Nevertheless, the latest surprise attack and the Sausage War had involved a considerable amount of their forces, and so to be prudent, it was decided to give the men one more day's respite before launching a major counter-attack.

TOLVAJÄRVI AND ÄGLÄJÄRVI

Colonel Talvela's counter-attack was to be divided into three parts. Major Jaakko (Jaska) A. Malkamäki led the two-battalion-strong Task Force M. He was to initiate the attack with a flanking movement on the north side of Tolvajärvi village. Once his troops had fully engaged the enemy, Pajari (who had sufficiently recovered) would launch the main thrust over the frozen lake with three more battalions. Major Erik A. Paloheimo would stay in readiness, keeping two battalions and one additional company as reserves.

Whilst the Finns made their preparations, the Soviet commanders again ordered the assault to continue despite the exhausted state of their men. At this point, they did not yet know about the Sausage War and the fate of the 718th Rifle Regiment, and instead sent orders for the unit to continue the attack. In reality, the bulk of these troops had already withdrawn at the north end of Lake Hirvasjärvi. Using strict discipline, the Soviet officers managed to eventually restore the regiment to some sort of fighting order, and were able to prepare their wide-fronted attack for the morning of 12 December.

Due to heavy snowdrifts and navigational errors, Major Malkamäki's men were late getting into position and consequently lost the element of surprise. His two battalions eventually started to advance over Lake Hirvasjärvi around 08:30. On the ice, they engaged the Red Army troops who had been preparing for a further flanking attack. Other Soviet troops, which had been passing further to the north, had earlier spotted the advancing Finns, but had assumed that they were friendly forces. This case of mistaken identity allowed the first Finnish attack to strike the command

Artillery captured at the battle at Tolvajärvi, at Värtsilä supply depot. Mannerheim's gamble was paying off, and he later reflected on the period prior to forming Group Talvela: 'In this situation, I had to make some of the weightiest and most important decisions of the Winter War. Everything pointed to our main position on the isthmus soon becoming the object of a general attack ... But the enemy's unexpectedly rapid advance on this front had compelled me to alter my plans. Instead, I directed a large part of my meagre reserves eastwards to Tolvajärvi, Kuhmo and Suomussalmi.' (SA-kuva)

post of the still disorganised 718th Rifle Regiment. In the ensuing battle, the regiment's commander was mortally wounded.

Despite their apparent success, for some reason Major Malkamäki was made nervous by the light Soviet resistance, and ordered his men to return to their earlier assembly area. Consequently, by lunchtime Task Force M had to inform Pajari that the attack on the north side had been unsuccessful. The failure seemed to result more from the lack of proper leadership than any enemy resistance, as the Soviet 718th Rifle Regiment had also retreated from the area. For the time being, neither side left any men holding the objective.

Meanwhile, due to problems launching the preliminary bombardment, Pajari's own attack was also delayed. Only a few of the companies had started their advance on time. As planned, these men had begun the lake crossing towards their objectives at Kotisaari Island, near the southern end of the lake. By 09:00, the Finnish artillery and machine guns along the shoreline had finally commenced their preliminary fire missions. The wait was hardly worth it, as a mere 15 minutes later the shelling stopped and Pajari's force received orders to proceed.

The 16th Battalion, the first to cross the lake, suffered heavy losses on the ice. Despite this, it reached the opposite shore and proceeded to advance south along the road. The 16th Battalion's attack was finally halted when several enemy machine guns, positioned in the nearby hotel, sent a devastating volley into their ranks. Positioned on top of a hill, this imposing building provided the Soviets with a formidable stronghold. From this vantage point, they were able to keep the lightly armed Finns at bay. Not everything went their way, however, as a well-placed 37mm Bofors gun prevented three Soviet tanks from

Due to the Finnish lack of heavy weapons, this tourist hotel on the eastern shore of Lake Tolvajärvi provided the Soviets with an excellent fortified position. They defended this stronghold fiercely, but were finally overwhelmed by Finnish reinforcements. (SA-kuva)

supporting their infantry. Eventually the arrival of reinforcements allowed the Finns to coordinate attacks from multiple directions, thus splitting the defenders' fire. The Soviets in the hotel managed to hold out until about 14:30.

Further to the south, the Finns were finally able to send troops to help the two companies which had been, since early that morning, fighting almost non-stop near Kotisaari Island. By late afternoon, these forces had been reinforced to four companies, which then managed to completely occupy the island. In the process, they had killed over 100 Red Army troops and captured 60 prisoners as well as several important artillery pieces. An even bigger weapons' cache than this was seized by the troops fighting east of the hotel. The Finns had encircled and killed around 200 enemy soldiers, and had gained additional artillery and an incredible 20 armoured vehicles. If all of the tanks could be repaired and put into use, Talvela's men would have nearly doubled the size of the Finnish armoured forces.

In total, the Red Army lost around 1,000 men as well as much valuable weaponry. At the same time, 100 Finns were killed and nearly 200 more were wounded.

Colonel Talvela now insisted that his troops press home the attack so the enemy would be completely destroyed. Pajari managed to convince him otherwise by reminding him of the setbacks previously suffered by Task Force M in the north. Most of the men were ordered back to Tolvajärvi village for a period of rest, while lighter formations held the new positions on the east side of the lake.

On 12 December, Pajari sent the following dispatch to Talvela:

I have today attacked and struck back at the enemy at Tolvajärvi, forcing them to retreat with heavy losses towards the east. The flanking action to the north was a failure but my attack was an overall success mainly due to the success on the southern flank. Men there occupied Kotisaari Island and after a tenacious attack reached the Tolvajärvi Isthmus. I then moved most of my reserves into combat at 13:00 in order to break the centre of the enemy's resistance. This caused their defence to collapse and started a general retreat. This action was very demanding for and placed heavy strain on all my troops. Also our losses have been heavy, especially amongst the officers. (Kilin and Raunio, 2010)

After the battle, Talvela wrote in his diary: 'Great day of battle at Tolvajärvi. Pajari made a frontal assault capturing large areas. On the left flank, we fought an engagement battle. We gained many spoils of war. Attack failed at Ilomantsi. To celebrate this great day I am going to have a sauna tonight' (Talvela, 1976).

Finnish soldiers examining destroyed Soviet tanks. The *motti* the Finns created often contained tanks, although most were without fuel, or were so low on it that the Soviets chose to conserve what was left for keeping warm. However, even immobile tanks caused the Finns to worry about their desperate lack of anti-tank weapons. (SA-kuva)

Against Talvela's wishes, the Finnish troops spent the night and most of the following day regrouping before they continued their advance. In the afternoon of 13 December, the men of the 7th Bicycle Battalion were the first to sight the retreating enemy. The enemy gave ground without a fight and contact between the two forces was again broken. The battalion continued to advance up to the Ristisalmi Isthmus where they were relieved and moved back into reserve. For reasons unexplained, Pajari had not organised a proper night reconnaissance, and so the following morning the enemy's location remained a mystery. Meanwhile, the now disorganised Soviet 139th Rifle Division continued its retreat from the area.[6] Brigade Commander Alexander Stepanov's 75th Rifle Division was ordered to march north and to replace these beleaguered men.

On 14 December, the Finnish advance continued to progress slowly, as two Soviet tanks appeared and managed to halt the entire offensive. Eventually an anti-tank gun was brought to the front, the two enemies were destroyed and the attack resumed. By the following morning, Pajari ordered his men to stand down due to exhaustion; however, Talvela countermanded the order and made the troops continue the advance. Talvela also had other worries on his mind, as an enemy battalion had again appeared at their rear on the road near Ilomantsi. He gave orders to Colonel Per O. Ekholm's Task Force A to destroy the enemy in the area. When Ekholm complained that he did not have sufficient reserves for the action, Talvela ordered him to personally lead his headquarters staff in a counter-attack. Ekholm gathered what kitchen, communications and other support personnel he could find into a temporary strike force and proceeded to drive off the enemy.

The collapse at Tolvajärvi had become too much for the Soviet high command to stomach. Therefore, on 13 December, they made a decision to replace Baljalev as 139th Rifle Division commander, and on the following day also relieved Khabarov from command of Eighth Army in favour of Army Commander 2nd Class Gregory M. Shtern.

6 At this stage the Chief-of-Staff of the 1st Rifle Corps Brigade Commander Ponedelin was demoted to take charge of this decimated unit.

A Finnish patrol resting in Viena (White Sea) Karelia. The men have built a traditional *rakovalkea*. This kind of fire is made from two long, deadwood trunks, which are placed on top of each other. The fire is then kindled in between the two logs. This helps to keep the fire off the ground, and provides intense, near smokeless heat for hours with no need to add more fuel. (SA-kuva)

While the Finns attempted to push forwards, Shtern was trying to get to grips with his new post. The Eighth Army Prosecution Service described the condition of one of his new rifle divisions, the 139th, as 'terminally demoralised'. Subsequently, Shtern gave strict orders to implement harsh disciplinary action should the retreating continue. Despite the executions that were to follow, morale failed to improve.

On 16 December, the Finns ran into some 200 fresh troops from a Soviet Officer Candidate School. These young men were extremely well trained and very highly motivated. They sold their lives dearly in a day-long battle, buying time for their comrades to withdraw. It appeared that at least this forward element of the 75th Rifle Division had not been demoralised by the sight of the broken men they had passed on the road in. Meanwhile, the 139th Rifle Division continued its withdrawal from the combat zone.

At the end of the day, as a reward for all their achievements, Talvela relented and gave his troops the rest that Pajari had been requesting. This respite was cut short when contact with the enemy was about to be lost again. Having pursued the Red Army forces over a distance of 4km, the Finnish vanguard finally reached Äglájärvi.

The Finns now took stock, regrouped and planned the destruction of the Soviet troops in and around

ALEXANDER STEPANOV
BRIGADE COMMANDER, 75TH RIFLE DIVISION

In the Winter War, Stepanov commanded the 75th Rifle Division until 13 February 1940, when he was wounded leading his troops at the battle of Äglájärvi. The demoted 1st Rifle Corps commander, Panin, took control of his troops from that point.

(1893–1941)

From May 1940 onwards, Stepanov led the 27th Rifle Division. When the Red Army reinstated the old general ranks after the Winter War, Stepanov was promoted to major-general on 4 June 1940.

He died leading the 27th Rifle Division against the Germans at Smolensk on 11 August 1941.

Ägläjärvi village. Meanwhile the Red Army had concentrated all of the 75th Rifle Division's combat-ready troops in the area, although it is worth noting that two of its regiments had already suffered heavily during the fighting retreat of the previous days. Any elements of the 139th Rifle Division that could still fight were also returned to the front.

On 18 December, the Finns launched attacks against Ägläjärvi village from three directions. Some troops from the northernmost, 10th Independent Battalion, managed to reach and make contact with the enemy within the village. Nevertheless, by nightfall all Finnish forces were forced to return to their staging areas.

During the day, Mannerheim telephoned Talvela; he promoted Talvela to the rank of major-general and Pajari to colonel for their achievements in bringing about Finland's first major victory. He stressed that Talvela was to avoid any further action that could result in heavy losses. Despite Mannerheim's caution, Talvela remained of the view that it was strategically important to move the battle line to the east side of the village. He considered it prudent to stop the offensive only after this objective had been secured. Therefore, against the wishes of the supreme commander, his orders were to continue the attack again the next day. This attack made little progress, and the only gain was that the Finns spent the night in the dugouts the Soviets had held the previous day. The Red Army, however, still held the village.

On the morning of 20 December, the Soviets launched their own surprise attack. Nine tanks led a battalion of infantry straight at the Finnish lines, reaching them at such speed that the first anti-tank gun was destroyed without managing to fire a single shot. Here the Finns again showed their determination by destroying the leading tank with satchel charges and the last one in the line with a 37mm Bofors anti-tank gun. This effectively blocked the road for the rest of the column. The anti-tank weapons then started working up the line, destroying tank after tank; the Soviet crews that were still alive ran away in panic. This early victory encouraged two of the Finnish captains to continue with the day's planned attacks. By late afternoon, they had reached the southern shores of Lake Ägläjärvi, near the village. There, all their consequent attempts to cut the remaining Soviet south-easterly supply road were unsuccessful, and the troops had withdrawn back to their own lines by nightfall.

By now, the exhausted Finns had managed to squeeze the Red Army forces into an ever-diminishing area around the village itself, and their only escape route along the road was close to being cut off. Meanwhile, the Soviets continued their air strikes behind the front lines. Although the coniferous forests provided good concealment, the lack of Finnish air cover was keenly felt.

Talvela had originally ordered that 21 December would be used for rest, but after consideration he instead ordered Ägläjärvi village to be captured by the end of the following day.

Supported by artillery, the main Finnish attack finally managed to cut the road by late afternoon. To the north of the village, the Finnish battalions started their advance shortly after dark. An absence of hostile forces meant that they had reached the village edge by midnight. There they encountered the entrenched Soviets, and were held at bay by fierce resistance.

The main Finnish attack continued alongside the road. As the Soviet defence stiffened, the group reserves were committed to the assault. By the end of the night, a total of three battalions had joined in the fray.

At this stage, Talvela sent the following report to headquarters explaining why he had continued the attack:

> Despite the endless, demanding fighting and the great strain this has had on the troops, by taking the initiative and by continuously advancing we have managed to create such a spirit of success that we have in the end succeeded in advancing. Our seven worn battalions and four artillery batteries now face the whole Soviet 1st Rifle Corps. How we are going to deal with them in the end is unclear. But it is absolutely necessary that as soon as we reach a suitable line, we dig in and defend so that the men can rest. It is still a big question mark for us how we are going to deal with the 155th Rifle Division on the Ilomantsi front. So far, the freezing weather and heavy snowfall have been doing our job there. (Talvela, 1976)

On 21 December, due to the perilous condition of their divisions, the Soviet Eighth Army command gave orders for a general withdrawal to the Aittojoki River. The Finns further accelerated these plans through their surprisingly early and aggressive assaults. The retreating troops had to beat off the advancing Finns repeatedly, but it seems that the order for the evacuation had been issued just in time. Thus, these men avoided being completely surrounded, and destroyed, by the narrowest of margins.

The war diary of the 2nd Sissi Ranger Battalion, which had been transferred to Talvela for the battle of Ägläjärvi, recounts the following events of the day:

> 16:45 following message sent to Group Talvela: At 10:00 am a strong and accurate artillery barrage from the enemy began, aimed at our field supply depot, which is located on a path about 3km from the southern tip of Lake Vegarusjärvi in the direction of 47-00. After this the enemy started a strong attack along the same path and also south from it. A flanking attack to the right by our vanguard company forced the enemy advance to halt for approximately half an hour. After the attack had begun, the enemy artillery shifted its focus along the path from the depot to a depth of 2.5km west, holding the road in question under constant fire.
>
> At 13:30 we received an alarm from Rupisuo depot that a large enemy formation was advancing on the south side of Lake Kalatanlampi westwards. The depot only held light sentries at the time as the majority of the men were taking part in the counter-attack in the south-east. Due to this threat to our flank, the 3rd Company was given orders to secure the road to the north-west. While the enemy applied continuous pressure along the path the squad present from the 2nd company was ordered to perform a westerly flanking manoeuvre. We have not yet received word of the success of this strike to the flank, a detachment from the 3rd Company has been sent to overwatch both sides of the path parallel to the road. We do not yet know the magnitude of the losses.
>
> Strong enemy bombardment, continuous without breaks. In order to hold my current position I hope for a strong counter-attack from the south
> …
>
> 19:50 Towards the evening situation more or less cleared. Enemy suffered around 50 dead, our own losses for the day are 2 dead and 14 wounded.

On the morning of 22 December, the attack towards the village was renewed from all sides. By mid-afternoon, the Soviet rearguard had been defeated and the village was completely in Finnish hands. Two battalions were quickly dispatched to try to intercept the main Soviet forces that had managed to escape, and who were now retreating south along the roads. By nightfall, these troops had reached the Aittojoki River.

A captured BA-20M armoured car at Värtsilä. The Finnish Army would repair, reuse and cherish each and every vehicle it got its hands on. This armoured vehicle was built on the chassis of a regular car. A machine-gun operator would stand inside the cupola at the rear of the vehicle. The metal rim circling the car was actually a radio antenna. The use of Swastikas in Finland can be dated back to the early Iron Age. In the modern times the symbol was adopted first by the Finnish Air Force at its foundation in 1918, and then by the Armoured Corp, Lotta Svärd and is even depicted on the presidential flag. (SA-kuva)

That same evening, Eighth Army commander Shtern was forced to inform his commander-in-chief, Voroshilov, that his 139th and 75th Rifle divisions had retreated from the Äglajärvi area in front of a numerically inferior enemy. After reaching the Aittojoki, the Finns set up defensive positions. This line would become quieter from this point on, and remain so for the duration of the war.

During the battle for Äglajärvi, the Finns had lost a total of 748 men, of whom 274 were killed, 445 wounded and 29 missing. According to the Soviet Eighth Army's casualty statistics, in December alone they had lost a total of 6,490 men in the area. The 139th Rifle Division had suffered 761 killed, 1,715 wounded and 1,076 missing. Stepanov's 75th Rifle Division had accumulated, in its few short days at the front, 747 killed, 957 wounded and 1,234 missing. Some Soviet documents list considerably higher numbers of casualties than these. Stepanov himself was wounded on 16 December, and the unit was then led by the former commander of the 1st Rifle Corps, Roman Panin.

Talvela's limited number of battalions had pushed back 36,000 Red Army troops, incalculably boosting the morale of the whole Finnish Army, and providing the victory Finland's political leaders so sorely needed. In doing so, Talvela had also destroyed a large portion of Eighth Army's reserves, thus giving the men of Hägglund's IV Army Corps, to the south of his positions, a fighting chance. In the process the Finns had captured a total of 59 tanks, 3 armoured cars, 31 artillery pieces, 220 machine guns, 142 light machine guns and more than 3,000 rifles from Eighth Army. Much of this materiel would be needed for the defence of the Karelian Isthmus (Eagle and Paananen, 1973).

CHAPTER 6
NORTH FINLAND GROUP

At the start of the war, Major-General Wiljo Tuompo, the commander of the North Finland Group, had a vast area to control. His men were responsible for defending most of Finland's eastern border, stretching all the way from Lieksa in the south to Petsamo on the Barents Sea. In the south, Tuompo's troops initially bordered those of IV Army Corps, and from 7 December onwards the forces of the newly formed Group Talvela.

When the Soviet attacks began, a mere eight infantry battalions supported by only a few artillery batteries were guarding this roughly 800km-long front line. The Soviets, in comparison, had allocated seven full infantry divisions to this region.

On the morning of 30 November, three divisions of the Soviet Fourteenth Army invaded the area around Petsamo in the far north. Petsamo was of huge strategic importance, as it

A young messenger boy and his dog. (SA-kuva)

The communications centre of North Finland Group in Kajaani, in a photo dated 8 December 1939. Here the men had four Morse code and two Hughes machines, along with radio communication equipment. This allowed Major-General Tuompo to keep in touch with his front-line troops along such a massive stretch of border. (SA-kuva)

was Finland's only port on the Barents Sea. In addition, the area was mined for precious nickel ore. The task of defeating the Soviets on this front was given to a separate force, Group Lapland, which Finnish headquarters took direct command of.

Further to the south, in central Finland, Corps Commander Michael P. Duhanov's Ninth Army, comprising the 47th Rifle Corps and the Special Corps headquarters, was tasked with cutting the country in half at its narrowest point by advancing rapidly all the way to Oulu on the west coast. To this end, the 122nd Rifle Division attacked first towards Salla, while the 163rd Rifle Division was to take the shortest route across Finland and pushed directly towards Suomussalmi. On the border of Eighth Army's sector, these two attacks were supported by the 54th Mountain Rifle Division, which was to perform a massive pincer movement towards Kuhmo. Soon the situation dictated that the Ukrainian 44th Rifle Division be sent to reinforce the Ninth Army.

The scale of Ninth Army's attack took the Finnish high command by surprise. Due to the lack of a decent road network, the Finns did not believe that the Soviets would amass such strong forces along this front. Nor did Mannerheim think it possible or strategically logical for the Red Army to try to cross the vast virgin forests, stretching for hundreds of kilometres, that lay between the eastern border and the fertile lands of the west coast. It would fall to North Finland Group to show the Soviet strategists the errors in their planning.

✚ WILJO TUOMPO
MAJOR-GENERAL, NORTH FINLAND GROUP

A former Jäger and chief of the Border Guards, Tuompo served as the commander of the North Finland Group during the Winter War. After the conflict ended, Tuompo returned to lead the Border Guards.

(1893–1957)

He was promoted to lieutenant-general in 1941. At the start of the Continuation War, he took up the position of chief of the command staff at General Headquarters. Tuompo was to remain in this role until December 1944. Tuompo resigned from the Finnish Army in July 1945.

THE BATTLE FOR SUOMUSSALMI

On 30 November, at 08:00, the main forces of the 163rd Rifle Division, under the command of Brigade Commander Andrew Zelentsov, launched their attack near the hamlet of Lonkka. Zelentsov's initial objective was to capture Suomussalmi by means of a two-pronged attack.[7]

By 4 December having advanced some 15km, the main body of his troops – the 662nd Rifle Regiment and the 81st Mountain Rifle Regiment (from the 54th Mountain Rifle Division) – had already reached a point halfway to their objective at Palovaara. Meanwhile, Zelentsov had sent 3,000 men, namely the 759th Rifle Regiment, supported by six 76mm cannons, to perform a southerly pincer attack along the Raate road. The rest of the division's artillery had remained with the northern pincer advancing on Palovaara.

By evening of the first day of the war, the southern-pincer troops had encountered the Finnish defensive lines at the Puraksenjoki River. Over the next two days, the Soviet 1st Rifle Battalion (from the 759th Rifle Regiment) launched a total of four unsuccessful assaults against the defending Finnish 15th Independent Battalion. Finally, on 3 December, the Soviets managed to send forces to encircle the defenders, whose positions were by now close to collapse. The Finns were granted orders to retreat, and quickly gave ground before ending up completely cut off. However, the opportunity to surround them was lost to the Soviets, who did not even realise that the enemy had fled. Instead, they spent a whole day waiting for their supporting artillery to arrive. When the guns finally showed up on 5 December, they commenced a brief preliminary bombardment, after which the infantry occupied the deserted Finnish positions.

(1896–1969)

MICHAEL DUHANOV
ARMY CORPS COMMANDER, NINTH ARMY

Michael Pavlovitch Duhanov graduated from Russian Ensign School in 1916. He was promoted lieutenant during World War I. In 1921 Duhanov graduated from the Military Academy and from 1934 to 1936 he acted as the principal of the School for Armoured Warfare.

On 21 November 1939, the eve of the Winter War, Duhanov was made commander of Ninth Army. However, a month and a day later, he was dismissed due to his army's poor performance. Corps Commander Basil Chuikov was his replacement.

From 9 May 1940, Duhanov was made responsible for the military schools of the Leningrad Military District. During the Great Patriotic War, Duhanov was given his next front-line command at the head of the 10th Rifle Division. This time his force was more successful, and from 9 October 1942 onwards Duhanov led the Sixty-Seventh Army. Towards the end of the war he took over as the acting commander of the Eighth Guards Army in the 3rd Ukrainian Front army group.

Between 1945 and 1953 Duhanov headed the department responsible for the military schools in the Leningrad Military District. He resigned from active service due to health reasons on 16 April 1953.

7 See map on p.144

The Finnish defensive line near the summer ferry-crossing site at Suomussalmi village. In a radio speech to troops recorded in the *New York Times* on 3 December 1939, Mannerheim declared: 'I undertake this task at an hour when our hereditary enemy once again attacks our country. Confidence in its chief is the first condition of success. You and I know the whole country is ready to fulfil its duty unto the death.' (SA-kuva)

HJALMAR SIILASVUO
COLONEL, 9TH DIVISION

After the Finnish Civil War, Jäger Captain Hjalmar Fridolf Siilasvuo continued to serve in the army. His roles included different posts at the Ministry of Defence, battalion and regiment commands and finally a regional military command from 1934.

(1892–1947)

In 1939, during the reservist manoeuvres, Colonel Siilasvuo was given command of the 9th Division. Alongside its men, Siilasvuo proceeded to win international fame for the tremendous blows he inflicted on the Soviets, first at the battles of Suomussalmi and then at Raate road.

After the Winter War, Siilasvuo was given command of the peacetime V Army Corps and promoted to the rank of major-general. In the Continuation War, Siilasvuo took over III Army Corps, which in turn was subordinated to the German Army of Lapland. In 1942, Siilasvuo was promoted to the rank of lieutenant-general.

After the armistice with the USSR, Mannerheim made the expedient Siilasvuo commander of all the forces in Lapland. For his army's success at the battle of Tornio, Siilasvuo was awarded the Mannerheim Cross on 21 December 1944. He remained in his role until the last of the foreign forces had been driven out of Finland in 1945.

While Zelentsov's southern detachment lost nearly two days in capturing undefended fortifications, the northern part of the division chose to split its forces. The 662nd Rifle Regiment was sent north towards Peranka village, while the 81st Mountain Rifle Regiment proceeded south towards the key objective of Suomussalmi. Although everything seemed to be going well for the Soviets at this stage, this splitting of their forces was to later prove a costly mistake.

The Finns held out at Suomussalmi village until 7 December, when they finally chose to retreat towards the south side of Lake Kiantajärvi. Before withdrawing, the whole settlement was put to the torch in order to deny the enemy its resources. The 81st Mountain Rifle Regiment thus occupied the burning village with relatively few casualties. The following day the units from Zelentsov's southern pincer movement also arrived, using the Raate road.

Finnish officers studying a map during the battles around Suomussalmi. Navigating in the snowy wilderness was often difficult. Both Soviet and Finnish forces found it problematic to pinpoint their exact locations with all the landmarks covered. (SA-kuva)

Despite this significant victory, the situation was soon to become perilous for Zelentsov's troops. Frostbite had combined with skirmishing casualties to cull nearly 20 per cent of his men, and now his forces in the Suomussalmi area were about to be cut off. The Finns managed the first stage of this feat on 13 December, when they severed the 163rd Rifle Division's lines of communication to the south and east of the village. On 15 December, the last remaining supply road, and the connection between the men in the village and the rest of the division's forces to the north, was cut. Zelentsov had lost the initiative, and from now on his troops found themselves permanently on the defensive.

ANDREW ZELENTSOV
BRIGADE COMMANDER, 163RD RIFLE DIVISION

Andrei Ivanovitch Zelentsov volunteered for the Red Army in 1918 as an aviation instructor. From there his career took a more earthbound focus, and prior to the Winter War, Brigade Commander Zelentsov had risen to being responsible for all the armoured forces of the 3rd Rifle Corps.

(1896–1941)

He was given command of the 163rd Rifle Division on 14 August 1939. This was to be an ill-fated assignment, but despite the demise of his command at the battle of Suomussalmi, Zelentsov was asked to lead the 88th Rifle Division during the Interim Peace. He was promoted major-general on 14 June 1940.

Zelentsov died on the Finnish front, while leading his 88th Rifle Division at Louhi, in an airstrike by a German dive-bomber, on 14 August 1941.

On 8 December, Colonel Hjalmar Siilasvuo and his 27th Infantry Regiment relocated to the Suomussalmi area. There he was to assume command of all the troops on this front, forming Task Force Siilasvuo, roughly at brigade strength.

Siilasvuo's commanding officer, Major-General Tuompo, in Kajaani passed on Mannerheim's strict orders to recapture the lost village. This seemed a tall order, as the enemy had superior numbers of men, and plenty of tanks and ammunition. In contrast, Siilasvuo's men were very lightly armed. The only advantage Siilasvuo appeared to hold was the mobility of his ski-troops in the dense, snow-covered forests.

The Finnish counter-attack for the recapture of Suomussalmi was set to begin on the morning of 11 December. Siilasvuo had deep concerns about the quality of the two battalions he had inherited with his command. These men had been fighting a losing battle against the Soviets since the beginning of the war, and just before his arrival, one of the company commanders had committed suicide. In order to raise morale, he circulated a rumour that his own regiment was only the vanguard of a whole division sent to help them out. In the end, this is exactly what did happen, as a couple of weeks later Mannerheim sent reinforcements, adding practically the whole 9th Division to his command. However, at the time Siilasvuo could not have known this and was merely hoping that his ruse would give the men the boost they so sorely needed.

The Finns employed both industrially manufactured and homemade 'field' versions of satchel charges. Normally, 2–4kg of explosives were tied around a wooden handle, and a hand-grenade detonator would be used to ignite the whole payload. When discharged next to a tank's lead wheel, or on top of its tracks, this would be enough to immobilise it. During the Winter War, the Finns developed the Molotov cocktail anti-tank weapon. These were made by mixing high-proof alcohol, petroleum and tar in a 0.5l glass bottle. The sticky, flaming liquid would pour through any open hatches, or could be used on the air vents, choking the tank's engine. (SA-kuva)

Siilasvuo planned his initial attack to hit the road at a natural choke point on the narrow isthmus between lakes Kuivasjärvi and Kuomajärvi.[8] The staging area was at Kuivassalmi, a position that lay just outside the Soviet patrol zones. From there the Finns were able to reconnoitre hidden paths leading to their target, setting up pickets of ski-troops along the way.

Eventually, Siilasvuo sent forth three of his battalions from the 27th Infantry Regiment, led by Lieutenant-Colonel Johan Mäkiniemi. Mäkiniemi's primary objective was to cut the road running south-east towards Raate. Controlling this road would prevent any Soviet reinforcements coming from that direction and would be the first step in isolating Zelentsov's 163rd Rifle Division.

Due to a navigational error during the night, the attack was delayed by a couple of hours. Despite this and the loss of the cover of darkness, the Finns soon captured the unguarded section of road. Two companies were immediately set into defensive positions across the road on the narrow isthmus shielding against any enemy reinforcements arriving from the east. The remaining battalions looped back west towards Suomussalmi.

8 See map on p.144

JOHAN MÄKINIEMI
COLONEL,
27TH INFANTRY REGIMENT

Johan August Mäkiniemi joined the *Pfadfinder* course in 1915. After the Finnish Civil War, he served for a short time as a company and battalion commander, before being promoted to the role of Civil Guard district commander.

(1888–1961)

During the Winter War, Mäkiniemi led the 27th Infantry Regiment in the famous battles of Suomussalmi, Raate and Kuhmo. His defence of a narrow isthmus against a whole Soviet division is still a widely studied feat of arms.

Throughout the Continuation War, Mäkiniemi led the 33rd Infantry Regiment in northern Finland. From 1943, he was the commander of the Perä–Pohjola Military District and the Northern Civil Guard District. He remained in this role until the end of war, whereupon he resigned from active service.

The Soviets, apparently, had not yet understood the magnitude of the threat they were facing. En route, the Finns had intercepted and destroyed a convoy of six trucks which had been sent to investigate, and if necessary, to stop a Finnish attack. Near Lake Pihlajalampi, the two Finnish battalions, arriving by different routes, both encountered the same robust Soviet defence of a nearby hill. By the evening, the Finns had managed to group a total of three battalions on the road below the hill; these all took part in repelling a Soviet counter-attack that ensued.

The troops of this Finnish vanguard were by now utterly exhausted after the long night advance, and the capture and subsequent defence of the road section. However, they were unable to rest, for they had no tents; all their camping gear had been accidentally left behind with the rest of the division's baggage train. Sleeping outside was impossible in the freezing temperatures.

After a long and wakeful night, the Finns renewed their attack against the positions at Pihlajalampi. As the Soviets refused to either retreat or surrender, some of the fighting turned into fierce hand-to-hand combat. By lunchtime, the three weary battalions managed to capture the hill.

Eventually Mäkiniemi's battalions were able to proceed towards Suomussalmi. By nightfall, they were finally in control of a large enough landing zone, allowing the troops on the opposite shore of Lake Haukiperä to open a supply route over the frozen surface. The long-awaited tents and hot food finally reached the men leading the attack.

On 12 December, Siilasvuo ordered his men to attack Suomussalmi village both from the east along the Raate road and from the west over the Hulkonniemi Peninsula. The day's fighting did not go well for the Finns, as little progress was made.

The following morning, a Soviet counter-attack was launched from within the village, aimed at reopening the supply road east towards Raate. The Soviet infantry was to be supported by all available artillery and five tanks. Despite the total lack of heavy weapons, the Finns somehow managed to halt the advancing infantry and tanks, and after several hours of fierce fighting pushed them back to Suomussalmi.

Siilavuo's troops once again went on the offensive, but on the edge of the village, the lack of heavy firepower was to thwart them again. Most of the Red Army troops had established strong positions among the buildings, basements and ruins of the village, which they defended fiercely. The Finns were unable to penetrate these strongholds, and eventually were forced to retreat back to the shelter of the surrounding forest edges. Meanwhile, as planned, one Finnish battalion had moved north to the Kannuslampi area. There the men dug in to guard this possible route of escape. Now, only the road north remained open for the Soviet troops at Suomussalmi.

On 14 December, the Finns continued to exert pressure on Zelentsov's forces in the area, in particular the 759th Rifle Regiment that was still holding the village proper, and the 81st Mountain Rifle Regiment just to the west of it. Finnish casualties had by now started to mount; the Soviets had learnt to open fire from basements and foxholes after the attacking troops had already passed. The victory that for a while had seemed so inevitable was denied to the Finns by a timely Soviet counter-attack, and by nightfall the Finns had once again been forced to withdraw from the village. The Finnish high command seemed to be unaware of this setback and instead somewhat prematurely announced the news of victory at Suomussalmi to all of its forces.

East of Suomussalmi, the two-company strong Finnish rearguard, led by Captain Eero A. V. Kontula, repelled an attack by the forward elements of the 44th Rifle Division. The Soviet Ninth Army command had ordered these troops to advance along the Raate road, with the aim of relieving their trapped comrades of Zelentsov's 163rd Rifle Division.

On 15 December, Siilasvuo made a slight change to his tactics. This time he sent a reinforced battalion to cut the northern road further away

OPPOSITE
Portable and warm, squad-sized tents were essential for survival in the Arctic temperatures. During the Suomussalmi battles, the men of the Finnish vanguard realised to their dismay that their camping gear had not followed in their wake, and that they were in for a very cold, miserable night. The same model of tent is still used by the Finnish military today. (SA-kuva)

Finish soldiers test the condition of a captured 45mm Soviet anti-tank gun at Hyrynsalmi. Such weapons were often immediately employed against their previous owners. The light guns were dragged into position on purpose-made ice roads. Then, after a couple of quick shots, before any retaliation could occur, they would be relocated to an alternative position. (SA-kuva)

from the village. These men managed to hold down a section of the road under suppressive fire, but could not wrest control from the defenders. The renewed attacks against the entrenched Soviets at Suomussalmi did not fare any better, and by the night of 18/19 December, Siilasvuo was so discouraged by the failure of the road-cutting attempts that he decided to pull back all troops from the area around Hulkonniemi. This again allowed the 163rd Rifle Division to regain contact with its various regiments. Nevertheless, the Finns kept up their pattern of aggressive reconnaissance by sending out small company-size task forces both in the Hulkonniemi and Raate road sectors. These actions helped delay and disrupt the preparations the Soviets were making for further counter-attacks.

To the east of the village, Captain Simo I. Mäkinen was given charge of the rear-guard defences towards Raate. On this flank, the Finns were still unaware that a whole new enemy division was heading their way, although increases in enemy concentrations had been noted.

Siilasvuo had chosen this narrow isthmus with care. He surmised that the Soviets would not dare abandon their heavy equipment in order to try an attack through the dense forests. This only left them with two options. They could either try crossing the frozen lakes Kuivasjärvi or Kuomajärvi, which would then leave them completely exposed to Finnish fire, or they would have to keep on pushing directly ahead on the narrow road between the lakes. As he correctly guessed, the Raate road was to form the 44th Rifle Division's sole axis of attack.

On 17 December, Mäkinen received one howitzer to strengthen his positions; he decided to immediately deploy it into a forward position where the gun could used in the direct fire role as an anti-tank weapon. This firepower addition seems to have arrived just in time, as the following day three tanks were destroyed by this new gun. Their defences were bolstered further on 19 December by the arrival of an additional machine-gun company. In this grim, modern-day version of the battle of Thermopylae, Mäkinen's 350-strong force continued to deny access along the road to nearly 14,000 Soviet soldiers.

Zelentsov had begun to reflect that the situation was getting unbearable for his troops at Suomussalmi. On 16 December, he had requested permission from his superiors for the 163rd Rifle Division to retreat and regroup. However, Ninth Army's headquarters decided to keep his troops in place, surrounded or not, and informed them that the 44th Rifle Division had already been sent on its way to relieve them.

Ninth Army's headquarters also gave further orders for the 163rd and 44th Rifle divisions to begin simultaneous, aggressive attacks starting on 22 December. This action ended up being postponed until the 24th, as Stavka had decided to replace Ninth Army's current commander Duhanov with Corps Commander Vasily I. Chuikov. This change in leadership was justified by the lack of progress the army had made, while the mounting casualty figures also did little to help Duhanov's cause. By 20 December, the 163rd Rifle Division had lost 1,501 men whereas the Finnish 27th Infantry Regiment, which had borne the brunt of the fighting for Task Force Siilasvuo, had lost a total of 216.

For the next attack phases, the Soviets wanted to reinforce the two infantry regiments, the divisional artillery and the headquarters already located at Suomussalmi. This was to

VASILY CHUIKOV
ARMY CORPS COMMANDER, NINTH ARMY

(1900–1982)

Vasily Ivanovich Chuikov's military career began humbly as a ship's mate in 1917. Two years later, he had already risen to be a regimental commander during the Russian Civil War.

After the Civil War, Chuikov graduated from the Frunze Military Academy in 1925. He then served as a military advisor to Chiang Kai-shek in China from 1927 to 1929. When the Red Army invaded Poland, Chuikov commanded the Fourth Army.

From 22 December 1939 onwards, Chuikov assumed command of the Ninth Army fighting on the northern Finnish front. Despite the changes in leadership, the situation did not greatly improve for the now threatened Soviet forces.

After the Winter War, Chuikov spent time as a military attaché to China until 1942, whereupon he was recalled to take over the Sixty-Second Army at Stalingrad. Chuikov went on to secure victory and his command received the honorific new title of Eighth Guards Army. From Stalingrad, the Eighth Guards Army continued its relentless march all the way to Berlin. In May 1945, Chuikov personally accepted the Berlin garrison's surrender. He was twice named a Hero of the Soviet Union.

Chuikov was promoted to the rank of marshal of the Soviet Union in 1955. From 1961 until his death on 18 March 1982, Chuikov remained a member of the Central Committee of the Communist Party.

The front line at Lake Joutsijärvi in early January 1940. The winter of 1939/40 was bitterly cold and the snow was deep. The Finns were able to use this to their benefit by advancing to point-blank range before launching their surprise attacks. (SA-kuva)

prove very difficult, as the Finns now controlled a 5km section of the road between the 163rd and 44th Rifle divisions. As a result, the reinforcement battalion sent by the 44th Rifle Division had to circle the Finnish positions and embark on an almost 200km-long march through the Lonkka–Palovaara area. This route was still considered safe, as the Soviets had controlled the sector since their initial offensive. At the same time, headquarters decided to send one more battalion from the 662nd Rifle Regiment back to Suomussalmi. These men had previously pushed northwards towards the Peranka crossroads, but so far had not managed to break down the hasty resistance the Finns had rushed into the area. It was fully expected that in order to reach their comrades at Suomussalmi, these reinforcements arriving from a northerly direction would have to fight their way through the Finnish lines on the Hulkonniemi Peninsula.

Despite the fact that most of the 44th Rifle Division's troops were still in transit, those men that were already present were ordered to commence a simultaneous assault with their comrades in Suomussalmi. The 44th Rifle Division's commander estimated that they would not be ready for this mission until after 25 December, and therefore the 168th Rifle Division was to launch the attack alone. This effort soon dwindled, and the attack had come to a complete halt by Christmas Day. The frustrated Ninth Army headquarters blamed the 44th Rifle Division's lack of activity as the main reason for its failure. It seems plausible that a determined attack launched simultaneously from both directions, as was planned, would have led to the Finnish defenders being crushed.

Unknown to Ninth Army's command, what would become known as 'Finn terror' had already started to spread through the 44th Rifle Division. A few days before, on 23 December, two Finnish companies had made a surprise raid in the Haukila area against the division's supply troops. This attack resulted in 70 Soviet dead, while the Finns took off with over 100 horses. In another incident further to the east, a battalion from the 27th Infantry Regiment hit the Raate road near Lake Kokkojärvi. They destroyed a tank and killed nearly 100 Soviet troops for the loss of only two men. The men of the 44th Rifle Division were unnerved by how the Finns could silently ski in to attack them from unexpected directions. This soon riddled the Ukrainian ranks with an almost paranoid sense of terror. Some troops deserted their positions when they thought they had heard the sound of skis coming from the woods; commissars inspecting the area afterwards found no evidence of any ski tracks for several hundred metres. The indecisiveness of its leaders and the reluctance of the troops meant that the 44th Rifle Division achieved practically nothing before the Finns took the initiative once again.

After the war, Khadzehen Mamsurov, who had been a regimental commander in the Ninth Army, gave the following commentary on the Red Army's restrictive political structure:

> When carrying out ski missions, I saw abnormal situations in the work of battalion commanders with my own eyes. Some ten men stood around and monitored the actions of the battalion commander and his subordinates. There was always somebody from the divisional headquarters, someone from the Ninth Army's political directorate, a man from the army newspaper … a dozen men besides the commander himself. I remember two cases when the battalion commander stepped aside and said to me, 'I don't know what to do, shall I quit and let them run things themselves?' (Edwards, 2006)

On 19 December, Mannerheim gave Siilasvuo something of an early Christmas present: his task force was to be returned to full strength again under the old 9th Division banner. Consequently, the following day, two poorly armed infantry regiments were sent to support the North Karelian Group. One regiment was directed to the Suomussalmi area, while the second was sent north to Lake Piispajärvi, where a newly formed Task Force Susi was gathering under Lieutenant-Colonel Paavo Susitaival. North

A Finnish ski patrol on a hill near the Ahvenlahti–Jelettijärvi lakes during the winter of 1942. (SA-kuva)

Battle for Suomussalmi, 27–28 December 1939

Finland Group headquarters also sent the 6th Bicycle Battalion, commanded by Major Arvo A. Järvinen, to further bolster Task Force Siilasvuo, on 23 December. This battalion had originally been meant for Susitaival, but was now deemed more useful at Suomussalmi.

Both task forces Siilasvuo and Susi were to start their attacks on 26 December. Susitaival was to use four battalions to take control of the Kuusamo–Suomussalmi road, and then to follow the road south to Palovaara. This was the very same spot where the Soviets had earlier split their

(1897–1944)

✠ KAARLE KARI
MAJOR, TASK FORCE KARI

Kari commanded Task Force Kari, drawn from the 9th Division, during the battles of Suomussalmi and Raate road. After the rest of Siilasvuo's division transferred to Kuhmo, Kari remained behind to command the garrisoned troops in the Suomussalmi area.

In the Continuation War, Kari began as the commander of the 1st Sissi Battalion. He subsequently held several regimental commands, and was promoted lieutenant-colonel in November 1940, and then to the rank of colonel in April 1943. He was made a Knight of the Mannerheim Cross, the 66th person to receive this.

On 19 January 1944, Kaarle Kari was killed in action while leading the 45th Infantry Regiment in the fighting in Lampero.

forces. Once they reached this objective, Task Force Susi was to complete surrounding the Soviet forces in the area by retracing their earlier route of attack to Juntusranta.

Meanwhile, Siilasvuo's 9th Division was to complete the destruction of Soviet forces in Suomussalmi village with a strong easterly attack. However, as the 44th Rifle Division seemed to be massing more troops, the plan was quickly amended. Not wanting to risk an attack to his rear, Siilasvuo instead ordered the village to be taken by the main body of the division from the

Bristol Blenheim Mk IV bombers participated in chasing the 168th Rifle Division across the ice of Lake Kiantajärvi. The yellow stripe at the tail of this Finnish plane was the designation for the German Eastern Front. The British-made Bristol Blenheim light bomber represented the 1930s mindset that newer bombers would be protected from fighter attack by their increased speed. Finland's interest in this model grew during the early 1930s and they received their first Blenheims in 1937. By that time it had become apparent that the Blenheim's speed advantage, compared to modern fighters, had already vanished. Additionally, the plane's defensive armament, consisting of one or two wing-mounted, forward facing machine guns, and one machine gun operated by a rear gunner, was insufficient for the demands of the time. (SA-kuva)

west. The men would assault along the Hulkonniemi Peninsula, while the 27th Infantry Regiment would continue to maintain its position as a wedge between the two Soviet divisions.

However, surprising Soviet counter-attacks west from Hulkuonniemi and from within Suomussalmi village, as well as the late arrival of promised reinforcements meant that Siilasvuo's own attack was delayed by a day. Finally on 27 December, Siilasvuo ordered his troops into action. On his northern flank, the 6th Bicycle Battalion was ordered to participate in the attacks south, towards Kylänmäki. Unfortunately, the battalion had already spread out across a wide frontage on a much longer stretch of the Kuusamo–Suomussalmi road, and therefore could only spare one company for this attack. The rest of the battalion attacked further north up the road, near Käkimäki. There, on 28 December, the Finns halted the advance of a motorised enemy column. By nightfall the troops in the column had abandoned their vehicles by the roadside, and made their escape across the wilderness back to the Soviet Union.

Meanwhile, the four battalions comprising what was known as Task Force Kari, under the command of Major Kaarle Kari, performed the main push towards the Hulkonniemi Peninsula. After a preliminary bombardment by the division's artillery battery and a mortar company, the troops launched their assault over the frozen Lake Oraviselkä. Task Force Kari made good progress initially, reaching the houses in the centre of Hulkonniemi. There, fire from the Soviet 81st Mountain Rifle Regiment finally halted their advance.

Although they had stopped the Finns, the situation was now becoming perilous for the men of the 81st Mountain Rifle Regiment. After suffering severe losses, they were forced to retreat into the area containing the 163rd Rifle Division's headquarters. There, the Soviets continued to offer fierce resistance until the early hours of the morning.

Although his attack had been halted, Siilasvuo was pleased to note that morale was high among his troops, and that despite their heavy losses, the two new poorly armed regiments had acquitted themselves well in the fighting. The Soviet assessment contrasted heavily. Earlier that evening, Ninth Army headquarters had understood finally how vulnerable its forces were and had informed Stavka of the difficult situation. It had stressed that the troops at Suomussalmi were in danger of being completely surrounded, which would result in their destruction. Stavka gave them immediate permission to withdraw northwards towards Juntusranta. The retreat began in full at 05:00 on the night of 28/29 December.

Finnish observers positioned on the higher ground could do nothing but monitor the massive Soviet formations escaping along the ice of Lake

Kiantajärvi to the north. The infantry were protected by the accompanying tanks, and Soviet fighters strafed any Finns visible along the shoreline. Siilasvuo had only a light reconnaissance formation in the area, and against such overwhelming force this unit could do nothing; its troops became pinned down in skirmishing with enemy patrols. Thus, the remaining Soviet forces managed to withdraw almost without loss.

In the morning, the advancing Finns experienced only light resistance from the rearguard formations in the Suomussalmi area. This thankless task had fallen to a force consisting mainly of supply troops and clerical personnel.

On 29 December, the last pocket of these defenders tried to break out by launching desperate attacks in all directions. They were destroyed by the 6th Bicycle Battalion; the latter took only light casualties, while leaving around 300 dead Soviet troops on the field. However, the sacrifice of the rearguard had managed to slow the Finnish pursuit considerably. Siilasvuo quickly dispatched troops to pursue the fleeing Soviets and even had the luxury of heavy air support for the first, and last, time in the entire campaign. The efforts of both the few planes and his troops were largely in vain: the Soviets had made their escape.

On 31 December, Mannerheim awarded Colonel Hjalmar Siilasvuo the Finnish Cross of Liberty 2nd Class for his tenacity over the three weeks of fighting, thanking him and his troops for their vigorous action and major

Narrow roads with treacherous snow banks on either side forced vehicles into single file. This greatly reduced their manoeuvrability and enabled *motti* to be formed. Men at the back of the column had no way of helping their comrades further up the line. (SA-kuva)

accomplishments. The capture of Suomussalmi had not happened a day too soon, as by now Finnish aerial reconnaissance had confirmed that an entire, well-armed division was amassing on the Raate road.

TASK FORCE SUSI

Paavo Susitaival was a member of the Finnish parliament when the Winter War broke out. He requested a front-line command and was given leadership of the 16th Independent Battalion, ranked lieutenant-colonel. Susitaival's initial involvement in the war came with securing the Kuusamo–Suomussalmi road in order to prevent Soviet forces from reaching the village of Peranka.

Susitaival's responsibilities grew considerably when he was asked to lead the newly formed Task Force Susi against the Soviet Ninth Army at Juntusranta, near the Finno–Soviet border. For this purpose, his 16th Independent Battalion was further reinforced with the 65th Infantry Regiment, one reinforced motorised pioneer company and two reconnaissance squads.

Task Force Susi's objective was to secure the critical Kuusamo–Suomussalmi and Juntusranta crossroads. From there, Susitaival's force would create a distraction and help entrap the enemy at Suomussalmi while proceeding towards Juntusranta. Susitaival himself judged his force to be of poor quality, suffering from weak leadership and being ill equipped. Indeed, initially the regiment's artillery battery had no weapons at all. Considering these factors, Susitaival's view was that the original plans for a wide-fronted attack would never succeed. Instead, he decided to concentrate the main body of his forces on the Kuusamo road, and advance southwards towards the Palovaara crossroads.

As the main body of Susitaival's force slowly made its way along the road to Palovaara, the forward elements of the 16th Independent Battalion had already managed to occupy the crossroads. This small force had travelled swiftly without its supplies cross-country, and launched a surprise attack against the inadequately defended junction. However, due to the extremely cold weather, these lightly equipped troops could not remain in the open to guard the position, and the whole unit had to be withdrawn into prepared shelters the following evening. The Soviets thus temporarily regained control of the crossroads; the Finns, wishing to avoid repeating this mistake, set up a new supply depot nearby. By 23 December, the critical crossroads was recaptured by one of the Finnish companies who had been ordered to 'rest in the area'.

At this stage, the commander of the 47th Rifle Corps (Ninth Army), Ivan Dashitsev, had just received orders to withdraw the 662nd Rifle Regiment back to the vicinity of Suomussalmi. However, Dashitsev was in no hurry to obey this order, as he seemed to have perceived no immediate threat to his troops.

The North Finland Group commander gave orders for both Susitaival and Siilasvuo to attack Suomussalmi from their respective positions. Susitaival tasked Lieutenant-Colonel Karl R. W. Mandelin's 65th Infantry Regiment with spearheading the attack on 25 December.

The forward elements of Mandelin's regiment stopped just in front of the positions of Task Force Sharov (from the 662nd Rifle Regiment, and under the command of Colonel Sharov) whose mission had been to secure the division's route of supply to Juntusranta through the crossroads, near the southern edge of Lake Piispajärvi. Mandelin had his men spend the whole of the following day preparing for a night attack. When the appointed time finally came, the Finns found only abandoned enemy positions. The following morning, a fresh battalion continued the pursuit, managing to advance nearly 5km without meeting any resistance. The unit was eventually ordered to halt for the night, just south of the Mustajoki River.

PAAVO SUSITAIVAL
LIEUTENANT COLONEL,
TASK FORCE SUSI

(1896–1993)

Paavo Susitaival, born Paavo Sivén, was a right-wing radical and a devout Civil Guard soldier. Together with his brother Bobi, they were probably two of the first boy scouts in Finland. Paavo was active in the Jäger movement, but was unable to make it to Germany for training, as both Russian and Finnish officials were monitoring the movements of his family closely.

During the Finnish Civil War, Susitaival served as a company commander. In 1921, Bobi committed suicide as a political protest over the lands lost following the Treaty of Tartu. Paavo resigned from the armed forces in order to continue his brother's work of fomenting an uprising in the lost territory of Repola.

As a lieutenant-colonel, Susitaival participated in the Mäntsälä Rebellion, which resulted in him being discharged in 1932. The following year he took up a position as section commander in the Isänmaallinen Kansanliike (IKL – Patriotic People's Movement), an anti-communist, nationalistic party. In 1934 his overt contempt for the government earned him a short prison sentence. Despite his convictions and previous record, Susitaival was elected as a member of parliament as a representative of the IKL in 1939.

Although politicians rarely served on the front, Susitaival was made the leader of Task Force Susi upon his own request.

In the Continuation War, Susitaival led the 29th Infantry Regiment in the offensive phase of 1941. Following this, he became the vice commander of the garrison in the captured city of Äänislinna.

He never progressed past the rank of lieutenant-colonel due to his abrasive personality and resulting personal feuds with prominent officers, including Mannerheim himself. According to Susitaival's own words, his life consisted of, 'Three wars, two rebellions, four trips to prison and regrettably one stint in Parliament'.

After the war, he retired from the army and focused on writing. An avid pipe smoker, he took his last puff at the ripe old age of 96.

By 28 December, it came clear that both Task Force Tchaikovsky (also from the 662nd Rifle Regiment, and under the command of Captain Tchaikovsky) and Task Force Sharov were in imminent danger of being cut off. As Finns of unknown strength were already in control of the junction, both formations were given permission to withdraw past this area, cross-country, towards Juntusranta.

Lieutenant-Colonel Mandelin of the 65th Infantry Regiment in his command tent during the battles at the Raate road on 8 January 1940. (SA-kuva)

Although the withdrawal began early in the day, while Sharov's men were still fighting their rearguard action, the Soviets were forced to leave behind all their motorised vehicles and heavy equipment. Finnish reports state that the Soviet forces which retreated from Hyövynvaara left behind 11 field howitzers, 6 anti-tank guns, 2 anti-aircraft cannons, 150 trucks, 11 tanks, 250 horses and 12 field kitchens. In addition, a large quantity of small arms and ammunition were repatriated.

Apparently, Sharov and his leading commissar A. A. Podhomutov had abandoned their troops and made their own way home. Out of Sharov's task force, only 300 men managed to make it back to Soviet territory. There, on 16 January, they were rewarded with the executions of Sharov and Podhumutov in front of the assembled ranks.

Following this impressive victory, the Finnish 65th Infantry Regiment continued southwards, finally joining forces with the 16th Independent Battalion, which had earlier captured the Palovaara junction after a cross-country trek.

Meanwhile, the rest of the Soviet 662nd Rifle Regiment – comprising Task Force Tchaikovsky – continued its escape towards friendly lines. Things went wrong from the outset when three Soviet SB-2 bombers attacked the 662nd troops, causing further casualties. Shortly after this, the unit ran into Finnish forces on the road near Lake Kivijärvi. The leading officer, Captain Tchaikovsky, ordered one company to encircle the Finnish positions from the west while he himself led a separate pioneer company in a flanking attack from the east. The remaining troops were to wait on the road for these two detachments to clear the road.

During his manoeuvre, Captain Tchaikovsky deserted his command, and made directly for the border with only six men escorting him. When it became clear that Tchaikovsky would not return, a leadership crisis ensued amongst the remaining troops. Battalion Commissar Buturin tried to take command of the situation, but was shot on the spot by one of the junior political officers. It was impossible to find a natural leader after this, and the remaining force split into two. Both groups attempted to make their own way along forested roads and unused paths. A total of 617 men made it, while 150 lost their lives during the trek.

The battles for both Suomussalmi village and the road to Kuusamo ended in resounding Finnish victories. The Soviet Ninth Army headquarters held the 47th Rifle Corps Commander Ivan Dashitsev solely responsible for the catastrophe that befell the 662nd Rifle Regiment. Had he followed the earlier orders to withdraw the regiment into the vicinity of Suomussalmi, this debacle could have been averted. In January 1940, Dashitsev was demoted and removed from corps command.

There are no precise records of how many Soviet troops died during the battle of Suomussalmi. Some researchers estimate the number to be as high as 5,000 dead, over 500 taken prisoner and many more missing.

THE RAATE ROAD

While Task Force Susi was advancing from the north and dealing decisive blows to the troops of Captain Tchaikovsky, it became clear to Siilasvuo that an entire, newly arrived division was advancing towards his men on the Raate road. Their passage, however, was still blocked at a narrow isthmus by the meagre forces under the command of Lieutenant-Colonel Johan Mäkiniemi.

It seems likely that had Brigade Commander Alexei Vinogradov, the commander of the 44th Rifle Division, acted with determination and haste, he could have joined forces with 163rd Rifle Division commander Zelentsov at Suomussalmi. However, due to his tardiness, the Finns had been able to reinforce and repel each attack that was launched from 16 December onwards. Vinogradov's highly mechanised and mobile armoured division had become bunched up and now simply did not have enough room to manoeuvre on the small forest road to Raate. Just prior to crossing the border into Finland, Vinogradov's troops had been supplied with thousands of pairs of skis. The problem was that very few of the Ukrainians knew how to use them, so most of the men resorted to wading through the waist-deep snow. The few who could ski were sent into the forests on patrol missions, often never to be seen again.

Furthering Vinogradov's dismay was the fact that his men were by now convinced that at any moment a flurry of snow-white

Although the Red Army had plenty of skis at its disposal, its troops lacked the skills to use them properly. Many pairs of skis were captured from the Soviet supply wagons at the Raate road. Nikita Khrushchev recalled in his memoirs: 'We tried to put our own troops on skis too. We started intensively to recruit professional sportsmen. We had to bring them from Moscow and the Ukraine as well as from Leningrad. They left in high spirits. The poor fellows were ripped to shreds. I don't know how many came back alive.' (Khrushchev, 1971; photo SA-kuva)

ALEXEI VINOGRADOV
BRIGADE COMMANDER,
44TH RIFLE DIVISION

(1899–1940)

Aleksei Nikolajevitch Vinogradov participated in the Russian Civil War on the eastern front as a common soldier. He completed the Ukrainian Infantry School in 1922, and proceeded to take a higher course in chemistry, graduating in 1924. From 1923 to 1937 Vinogradov served as squad leader, company commander and regimental chief of staff. He held a short regimental command from 1937 to 1938.

In January 1939, Vinogradov was handed command of the 44th Rifle Division. Under his leadership, the division took part in the conquest of eastern Poland in September 1939. From there the unit transferred by rail north to the town of Vienan Kemi. The plan was that Vinogradov's men would then join forces with the 163rd Rifle Division for the capture of Suomussalmi. Their ultimate goal was to cut Finland in half by advancing towards the city of Oulu.

What followed was one of the most remarkable military defeats in modern history. Vinogradov's division, advancing along the narrow Raate road, ended up first surrounded and then all but destroyed by the Finns.

Vinogradov himself escaped the *motti*, and made it back to Russia in January 1940. According to Stavka's investigators, the division's command was instrumental in its defeat. As a result, Vinogradov was executed by a firing squad in front of the decimated ranks of his former command.

He was posthumously rehabilitated by the Leningrad Military District on 17 November 1990.

Finns would fall on them from the nearby forests, showering them with grenades. Often, these attacks were supported by snipers, who had orders to take out the officers first. Then, Suomi submachine-gun fire would rake the nearby tents and foxholes. Before the Soviets could muster any reinforcements or organise resistance, the woods would go quiet again: the Finns had left as rapidly and silently as they had arrived.

Siilasvuo also seemed convinced that Vinogradov, who had been trained to fight on more open European battlefields, would no longer dare to send large forces into the woods to loop around the blockade. This turned out to be correct, as in spite of the deep and uncontested reconnaissance mission that Vinogradov's 146th Rifle Regiment carried out, moving well past the Finnish positions, any plans for future attacks through the wilderness were cancelled. Such a manoeuvre would have allowed the Soviets to use a much larger proportion of their forces, and when combined with their massed artillery, might have been able to blast a way through on the road. One captured Ukrainian officer, who had been attacking Mäkinen's roadblock, stated: 'of course we tried to open the way, but it was like … butting your head against a stone wall … it was unbelievable' (Trotter, 1991). This officer's account of the 44th Rifle Division's passage to Finland was equally negative:

From Murmansk, we marched almost 350 kilometres in eleven days which I am sure you Finns would have been proud to accomplish. The only thing we received was a scolding from headquarters because of our slow tempo of advance. During this march we began to wonder about the whole war … we lost 10 per cent of our strength mainly due to frostbite. When we

crossed over to Finland we could no longer make campfires because as soon as we did bullets and grenades could have started popping in the middle of our encampment. Such cold … such endless wilderness and darkness. We tried to keep together so we would not get lost. Soldiers crowded shoulder to shoulder in some areas. (Eagle and Paananen, 1973)

For now, the initiative lay firmly with Siilasvuo, and he knew just how to make best use of it. As the intensity of battles at Hulkonniemi and Suomussalmi decreased, more troops were sent to reinforce Mäkiniemi's positions.

On 30 December, Tuompo gave Siilasvuo new orders: as soon as his 9th Division had rested after the battle for Suomussalmi, it was to push on and destroy the 44th Rifle Division along the Raate road. Tuompo also transferred the 1st Sissi Battalion to act as the division's reserve. This battalion specialised in guerrilla warfare; its ski troops were highly mobile and already well equipped for working behind enemy lines.

Upon its arrival the 1st Sissi Battalion was positioned south-west behind the front. From there, they were to loop around the enemy lines, attacking towards Haukila. The battalion started to advance as planned but encountered

A Finnish patrol returning after a successful mission in the enemy's rear. Finland managed to manufacture a mere 4,000 Suomi submachine guns prior to the outbreak of the war. However, as People's Commissar for Defence Voroshilov remembered: 'Only after the actual invasion did we recall, that way back in the early 1930s, we had acquired samples of the Suomi MG. This was tested by a commission specialising in infantry weapons. They found the weapon completely unsuitable for military operations. Now, having encountered the widespread use of submachine guns in the Finnish Army, we bitterly regretted these miscalculations.' (Eagle and Paananen, 1973; photo SA-kuva)

A captured T-26 M1933 tank at Suomussalmi. At the time of the Winter War, the Soviet tanks all had petrol engines. The severe supply issues often immobilised these tanks in the efforts to conserve fuel. (SA-kuva)

enemy positions earlier than expected at the southern edge of Lake Kuivasjärvi. After four hours of fighting, the Finns retreated to the staging area. The main thrust, directed towards the road, did not fare any better.

By 1 January, practically all of the combat elements of the 44th Rifle Division, comprising nearly 14,000 men, had reached the front. The Soviet artillery batteries included 38 76mm cannons, 28 122mm cannons and 12 152mm cannons. The division also fielded 48 anti-tank guns, 14 heavy mortars and a total of 44 tanks. All these men and this materiel clogged up the narrow Raate road; the conjestion was made worse by the presence of the division's transport elements, comprising 530 trucks, 103 tractors and 4,531 horses.

The 44th Rifle Division's commander and its political commissar did not even bother reaching Finland until after New Year, and so the leaderless divisional elements had taken up positions along the road wherever they could find space. Meanwhile, Siilasvuo's men performed a reconnaissance in depth, and were reorganised in light of the intelligence gathered. Mäkiniemi resumed command of the troops at the roadblock area, while the separate Task Force Kari was ordered to circle towards Ala-Vuokki proceeding in the direction of Raate from the south-east.

On 1 January, Mäkiniemi launched a frontal attack towards Haukila, the position immediately in front of the Finnish lines. Captain Eino E. Lassila's 1st Battalion (27th Infantry Regiment) and the 1st Sissi Battalion hooked around the southern end of the enemy positions. Lassila managed to advance close to the Raate road without detection, surprising the artillery batteries positioned there. As all of the enemy's guns were trained towards the west, the Finns were able to infiltrate them before they could be re-aimed. The gun crews were cut down within minutes while the Finnish combat engineers blocked the road by planting mines and felling trees using explosives. The 1st Sissi Battalion, advancing on Lassila's left flank, was not as successful. In the ensuing firefight, the battalion suffered heavy losses, losing its ability to function as a fighting unit.

By the afternoon, the men of the 1st Sissi Battalion had to be replaced by Captain Aarne G. Airimo's 3rd battalion (27th Infantry Regiment). The following day, Airamo's men managed to advance to within 300m of the Raate road and link up with Captain Lassila's troops. Although the Finns now were able to suppress all movement on the road, the Soviet resistance was too strong for it to be completely severed.

Things were not going well for the Red Army. That morning, they had launched one counter-attack after another, each stronger than the last, from both east and west, without being able to dislodge the Finns from the vicinity of the road. Worse still, in the course of the day several of their attacking tanks were destroyed or immobilised. Their burning bulks added further obstacles, rendering the road virtually impassable for any further relief attempts.

During the day's battles, Vinogradov, the commander of the 44th Rifle Division, reached the front line. There he informed his officers that their fellow troops had been forced to abandon Suomussalmi village. He also gave orders for the division to take up a hedgehog defensive formation. The 146th Rifle Regiment was given responsibility for defending the southern flank of the division.

To the south-east of the Ukrainians, the forward elements of Task Force Kari finally reached their designated forming-up point. The 22nd Light Detachment rested for the reminder of the night and then launched its own attack across Lake Vuokkijärvi. There, near Sanginaho, the entrenched enemy troops from the 146th Rifle Regiment were able to repel all their attempts to establish a bridgehead.

However, this action by the encircling Finns caused concern at Soviet Ninth Army headquarters. They promised the troops around Haukila that additional divisional forces would be sent to help clear the supply route to the east. In the meantime, the starving division was permitted to start butchering some of its horses. In addition to the food shortages, the cold weather was proving deadly in more ways than one. Ismail Akhmedov, a GRU (military intelligence) captain with the 44th Rifle Division, recalled that 'the battalion had been badly punished when the men had lit fires to warm themselves and heat what food we had. From among the treetops the Finns had machine-gunned every campfire, easily picking out the dark silhouettes of the men against the snow' (Troy, 1984).

The Soviets had been able to enjoy almost complete air dominance up to this point. Unfortunately, most of their fighters and bombers could offer little support, on account of the thick forests. From time to time, they would perform a sortie where they would fire into the trees at random. The thick foliage and good camouflage protected the Finns from all but the luckiest of shots.

Captured Soviet rifles. (SA-kuva)

On 2 January, North Finland Group decided to transfer the entire 65th Infantry Regiment of Task Force Susi, save for the 1st Battalion, to Siilasvuo's command. Having secured the arms left behind by the Soviets at the battle of Hyövynvaara, these troops had continued their advance further east towards Juntusranta. Despite the distance they now had to march back, most of the men arrived already on 4 January. They immediately proceeded to relieve the elements of the 27th Infantry Regiment from front-line duty.

Raate Road Battles, 5–7 January 1940

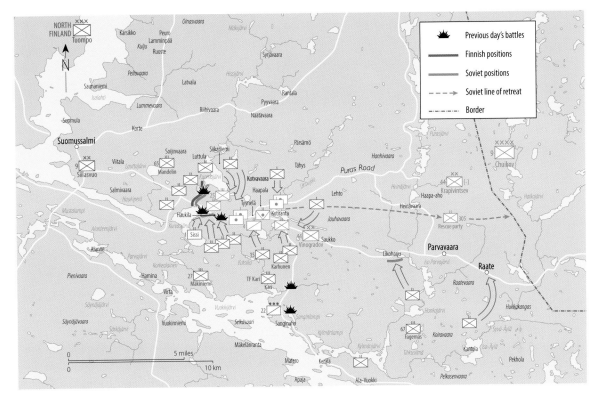

While the Finns awaited their reinforcements, the 22nd Light Detachment (64th Infantry Regiment) was ordered to capture the newly discovered enemy base at Sanginlampi. This base was being fortified as a strong point on the southern flank of the 146th Rifle Division. According to the intelligence, it was defended by at least several tanks and cannons.

Despite repeated attempts, the base at Sanginlampi proved too strong for the 22nd Light Detachment to overcome. Siilasvuo thus ordered Task Force Kari, which had been on a south-easterly march past the area, to lend its weight to the attack. On 3 January, Major Kari sent his 15th Independent Battalion directly north towards Sanginlampi, while a second battalion, led by Lieutenant Veikko E. Karhunen (4th Battalion of the Field Replacement Brigade), was to encircle the enemy base from the east.

In spite of the determined efforts by both battalions, the enemy positions held. By nightfall, the 15th Independent Battalion withdrew to their staging area, while Karhunen's battalion withdrew north to rest. Their new temporary encampment now effectively cut off any escape route for the Soviets.

Soviet columns on the Raate road. The dense forests on both sides of the road provided the advancing Finns with ample cover. They would simply surge forward, causing the greatest damage possible before vanishing into the protection of the trees once more. (SA-kuva)

The following day, around midday, Karhunen split his force in two and renewed the attack with a pincer move. A short and desperate battle ensued. The Finns made grim but steady progress as they were forced to clear one machine-gun nest and emplacement at a time. In just a few hours of fighting, the Finns lost 14 killed and 28 wounded. Soviet fatalities at the same time mounted to 260 dead and 40 men taken prisoner. All of the armoured vehicles appeared to have made their escape at some earlier point.

These vehicles soon reappeared, as the Ukrainians launched a relief attempt towards Sanginlampi. The Finnish 15th Independent Battalion halted this attack a few kilometres to the north of Sanginlampi, ensuring that the lands to the south were now solely in Finnish hands.

The threat to the sole Soviet supply route grew ever more menacing. The men defending the Puras crossroads were by now almost completely out of ammunition, food and fodder for the horses. Ninth Army headquarter tried to ease their plight by dropping three bags of ship's biscuits from the air. They managed to repeat this feat on 6 January, when the same quantity was parachuted in. This proved to be the last successful attempt of any kind to supply the struggling troops.

By the evening of 4 January, after their victory at Sanginlampi, the Finns had increased the pressure further by pushing the Soviet front line back closer to the road. This prompted Captain Pastuhov, commander of 2nd Battalion, 146th Rifle Regiment, to inform his divisional commander Vinogradov that without food and ammunition his troops were no longer fit to fight. Soon afterwards, parts of the regiment became completely surrounded by the Finns.

Ninth Army commander Vasily Chuikov informed the Army Supreme Commander, People's Commissar for Defence Kliment Voroshilov, that the 44th Rifle Division was facing a very difficult situation, and requested permission for it to withdraw into new positions east of Lake Kokkojärvi.

On 4 January, Siilasvuo gave orders to encircle and destroy the enemy in the area between Lake Kokkojärvi and Haukila. In preparation for these attacks, so-called winter roads were ploughed through the snow up to a distance of a few kilometres from the enemy positions. These functioned as jumping-off points, allowing the Finns to mass troops together quickly and without being detected. However, the combined efforts of both Task Force Kari and the rest of the 9th Division's battalions were not enough, and the Finns failed to occupy the road as planned. The situation had nevertheless decisively worsened for the Soviets, as from now on they would be fighting an enemy both to their south and to their north.

From their new positions the Finns were also able to suppress movement along the road, preventing the withdrawal of all the heavier equipment. During the night, the temperatures plummeted to below -35°C. Vinogradov sent scout parties into the dark to see if they could find a possible northerly escape route on little-used paths. He surmised that the virgin forests to the north were unsuitable for large formations and hence unlikely to hold strong Finnish forces. The scouting parties failed to return.

Siilasvuo ordered elements of the 9th Division to continue to attack throughout the night. Just before dawn on 6 December, Lieutenant Karhunen's battalion managed to capture a section of the road near Lake Kokkojärvi. There the Finns immediately dug defensive positions, with one anti-tank gun pointing towards the encircled enemy in the west and one guarding against any possible relief attempts from the east.

Later that day, on its third attempt, the 15th Independent Battalion finally managed to sever the road in the Tyynelä area, about a kilometre west of Lieutenant Karhunen's roadblock. There the battalion was able to halt the advance of an enemy motorised column escaping from the direction of Kokkojärvi.

Around Haukila, where Soviet forces were concentrated, the attacks from Mäkiniemi's 27th Infantry Regiment were largely ineffective. The Soviets themselves made a strong attempt to break through to the east. When

Dead Soviet soldiers and abandoned T-20 Komsolets artillery tractors towing 45mm anti-tank guns on the Raate road. General der Infanterie Waldemar Erfurth, the German Liaison Officer with the Finnish armed forces, noted: 'During the Winter War, the Finns learned, when the enemy broke through, to attack him from all sides, to encircle him, press him together and finally destroy him.' (SA-kuva)

RIGHT
Captured Soviet supply wagons on the Raate road. Mannerheim later commented on the *motti* in general: 'The fact that the surrounded units refused to surrender in spite of cold and hunger was largely due to the political commissars. Soldiers were prevented from surrendering by threats of reprisals against their families and the assurance that they would be killed or tortured if they fell into the hands of the enemy. There were innumerable cases where officers as well as men preferred suicide to surrendering.' (Mannerheim, 1954; photo SA-kuva)

their leading tanks drove straight into the Finnish mines at the makeshift roadblocks, the Soviets sent their pack animals forward in the hope that a stampede could clear a path through. However, the road to Raate remained cut, and by evening the Finnish troops located in the woods to the north noted tracks made by some of the Soviet troops escaping through the wilderness. It was thus decided that the noose around the Haukila *motti* needed to be tightened further. During the night, the Raate road was cut at multiple points, creating several smaller *motti*, which the Finns then proceeded to try to destroy.

On 6 December, the Ukrainians counter-attacked from the Haukila *motti* in an attempt to reconnect the division's fragmented forces. They failed, and by evening the troops in the area had lost all forms of contact with Ninth Army headquarters. Just prior to this loss of contact, the Soviet high command had given one final motivational radio message for the troops: 'Fight until the very last man.' At the same time, Vinogradov was allowed to act freely as he saw fit, with the proviso that no equipment was to be left to the enemy. He was also told to designate areas for forthcoming aerial supply drops.

Despite these orders to hold, Vinogradov ordered his troops to immediately begin organising for a rapid withdrawal to the east. All the

materiel that could not be taken with them was to be destroyed. If the road could not be reopened for wheeled and tracked vehicles, the men were to demolish all the heavy equipment and then escape on foot, heading north towards Lake Kokkojärvi and then turning due east.

As ordered, the troops gathered on the road in preparation for one last breakout attempt. The baggage train took position behind the leading infantry companies and two anti-tank guns, which had been loaded with shrapnel shells. This line of troops now waiting their turn to retreat included two batteries of the 122nd Artillery Regiment, a full anti-tank battalion, several supply units as well as numerous trucks filled with the wounded.

Immediately after the column set off, a hail of Finnish machine-gun fire and grenades stopped it in its tracks. Such was the suppressive effect of this attack that it prevented the Ukrainians from destroying most of their vehicles. As soon as they had spent the few remaining artillery shells, the Soviet troops fled towards Lake Kokkojärvi. They quickly discovered that this area was in Finnish hands, so the beleaguered soldiers had to continue east for several more kilometres through the dense woods.

What the Ukrainians had not known was that earlier on the same day, the artillery batteries at Lake Kokkojärvi had found themselves surrounded by the Finns on three sides. Despite their perilous situation, the men, weapons and transport had been organised into a marching column. Soon after their departure this column had run into a Finnish roadblock. The Soviets were soon defeated and the disorganised artillerymen fled into the woods, abandoning all their vehicles and artillery.

The following day, Battalion Commissar Krapivintsev managed to unify most of these runaway groups and lead them through deep snowdrifts towards the east. A couple of hundred men were still lost in the area and ended up prisoners of the Finns. Finally, a reinforcement battalion from the Soviet 305th Rifle Regiment was sent to Krapivintsev's rescue. They cleared a 9km channel from the border into Finland, thus enabling more men to make it back to their own side.

By the morning of 7 December, fighting in the area had petered out. The Raate road was littered with abandoned Soviet vehicles and heavy equipment. By now the rest of the Finnish forces were able to proceed to their designated areas mostly unopposed. The 27th Infantry Regiment alone captured more than 1,000 prisoners during the day. On 8 January, Mannerheim once again communicated his deepest gratitude to Siilasvuo and his men.

The aftermath was disastrous for the Soviets. Stavka's decision to force Vinogradov's 44th Rifle Division to remain in place, while they allowed Zelentsov's 163rd Rifle Division to retreat, was a costly mistake. Due to its heavy losses in men and equipment, the 44th Rifle Division could no longer function as a fighting unit. It would not be able to return to action before the beginning of March, by which time its ranks would be rebuilt with 1,198 replacements. The division would not have the opportunity to take part in any further action during the Winter War.

A destroyed Soviet tank convoy, waiting to be reclaimed for Finnish service. (SA-kuva)

Stavka conveyed its displeasure via official channels, pinpointing responsibility for the failure on three men in particular: 44th Rifle Division commander Vinogradov, his chief of staff Colonel Volkov and lastly Pahamov, the Leader of the Political Division. The three were summarily executed in front of their own men. The official entry on Vinogradov's record gives the reason for his execution as: 'The irrevocable loss of fifty-five field kitchens to the enemy' (Trotter, 1991).

According to Stavka's own investigation, the 44th Rifle Division lost 4,674 men, of whom 1,001 were killed 1,430 wounded and 2,243 missing. Amongst the materials abandoned to the Finns were 4,340 rifles, 252 submachine guns, 97 medium machine guns, over 70 field artillery pieces, 25 anti-tank guns, 43 tanks and 10 armoured cars and 20 tractors, as well as nearly 250 trucks and over 1,100 horses.

ENCIRCLEMENT AT KUHMO

The town of Kuhmo lies approximately 60km west of the pre-war Finnish–Russian border. In early December 1939, the 25th Infantry Regiment had managed to halt the advance of the elite Soviet 54th Mountain Rifle Division towards the town. The Finnish defenders had been ordered to conserve their troop numbers, and to focus on conducting small-scale guerrilla attacks against the Soviet flanks, while the bulk of North Finland Group's forces were engaged at Suomussalmi.

Once the Finnish 9th Division had secured victory over the Soviet 44th Rifle Division at Suomussalmi and Raate road, Siilasvuo was given orders to take on the entrenched 54th Mountain Rifle Division, under Brigade Commander Nicholas Gusevsky, in the Kuhmo sector. Gusevsky's troops were highly trained and were perhaps the best suited out of all the Red Army units to the terrain and the Arctic warfare conditions. This was an important consideration: according to the Finnish meteorological records from the time, 'It became so cold that even the reindeer were dying' (Ilmatieteellinen Keskuslaitos, 1953).

By the end of January – the point at which Siilasvuo's men arrived – the 54th Mountain Rifle Division had already dug defensive positions along a 45km stretch of the Riihivaara–Kuhmo road. In his book *Kuhmo Talvisodassa*, Hjalmar Siilasvuo recalls the following about the situation he faced:

When I examined the resources allocated for this task, I found them to be too weak. We had already given the enemy one month to dig

NICHOLAS GUSEVSKY
BRIGADE COMMANDER, 54TH MOUNTAIN RIFLE DIVISION

(1898–1941)

Nicholas Andrianovich Gusevsky started his military career during the Russian Civil War. He graduated from the Soviet Military Academy, and returned to his former school as a senior lecturer in tactics after the Winter War.

During the Winter War, he led the 54th Mountain Rifle Division in its attack towards Kuhmo. There, his men became surrounded and suffered tremendous losses, barely managing to hold until the end of the war.

Gusevsky held several special command duties in the Central Front during the Great Patriotic War. He went missing in action in August 1941. The only account of what might have happened to him comes from his fellow general, Dmitry A. Krutshikin, who claims that Gusevsky committed suicide whilst trapped in a *motti* that the rapid German onslaught had formed.

in. I knew from experience that the Russians had excellent entrenching machinery. At Suomussalmi, in much shorter time, they had managed to build fortifications and dugouts impervious to our light artillery … Also, there simply was not enough men for the planned mission … However, the enemy's penetration deep into the Kuhmo area had forced the high command to plan an offensive against this sector despite the uncertain prerequisites. (Siilasvuo, 1944)

On 26 January, the commander of North Finland Group Major-General Tuompo gave Siilasvuo his final attack orders. By now, his forces had finished taking up positions both north and south of the enemy's entrenchments. The latter had not been strategically planned. Instead, the Soviet troops had dug in wherever they happened to be when the orders to halt arrived.

Siilasvuo's men were by now highly experienced in the kind of *motti* tactics that were now called for. The nature of the terrain, with its narrow isthmuses, was once again to their advantage for such manoeuvres. In preparation for rapidly cutting off the enemy lines, the Finns made ice roads and established strategic supply stations near their designated assembly areas. As these preparations would take some time, Siilasvuo set the date of the attack for three days ahead. The 9th Division's first goal would be to complete the encirclement of the Soviet forces. When everything was ready, the men would move to their jumping-off points only at the last moment; this would prevent the (rare) Soviet patrols from detecting them, and more importantly allowed the soldiers to rest in the comfort of their warm tents for as long as possible.

Early on the morning of 29 January, Captain Heimo M. O. Murole's battalion set off from the north, making contact with the Soviet positions defending the road by lunchtime. By launching vigorous counter-attacks, the defenders were able to hold off Murole's men, a mere 400m from the road.

Further to the east, Lieutenant-Colonel Mäkiniemi led three battalions from his 27th Infantry Regiment abreast towards the rear of the middle part of the Soviet lines. His goal was to cut the 54th Mountain Rifle Division in two. Mäkiniemi managed to reach and sever the road, but failed to increase the breach to either east or west. However, his actions had forced the enemy to corral together into two *motti*, at Reuhkavaara and Loso.

To the south of the Soviet lines, Captain Eero Halonen's battalion also managed to sever the road leading towards Lieksa. The Finns tried immediately to crush the resultant Soviet *motti*, but practically all of the encirclements held.

Kuhmo sector *Motti*, February–March 1940

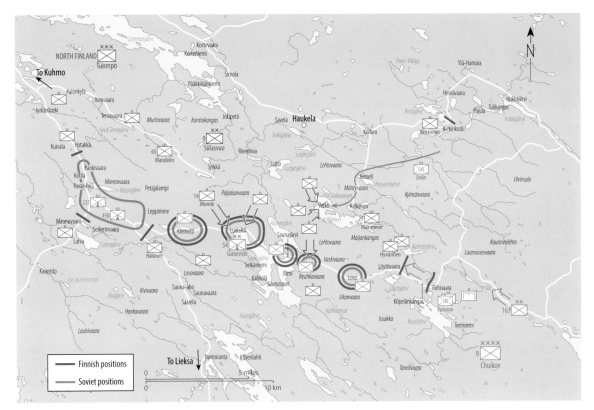

The following day, the bulk of 9th Division was engaged in pinning down the entrapped 54th Mountain Rifle Division forces. Siilasvuo then reassigned most of his limited reserves to Mäkiniemi, who was to use them to widen the breach at the road and to capture Löytövaara hill. If this could be achieved, any further Red Army relief attempts from the east would be virtually impossible. In the end, the hill was not captured until 31 January, and only after Siilasvuo had thrown his remaining reserve companies into the fray.

Upon hearing that the Finns now held the high ground, a Soviet task force was formed under Major Kutusov (deputy commander of the 54th Mountain Rifle Division) comprising two ski battalions and one pioneer battalion. Kutusov was ordered to perform a fierce counter-attack in order to dislodge the encroaching Finns from Löytövaara hill. A catastrophe ensued: Kutusov himself was killed on the way to meeting up with his men, and the lack of any radio equipment meant that the troops could not receive remote orders. Over the next few days, Finnish counter-strikes destroyed the ski battalions almost to a man.

Despite the destruction of this task force, the Soviet troops still continued to threaten the defenders at Löytövaara from positions a few kilometres further to the east at Kilpelänkangas. To eliminate this, on 6 February Major Salomon H. V. Hyvärinen received orders to lead his battalion on a raid against the enemy forces assembling in the area. The surprise attack turned out to be highly successful, and with the job done, the Finns retreated back to Löytövaara. As Kilpelänkangas was left unoccupied, the Soviets were eventually able to regroup and bring in further reinforcements. On 8 February, alarmed by this fact, Siilasvuo ordered a further attack to take place.

The following day, two battalions once again attacked the Soviet staging area at Kilpelänkangas. By evening, the defenders had finally begun to give ground, retreating towards Riihivaara. The Finns decided not to pursue the withdrawing enemy. North Finland Group headquarters reasoned that the attack on Löytövaara hill had already tied down too many of 9th Division's

Finnish positions in the Kuhmo area on 1 February 1940. The walls of the dugouts were often strengthened with thin timbers. This helped to prevent the sides from caving in during Soviet artillery strikes. (SA-kuva)

troops and that this was as good a position to hold and defend as they were ever likely to find.

Meanwhile, a third *motti* of 54th Mountain Rifle Division forces had formed further to the west. It contained the divisional headquarters, and was located on the narrow stretch of land between lakes Saunajärvi and Alasjärvi. The first Finnish attempt to destroy this Saunajärvi *motti* took place on 11 February. Three battalions circled in to attack the Soviet positions simultaneously from different directions. For a total of four days the Soviets managed to hold the Finns at bay; at this point Siilasvuo was forced to respond rapidly to a new threat, and so he ordered the attack to halt.

A Soviet ski brigade, led by Colonel Vjatseslav Dolin, had managed to break contact with the Finnish forces in the north. These men had now made a circuitous cross-country trek into the 9th Division area, appearing to the rear of Mäkiniemi's 27th Infantry Regiment. The Finns were anxious to pinpoint the location of this unit; having them attack from an unknown direction was not an option.

In a chance encounter near Mäntyvaara, about 5km north-east of the 54th Mountain Rifle Division's positions, a small Finnish patrol stumbled upon a group of Red Army troops at an isolated logger's cabin. In the subsequent fire fight, Dolin and some other senior officers of the ski brigade were killed. However, the Finns still had no idea where the main body of the brigade was.

On 13 February, the remainder of the ski brigade was able to cut the 27th Infantry Regiment's supply route, and attacked the provisions camp of one pioneer company. By that evening, the Soviet forward elements had already reached the winding Vetko land bridge at Lake Kälkänen. However, their earlier attack against the supply columns had made their position clear to the Finns, who had quickly scrambled all available troops to the area. The Soviets had been forced into a corner.

Siilasvuo recalled the following about the battle at Vetko:

> Lieutenant Saikku (1st Company 65th Infantry Regiment) started his attack even though it was clear that he was facing a superior enemy … the company was met with fire and grenades. The situation was slightly improved by the fact that, as we had all previously observed, the Russian automatic rifles would not work in such cold temperatures.[9] Often, when their weapons refused to function, the enemy would stand up and use a bayonet or just grabbed our men with their bare hands. (Siilasvuo, 1944)

The battle continued through the night. The Soviet troops took up fortified positions using the few houses on the Vetko land bridge, and refused to give in. By the following morning, the Finns had managed to bring forward a single piece of field artillery, which was then fired directly over open sights. When this failed to convince the remaining defenders, the Finns lobbed grenades into the buildings. When this too failed, the houses were put to the torch. With the buildings completely ablaze, the last surviving defenders rushed out; instead of surrendering, they attempted to break out. Those who tried to flee in a southerly direction across the ice were cut down by machine-gun fire. On the morning of 15 February, almost 400 Soviet bodies lay on the battleground. In the end, only a small group managed to escape

---

9   Soviet troops often used too much grease on their weapons and failed to clean them thoroughly afterwards, causing the mechanisms to freeze in temperatures that plummeted to nearly -40°C.

north-east during the night, uniting with the last remaining elements of Dolin's regiment at Kesseli.

At Kesseli, these elite soldiers continued to fight desperate defensive battles over the coming days. On 16 February, after four hours of fierce fighting, the Soviet forces there finally dispersed into small groups in order to try to escape. Most of these 'splinters' were dealt with immediately by the encircling Finnish formations. For several days afterwards, Finnish patrols, and supply troops in the rear, continued to come across small detachments of Soviet ski troops desperately trying to find a route back to their own lines.

The operation to contain Dolin's ski troops had tied up a large proportion of the Finnish forces in this sector. Many of these men had been removed from guarding the *motti*. Had the Soviets realised how thin the circle around them had become, they might have made good use of it by escaping. As it happened, the cold, hunger and their own passivity prevented them from seizing this opportunity.

When the Soviet Ninth Army headquarters finally found out what had happened to the ski troops under Dolin's command, they made the following simple statement: 'Dolin and his men had died without achieving honour.' It seems that the highly inaccurate maps they had been provided with were both the reason for their initial success in surprising the Finns, and the reason for their ultimate mission failure. Around 50 of the regiment's men were later rescued by plane, while a few more made it through the Finnish encirclement into the Luelahti *motti*.

Following this fiasco, the Soviets had to transfer further reinforcements to the area. This task fell to the now mostly rebuilt 163rd Rifle Division. It is difficult to imagine what the veterans of that unit must have been thinking at this point. It was not that long ago that they themselves had fled from Finnish forces at Suomussalmi.

On 25 February, the 163rd Rifle Division launched an attack westwards along the Saunajärvi road. Their objective was to liberate their comrades in the 54th Mountain Rifle Division, who were still trapped in *motti* from Loso to Luelahti. Despite launching several regiments into the fray, the 163rd Rifle Division again failed to impress Ninth Army's leadership. The Finns repelled their attacks almost on a daily basis. The most the division seemed to achieve was forcing the Finns to retreat a kilometre, in orderly fashion, from Kilpelänkangas to their earlier defensive positions at Löytövaara hill. The Finns would occupy these positions until the end of the war.

Meanwhile the Finnish 9th Division continued its attempts to crush the Soviet forces in the *motti* around Luelahti Bay. There, Siilasvuo's artillery

Positions in the Saunajärvi *motti*. Heavy machinery enabled the Soviets to dig their defensive fortifications into the frozen ground. At times, the Soviets even used the frozen bodies of their fallen comrades to create higher embankments. (SA-kuva)

launched the heaviest shelling that they had been able to undertake in the whole war. From 1 March onwards, some 4,500 shells were fired at the Soviet positions. Each day the Finns paid a high cost in lives in order to gain a little bit more ground from the dogged Soviet troops.

The defences near the 54th Mountain Rifle Division's headquarters were finally overcome on 8 March; according to estimates, around half of the troops managed to escape west to the next *motti*. The Finnish forces then proceeded to prepare for further attacks against this target. By 13 March, when the news of the Moscow peace treaty reached the combatants, the men had advanced to within just 40m of the Soviet dugouts. The attack was halted immediately, but both sides continued a fierce exchange of fire for the last two hours of the war. These operations ended up costing both sides dearly. Siilasvuo's troops lost an estimated 4,595 men. Of these 1,340 were dead, 3,123 wounded and 132 missing.

With peace agreed, the Soviet forces were finally freed from their *motti*. A total of 3,490 soldiers of the 337th Rifle Regiment were present in the westernmost *motti*. In Luelahti Bay, 2,933 men had survived the encirclement. However, at Klemetti *motti* there were only 150 survivors at war's end. In the *motti* at Kannas and Loso, a total of 2,500 Soviet troops still occupied their makeshift fortifications on 13 March.

During the Kuhmo battles, the 54th Mountain Rifle and 163rd Rifle divisions lost a total of 12,700 men, 3,200 of whom had been killed and 9,500 wounded.

Survivors from the Finnish 65th Infantry Regiment on their return march from Lake Saunajärvi on 16 March 1940. (SA-kuva)

CHAPTER 7
LAPLAND GROUP, 1939—40

In northern Finland, the Soviet Fourteenth Army, led by Army Corps Commander Valerian A. Frolov, tried to cut off Finland's only Arctic port, Petsamo. Frolou's operations were supported, further south by the 122nd Rifle Division of the Ninth Army striking towards central Lapland.

On 13 December, the Finnish high command had split the vast area controlled by North Arctic Finland Group into two parts. The divisions in Lapland were placed under the command of Major-General Martti Wallenius, as the newly formed Lapland Group. The situation in the region looked grim for Wallenius from the outset.

At Petsamo, on the shores of the Barents Sea, the near battalion-strength Task Force Pennanen was barely holding its ground against Fourteenth Army's 52nd Rifle Division. Fourteenth Army's advance proceeded slowly, as it was utilising

Captain Pennanen and his men fought a tiring campaign of attrition against the Soviet 14th Army. Although his troops were forced to retreat, the Soviets failed to secure a decisive victory. Instead, the small raids organised by the Finns and the Arctic winter eventually ground the Soviet advance to a halt. (SA-kuva)

 MARTTI WALLENIUS
MAJOR-GENERAL,
LAPLAND GROUP

(1893–1984)

Kurt Martti Wallenius began his career as a Jäger and eventually rose to the rank of major-general. His career was to be constantly overshadowed by the suspicion that before the war, he was behind the kidnapping of President Kaarlo Juho Ståhlberg, and that he supported the Lapua Movement and took part in the Mäntsälä Rebellion. At that time he had been part of the army's general staff. He was relieved from his duties following the kidnapping, and ended up being imprisoned for a year for the rebellion.

When the Winter War began, due to these political suspicions Wallenius was assigned to the reserves. However, he was recalled to lead the Lapland Group on 13 December 1939.

It is thought that Wallenius was the first to employ the so-called *motti* tactics at the battle of Pelkosenniemi from 17 to 19 December 1939. There, three of his battalions first surrounded and then split the Soviet 273rd Rifle Regiment. After the battle the surviving enemy soldiers escaped, leaving behind all their heavy equipment. This victory halted the Red Army's advance in the north.

On 28 February 1940, Wallenius was transferred and took up temporary command of the Coastal Group, in order to help with the defence of Viipuri Bay. However, he was replaced in this role a few days later.

After the Winter War, the politically radical Wallenius was returned to the army's reserves. When the Continuation War began, he repeatedly requested that he be given a front-line command. As his pleas were always rebuffed, Wallenius acquired a medical certificate that allowed him to be discharged and struck from the roll of officers. He then tried to again volunteer for the front lines as a regular infantryman, but was turned down on account of his age. Wallenius devoted the rest of his life to writing.

only one-third of the forces available, having already left one division to the rear guarding the port facilities. This, the 104th Mountain Rifle Division, had earlier spearheaded the attack from the direction of Kalastajansaarento and had been ordered to establish positions along the coast in order to deter any possible foreign relief force from landing. Wallenius did not know if any such help would ever arrive.

The Finnish high command did not expect to be able to hold the Petsamo region, with Soviet bases in such close proximity and having no naval vessels of their own. In their view, the loss of the nickel ore mines would be unavoidable and would just have to be endured. From the Soviet side, once these mines had been captured, they would be content to leave most of their forces and artillery trained towards the open sea, while a reduced force continued to attack south.

Soviet forces made slow progress on the push south along Finland's Arctic Highway. Temperatures had plummeted to below -40°C, and as the supply columns stretched out, the Finns would suddenly launch their small raiding parties. By the end of January 1940 the relentless winter and sniper attacks had more or less halted any Soviet attempts to advance.

A more dangerous situation was meanwhile developing much further south, where the Soviet 122nd Rifle Division, led by Colonel Peter Shevchenko, was rapidly progressing across Finland towards Salla. Major Vilho Roininen's harassed 17th Independent Battalion had been conducting a fighting retreat against this division all the way from the border. Soon his command was transferred to Task Force Roininen, with battalion-strong reinforcements arriving first on 6 December and again on the 12th. Despite this help and his best efforts, by 9 December Shevchenko's forces had already occupied Salla village nearly 50km in from the border. The ultimate goal of the 122nd Rifle Division was to sack the city of Rovaniemi, the capital of Lapland, and if possible continue all the way to the port of Tornio on the Gulf of Bothnia. By now, divisional headquarters did not believe the Finns could muster any significant defensive efforts before the town of Kemijärvi, a point that was almost halfway to the Swedish border.

In order to stall the relentless Red Army onslaught, the Finns scraped together all their available men. By 15 December, they had mustered four battalions under Task Force Roininen in the Salla sector. Although Shevchenko's 122nd Rifle Division comprised mostly reservists, it was further strengthened by the addition of the 273rd Mountain Rifle Regiment (commanded by Major Stephen Kolomiets), a machine-gun battalion and the 100th Independent Tank Battalion. Shevchenko decided to split his division's forces. He sent the 273rd Mountain Rifle Regiment towards the town of Kemijärvi along a northerly route past Pelkosenniemi village. From there they could proceed to cut off the Arctic Highway and deny supplies to any Finnish forces still fighting to the north in the Petsamo region. Meanwhile, the main body of his 122nd Rifle Division was to push directly toward Kemijärvi on the road through Märkäjärvi village.

PETER SHEVCHENKO
COLONEL,
122ND RIFLE DIVISION

(1901–60)

Peter Semnojovitch Shevchenko volunteered for the army in 1918, and fought in the Russian Civil War for the following four years. He graduated from the Siberian Infantry Academy in Tomsk in 1925, completing the senior officers' courses in 1927. Shevchenko fought in the conflicts over the Northern Manchurian Railway in 1929.

During the Winter War, he led the 122nd Rifle Division at Salla. Shevchenko was promoted major-general on 4 June 1940. He also briefly commanded the 42nd Rifle Corps against the Finns on the Northern Front during the Great Patriotic War.

In 1942, he was transferred to lead the 213th Marine Division in Central Asia. In 1943, Shevchenko became the chief of the Military Colleges, and after the war in 1946 he served as the deputy commander to the Vienan and the Turkestan military districts.

VILHO ROININEN
MAJOR,
TASK FORCE ROININEN

(1893–1960)

Following his service as a Jäger, Roininen took part in the Finnish Civil War as a staff sergeant in the ranks of the White Guard.

During the Winter War, Roininen first led the 17th Independent Battalion and then subsequently Task Force Roininen. He held this position through the Interim Peace, until being transferred to lead the 33rd Infantry Regiment and from there to lead the 5th Border Guards. He was promoted to lieutenant-colonel in 1940.

At the onset of the Continuation War, Roininen transferred to lead the 2nd Sissi (Ranger) Battalion. In 1942, he left the front line to take over the Perä–Pohjola Military District. A year later he was to head the 25th Infantry Training Centre. Roininen remained in this post until the peace, and upon leaving his post devoted himself to agriculture.

A reindeer patrol at Jäniskoski, on 20 February 1940. These sturdy animals were ideal for pulling weapon and supply sledges through the snowy forests. Such transport could silently cover long distances, allowing the Finns to surprise Soviet sentries and supply columns. (SA-kuva)

 ARMAS PERKSALO
MAJOR,
40TH INFANTRY REGIMENT

As one of the first volunteers for the Jäger movement, Perksalo received his baptism of fire on the Eastern Front of World War I. During the Finnish Civil War, Perksalo served as a company commander for the White Guard.

(1894–1968)

Perksalo was the commander of Oulu's 1st Civil Guard District when the Winter War began, but soon transferred to lead the 40th Infantry Regiment. In this role, he saw battle at Pelkosenniemi, Joutsijärvi, Lake Märkäjärvi and finally at Viipuri Bay.

At the start of the Continuation War, Perksalo led the 34th Infantry Regiment in the Hanko area, and later joined the battle with his unit at Aunus. He was promoted lieutenant-colonel in 1941.

In 1942, Perksalo moved from the front lines in order to command the Salo Military District, a post he then retained until the end of the war.

In the post-war period, Perksalo worked as managing director of a concrete company until 1951, and then as a school teacher from 1953 to 1955.

Major-General Wallenius decided that the Soviet advance had to be stopped well before the town of Kemijärvi, and especially in its drive towards Pelkosenniemi, where the Red Army was making worryingly good progress. To this end, he called on the 40th Infantry Regiment, under the command of Major Armas Perksalo. These troops began to arrive at Pelkosenniemi from 16 December, a battalion at a time. By then Kolomiets' 273rd Mountain Rifle Regiment had already advanced to the Kitinen River ferry crossing at the northern edge of Pelkosenniemi. The Soviets managed to establish a bridgehead on the west bank, despite the defenders' best efforts to prevent this.

Finnish sentries in the Petsamo area on 6 February 1940. (SA-kuva)

On 17 December, Perksalo received orders to strike back by encircling the Soviet forces. At 04:00 the following morning, in order to loop around Kolomiets' troops, Perksalo sent two battalions on a 2km northerly march. The first of these battalions, led by Captain Frans B. Lindberg, quickly encountered troops from the 273rd Mountain Rifle Regiment moving out from their bridgehead. Lindberg immediately assigned his troops defensive positions so that the advance could be contained. Meanwhile, the second battalion, under Captain Suoranta, continued to cross the Kitinen River further to the north, before swinging back towards the rear of the Soviet lines. From there, Suoranta hoped to attack the poorly defended Soviet artillery batteries and supply trains.

Things did not go well for the Finns at the Kitinen bridgehead. The

(1896–1970)

STEPHEN KOLOMIETS
MAJOR, 273RD MOUNTAIN RIFLE REGIMENT

Stefan Vladimirovitch Kolomiets began his military career as a scribe in an Imperial Russian regiment in 1915. By 1919, he had volunteered for the Red Army, and completed a commanders' course that year in Moscow. After serving as a squad leader during the Russian Civil War, he furthered his military education, graduating from the Military School in 1926, and with further periods of study in 1932, 1934 and 1936. He was promoted to the rank of major in 1938.

Kolomiets worked in different intelligence roles and as a battalion commander within the 18th Rifle Division from 1935 to 1939.

During the Winter War, Kolomiets commanded the 273rd Mountain Rifle Regiment, taking part in the heavy fighting in the Pelkosenniemi area. These battles ended in resounding defeat for his unit.

In the Continuation War, he first commanded the 1st Polar Division and then the 186th Rifle Division on the northern Finnish front. From 1942 to 1943 he led the 374th Rifle Division, and then finally the 34th Rifle Division until the end of the war.

Kolomiets was promoted major-general on 13 September 1944. After the Great Patriotic War, Kolomiets went on to share his considerable combat experience at the Frunze Military Academy, serving there until his retirement in 1966.

Reindeer and sledge teams advancing on the Lapland front. (SA-kuva)

Soviets pushed forward tenaciously in spite of 40th Infantry Regiment's manoeuvring and counter-attacks. Eventually two enemy tanks managed to ram straight through the defensive positions of Lindberg's battalion. This caused panic amongst the Finnish supply troops, who rushed onto the road in their flight to the south.

However, just as all seemed lost to the Finns, Shevchenko's forces suddenly began to retreat as well. In their hurry to escape, they left behind precious equipment, including 16 cars and 2 anti-tank guns. It turned out that Captain Suoranta's men had pressed on through the dusk, and succeeded in striking against the Soviet artillery positions and supply columns. Suoranta's battalion had managed to advance within 100m of the Soviet lines without being detected. From there his men had burst forth, routing the Soviet troops with ease. By the following morning, the enemy had withdrawn completely. The Finns came off worse in the casualty count, however, losing 250 men compared to a mere 94 dead on the Soviet side. Despite the heavy price, the 273rd Mountain Rifle Regiment's advance had been stopped, and the Finns still controlled Pelkosenniemi.

In the aftermath of the fighting, contact with the retreating Soviets was temporarily lost. They were not detected again until 21 December, when they were finally tracked down at Savukoski hamlet. From there they continued to fall back along their original route of advance, retreating all the way to Saija village. At Saija, frontal responsibility was subsequently transferred to the newly arrived 88th Rifle Division. The situation in this sector remained

relatively calm until the end of the war. The Finns concentrated on raiding Soviet rear positions, destroying vehicles and phone lines, and harassing the lines of communication.

LAKE JOUTSIJÄRVI

Since the fall of Salla, Task Force Roininen's four battalions had conducted a fighting retreat under pursuit by the 122nd Rifle Division. Shevchenko's troops had overrun Märkäjärvi village quickly and were making good progress towards Kemijärvi town. On 16 December, Wallenius issued the following order from Lapland Group's headquarters: 'The enemy is exhausted … your mission now is to stop its advance permanently. The defences at Lake Joutsijärvi must not be abandoned without permission!'

From 17 December onwards, the 122nd Rifle Division launched repeated attacks. However, the Finnish defences at Joutsijärvi held; despite the use of artillery and armoured support, the Soviets were unable to break through. Shevchenko's initial plan was to use the 420th Rifle Regiment along the road, while the 715th Rifle Regiment attempted to outflank the Finns cross-country. Despite support from the heavy artillery and the 100th Independent Tank Battalion, the 420th Rifle Regiment was badly mauled. By 20 December, this regiment had to be rested, and the responsibility for carrying on the offensive was passed to the 596th and 715th Rifle regiments. The plan was to split their battalions across a three-pronged attack that would encircle and then crush the Finnish defences.

LEFT
The fleeing men of the 273rd Mountain Rifle Regiment even left behind their brass section. These instruments had been intended for what was considered an inevitable victory parade. This picture was taken after the battle of Pelkosenniemi on 4 January 1940. (SA-kuva)

RIGHT
A Finnish line at Lake Joutsijärvi. The well-prepared dugouts gave enough protection for the men to repel the Soviet infantry, despite the presence of supporting tanks and artillery. (SA-kuva)

The Finns, however, had already begun to launch limited counter-attacks of their own on the south side of Lake Joutsijärvi. Before the main Soviet assault began, the battalion tasked with circling around on this route encountered the Finns and ended up withdrawing in disarray. The initial volley from the Finns had managed to kill most of the battalion's senior officers, including its commander. The Soviet troops panicked and, leaving behind a significant amount of weapons, fled eastwards. According to Finnish estimates, the Soviets lost around 250 men and the Finns 55.

Despite this serious setback, Shevchenko ordered the 122nd Rifle Division to continue with its assault. The Finns repelled the main body of the attack. Worse still, the battalion sent to encircle the Finns from the north was now in danger of being cut off. These troops managed to force their way out of the *motti*, but in the process had to abandon their machine guns as well as several dead or dying comrades.

On 21 December, Ninth Army headquarters gave orders for the 122nd Rifle Division to establish temporary defensive positions in its current location, in order to spend time regrouping and preparing for another push forward. That order to attack never arrived, however, and the division withdrew further under increased Finnish pressure. By this point, Lapland Group headquarters had decided that the Joutsijärvi region would become the main focus for its operations.

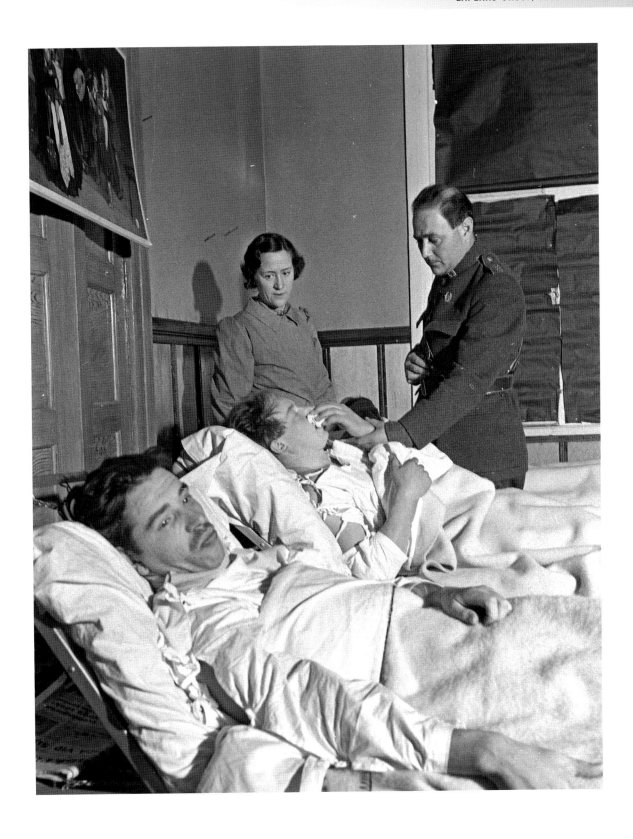

Finnish soldiers taking positions along the shores of Lake Joutsijärvi. The Suomi machine gun carried by the man on the left was an extremely reliable and accurate weapon, even when fired on fully automatic. (SA-kuva)

The regrouped Finnish forces were ordered to renew their attack against the Soviet positions at dawn on 2 January. After spending a freezing night under the stars, the men of the task force were sluggish in making their preparations. The assault thus suffered serious delays and did not commence much before lunchtime. Perhaps due to this, the attack was a failure and only one of the companies managed to reach their intended objective at Moitavaara hill. Realising that they were now cut off from the rest of the Finnish forces, they made a circuitous escape back to their own side of Lake Joutsijärvi. Enemy tanks had prevented their compatriots from reaching their goals elsewhere. These attacks were unsuccessfully repeated over the next few days. On 5 January, the Finns were in turn forced to repel an attempt by Soviet forces to break through; the Red Army had been emboldened by the lack of progress the Finnish assaults made.

By this stage, news of the staggering Soviet defeats at the battles of Suomussalmi and Raate road had injected considerable caution into Ninth Army's planning. To prevent a similar fiasco from occurring on the northern front, Army Commander Chuikov ordered the 88th Rifle Division to be transferred to the area from Archangel. Their march over the frozen White Sea inlet ended up taking much longer than expected, and these troops failed to arrive in time to have any impact on the fighting. In fact, some of the units would not even complete the long transit before hostilities ceased.

On 13 January, as no help would be immediately forthcoming, Stavka issued new orders to the 122nd Rifle Division. They were to withdraw towards the border and into positions that were more defensible at Lake Märkäjärvi. This division, which of all the Soviet forces had penetrated the furthest into Finland, was forced to turn around and retreat. At the height of their offensive, they had extended the front line forwards by some

General duty at Kemijärvi. At this latitude, during winter the sun would not climb over the horizon before 11:00, and would then remain visible for only a couple of hours. In this brief, sunny phase, it was easy to get whiteout, a form of temporary blindness, as the light reflected directly back from every surface. During the rest of the 'day', a ruddy dusk prevailed. Even during the night some visibility remained, as the eerie blue nimbus created by the moon and the stars shone on the white canvas. (SA-kuva)

Swedes from Task Force SFK (Svenska Frivilligkåre – Swedish Volunteer Corps) practising assembly of a light mortar in the snow. The mortar would be dragged into position on a sledge by a single soldier. Another sledge might be used to haul the rounds. This enabled the mortar squad to rapidly redeploy and to keep up with the attacking infantry, giving accurate close-range support. (SA-kuva)

145km. As the Soviets conducted their orderly retreat, the Finns pursued them along the road network.

The Soviet forces proceeded to fortify positions on the west bank of Lake Märkäjärvi, while the Finns set their troops into an extended semicircle in front of these defences. On 26 January, Lapland Group's headquarters passed responsibility for the front line to Task Force SFK (Svenska Frivilligkåre – Swedish Volunteer Corps). This force mostly consisted of Swedish and Norwegian volunteers and was commanded by the Swede Lieutenant-General Ernst Linder. He had already played a role in the 1918 Finnish War of Independence and had been promoted to his present Finnish rank in 1938. Linder's task force also utilised a Swedish volunteer aviation group, comprising six fighters and four light bombers. Task Force SFK had completed taking over front-line responsibility by 28 February. The positions they took over were excellent and helped greatly at repelling any further attacks by the Soviets, but Linder lacked sufficient forces to encircle

and destroy the enemy. Thus, the Märkäjärvi sector remained quiet, and out of Task Force SFK's 2,500 men, only 70 were to fall in action.

Lapland Group had managed to contain Soviet forces on all the northern fronts. Despite the deep and threatening advance into Finnish terrain, only Petsamo and several significant crossroads had been lost. Finnish Lapland was largely devoid of any vital infrastructure elements, and as long as the Soviets were kept far away from key objectives, there was relatively little damage that they could do.

Laplanders in Koivu on 8 February 1940. Although the Soviets did not manage to achieve a strategic victory on the Lapland front, many of the indigenous people were still displaced. These experienced woodsmen served as valuable scouts and trackers for the Finnish patrols. (SA-kuva)

CHAPTER 8
A WATCHING WORLD

Only Finland – superb, nay, sublime – in the jaws of peril – Finland shows what free men can do. The service rendered by Finland to mankind is magnificent … Everyone can see how Communism rots the soul of a Nation; how it makes it abject and hungry in peace, and proves it base and abominable in war. We cannot tell what the fate of Finland may be, but no more mournful spectacle could be presented to what is left of civilised mankind than that this splendid Northern race should be at last worn down and reduced to servitude worse than death by the dull brutish force of overwhelming numbers.

Winston Churchill, broadcast speech, 20 January 1940

The ammunition works at Vanhakaupunki during January 1940. Women joined the volunteer Lotta Svärd organisation, or worked in industry, in order to help the Finnish war effort. (SA-kuva)

By early January 1940, the Finns had succeeded in stalling the Red Army on all fronts. The freezing winter conditions had favoured the defenders, with Soviet weapons rendered useless and vehicles immobilised by the plummeting temperatures, and further strain placed on the already stretched supply routes. In these conditions, Finnish forces were able to play to their strengths of highly mobile, small-group actions. In many places the Red Army had been turned back with significant losses, and equipment, including tanks and other heavy weapons, had been salvaged by the Finns in greater numbers than they had possessed at the beginning of the war. Despite these gains, the Finnish Army was still woefully underequipped and especially lacked the means to deal with Soviet armoured forces. By contrast, Stauha was learning from his earlier mistakes and was now gathering more troops to send to the front.

The whole world, and the Finnish government, thought it miraculous that the nation had lasted this long. Now that there seemed to be a lull in Soviet operations, Finland's ambassadors and ministers sought to maximise this gift of time they had been granted. In January 1940, Finnish foreign policy had three clear goals:

1. Establish communications with the Soviet Union.
2. Draw Sweden into the conflict, ideally to the point where they would join the war on Finland's side.
3. Lobby for Western intervention, material support and volunteer fighters.

It turned out that establishing contact with the Soviet high command would be very difficult. It was not until the end of January that Swedish mediators received their first correspondence from the Soviets, stating the following:

> The Soviet Union is willing to negotiate with the Finnish government. However the Finns must first let it be known which land concessions they are proposing to make. It is also necessary to note that the new Soviet demands will not be limited to those given in Moscow in the autumn of 1939, and also that no previous promises given by the Soviet government still apply. (Edwards, 2006)

It was clear that the Soviet Union was not willing to let go of their demands. In their counter-offer, the Finns proposed that they would give the Soviet Union most of the lands they had initially demanded, especially the critical

LEONIDAS

St.-T. återger här en av den kände politiske tecknaren Louis Rae
maekers teckningar ur den holländska tidningen De Telegraa,

Stalin: Mina flygmaskiner skola förmörka solen.
Mannerheim: Gott, då få vi strida i skuggan.

One of the renowned political cartoonist Louis Raemacker's drawings from the Dutch newspaper *De Telegraaf*. It reads:
'STALIN: My fighters and bombers will block out the sun!
MANNERHEIM: Great, then we can fight in the shade!' (SA-kuva)

HJELP FINSKE BARN
send Bidrag til
FORENINGEN NORDEN
MERKAT NR. 331.

A Norwegian stamp from 1939 seeking support for Finnish children: 'Help the Finnish children. Send your aid to the Nordic Union.' During the war Sweden, Denmark and Norway sent supplies to Finnish children and also offered them homes until the hostilities had ended. Between 1939 and 1944, nearly 80,000 children were relocated to safety across Scandinavia. (SA-kuva)

buffer area near Leningrad, but proposed that these would be traded for similarly sized areas elsewhere. Furthermore, they stipulated that both sides should pay compensation for any private properties lost in this trade-off. When Prime Minister Risto Ryti asked Mannerheim how long his forces would last, he responded: 'In war one never really knows how it is going to turn out in the end, but at the moment the situation is good and gives no grounds for panic' (Tanner, 1950).

The Soviet Union had rejected all these Finnish proposals by 5 February. The next Soviet offensive on the Karelian Isthmus began soon after.

Meanwhile, Finnish negotiations with Sweden failed to progress with any greater degree of success. Despite a sense of growing sympathy and a desire to help the Finns among many Swedes, its government maintained the nation's mantle of impartiality. To the Finns' benefit, however, materiel and weapons began finally to flow across the border from Sweden. Artillery pieces, ammunition and even some aeroplanes were acquired from France,

Great Britain and the United States. Due to the long, indirect routes taken, much of this material did not reach Finnish front-line troops before the end of February 1940. For example, some 12 Hawker Hurricane aircraft – which the Finns had purchased for an exorbitant sum – arrived just before the war ended. In response to the criticism concerning their sale, the British Prime Minister Neville Chamberlain later wrote:

> [The Finns] began by asking for fighter planes, and we sent the surplus we could lay hands on. They asked for [anti-aircraft] guns, and again we stripped our own imperfectly armed home defences to help them. They asked for small-arms ammunition, and we gave them priority over our own army. They asked for later types of planes and we sent them 12 Hurricanes, against the will and advice of our Air Staff. (Feiling, 1970)

The British and French governments approached Norway and Sweden to see if they would provide transit facilities for an expeditionary force. On 7 March, just one week before the end of the Winter War, and even though these requests had already been denied, General Sir Edmund Ironside, Britain's Chief of the Imperial General Staff, informed the Finns that a force of 57,000 men was ready to be deployed. The first division of 15,000 men could be in Finland by the end of the month. This task force, codenamed Avonmouth, was drawn from the Guards regiments, the French Foreign Legion, the Polish Independent Rifle Brigade and the Chasseurs Alpins. However, the ships carrying these troops never departed their loading areas. The refusal of the Swedes and the Norwegians to allow passage had scuppered the process. It appears both countries feared that once the British and French forces had gained control of the northerly sites of iron and nickel ore deposits, they would have been unwilling to depart. The shadow of this Allied intervention did, however, increase the pressure on the Soviets to bring the conflict to a close quickly.

Around the world, Finland could count on the support of popular opinion. The presence of many 'front-line reporters' brought stories of the Finns' valiant defence of their country into homes around the globe. In reality, many of these reporters never saw the front, and ended up concocting their stories from the safety of the bar in the Hotel Kämp in Helsinki. After one irate editor demanded that his journalist source a real story involving the venerable Field Marshal Mannerheim, he received the following cable with a frank appraisal of Mannerheim's

On 20 October 1939, on the eve of the Winter War, an initiative was launched for the women of Finland to exchange their wedding bands for a simple steel ring (*Rautasormus*) from the government. The money raised this way would then be used to improve the air defences of Finland. Wearing the *Rautasormus* was something to be proud of. A total of 315,000 gold rings and 19,100 other pieces of jewellery were exchanged. Altogether the defence budget was bolstered by 1,750kg of pure gold. This would have been enough for the purchase of 30 new fighter planes. Unfortunately, the process for smelting and transferring these gifts to internationally accepted gold bars was surprisingly complicated. Due to many reasons, and despite the best intentions, this money was not used before the war ended. (Sotiemme Veteraanit)

In February 1940, the British magazine *War Illustrated* featured several spreads on the situation in Finland. (*War Illustrated Compilation*, vol. 2, Amalgamated Press, London)

availability for interview: 'Mannerheim impossible. Shall I try Jesus Christ instead?' (Trotter, 1991).

Inspired by the stories they had heard, volunteer soldiers from a variety of countries, but especially from Sweden, Denmark and Hungary, began to arrive in January 1940. However, these men had to be trained, and then assembled into units, which meant that for many their participation in the war turned out to be largely symbolic. In theory, the Swedish government had given permission for the assembly of volunteers in Sweden, but in practice these men did not form cohesive units, and had received little training prior to arriving in Finland.

After much lobbying, on 10 December the United States government gifted Finland 2.5 million dollars. However, there was a catch: this money could only be used for agricultural and civilian aid. This prompted one congressman to comment bitterly: 'because of these limitations brave Finland cannot buy anything but powder-puff and panties. Finland asks for ammunition – we send them beans. When they ask for explosives, we send them tea. When they ask for artillery, we send them broomsticks' (Eagle and Paananen, 1973).

Similar sentiments were expressed in American newspapers. The *Washington Post* commented: 'Finland cannot expect any other help from the U.S. except formal applause.' And the *New York Times* editorial predicted: 'After their work is done in Finland, the Soviets will find, among other things, that they have earned the lasting distrust and contempt of the American people.' In the end, the opposite occurred: barely a few years later the US poured millions of dollars into the Soviet Union and finally severed all diplomatic ties with Finland.

Soviet commanders had erroneously predicted that the Finnish proletariat would rise up against its oppressors and support their efforts. This was based upon the impressions gained from the Civil War of 1918. However, since that time living conditions for each class of Finnish society had been gradually improving. It was actually the Soviet threat to Finnish independence that finally allowed old hatchets to be buried, and spurred the nation to share a common goal of repulsing the old eastern enemy.

Examples of the *puhdetyö* (handicrafts) the Finnish troops would make in their dugouts during idle hours. Shown here are some items made out of birch bark, including a pair of slippers, a knife scabbard and a holder for a fishing rod. (SA-kuva)

Nevertheless, the Soviet propaganda machine kept its presses hot throughout the war. Aeroplanes dropped leaflets on the Finnish troops, or makeshift rockets were launched over the front lines to distribute propaganda. One such leaflet read:

SOLDIERS!
The Red Army has breached your defences. You have been surrounded! Your resistance is both hopeless and useless. Thousands of tanks, guns and planes of the Red Army will sweep away anyone who tries to resist.
Think hard! Why die for the benefit of the sell-out ministers, generals, capitalists and landowners? Your wives, children, fathers and mothers are back at home waiting for you.
There is still an option to save your lives. Stop this war and disarm your officers!
Join the Red Army and you will have saved your life!

In the Soviet Union those caught listening to Finnish radio propaganda were severely punished. In contrast, Finnish soldiers enjoyed the over-the-top statements and entertainment that the Soviet radio propagandists provided.

The best known of all these Soviet provocateurs was the so-called *Moskovan Tiltu* (Moscow's Tiltu). Many Finnish soldiers came to love listening to this famous Soviet female broadcaster and traitor. Mostly the men just made fun of her and the blatantly over-the-top propaganda claims she peddled.

OPPOSITE TOP
Morane-Saulnier MS.406 fighters at Viitana base, near Äänislinna in 1942. A more modern type of Finnish fighter that saw service during the Winter War was the heavy Morane-Saulnier MS.406, which was slow and lightly armed. France donated 30 of these aircraft. They reached combat readiness in February 1940 and achieved 14 aerial victories. During the Interim Peace and Continuation War, a further 57 were purchased from Germany. The MS.406 suffered heavy losses due to its poor performance, and was recommended for shelving as early as 1942. This was unfeasible because of the overall lack of aircraft, so modification and modernisation efforts were undertaken instead. The results were underwhelming, to say the least. (SA-kuva)

OPPOSITE BOTTOM
16th Flight Squadron's base at Äänislinna in March 1942. In December 1939, a deal had been struck between Finland and Great Britain for 20 outdated Gloster Gladiator biplanes the British had been planning to retire. These planes were sold at an outlandish price to the desperate Finns. With great pomp, Great Britain donated an extra ten Gladiators to Finland for free – a gesture purely aimed at bolstering the government's domestic reputation, as the public viewed Finland's cause very favourably. Subsequently, the British government pressured South Africa to donate a further 29 used Gladiators. (Courtesy of the private collection of Esa Muikku)

LEFT
A Soviet propaganda poster from 1940, 'Mannerheim the Executioner'. The caption translates:
'1910: Servant of the Russian Emperor, Nikolai the Bloody.
1918: Murderer of tens of thousands of workers, executioner of the Finnish peoples.
1939: Gold that Mannerheim distils from the blood of the Finnish peasants and working classes.
1940: Lackey of the English bankers, main provocateur of the war against the Soviet Union.'

Maintaining the engine of a Fiat G.50 fighter at Pyhäniemi airbase on the eve of the armistice. Finland purchased 25 Fiat G.50 fighters from Italy during the Winter War, and received ten more during the Interim Peace. As with many other models, the Fiats were purchased because no better ones were available, although they were considered an adequate model. The Great Powers refused to sell the best they had to offer for varying reasons, so Finland had to make do. The fighters joined the war in February 1940. At first, the Fiats suffered from major malfunctions due to the Arctic cold. Italian instructors also took part in the war, flying combat missions for Finland. (SA-kuva)

CHAPTER 9
THE BATTLE FOR LADOGA KARELIA, 1940

ENCIRCLEMENT: THE 18TH AND 168TH RIFLE DIVISIONS

During December, Major-General Woldemar Hägglund's IV Army Corps had managed to halt the Soviet offensive north of Lake Ladoga on a line running through the villages of Kitilä, Ruokojärvi and Syskyjärvi. Now he assigned the 13th Division the task of encircling the two enemy divisions in front of this makeshift defensive line. Colonel Bondarev's 168th Rifle Division's positions stretched along the Pitkäranta road and the shores of Lake Ladoga, while Brigade Commander Kondrashev's 18th Rifle Division had occupied the terrain north-east of them in the Lemetti area and along the only other passable road towards Uomaa village. In addition to the large number of artillery and tanks already present, the 34th Light Tank Brigade had joined the two infantry divisions in the area.

A Finnish sentry at his guard post. (SA-kuva)

In order to free up more troops for the planned encirclement, Task Force Jousimies, which was to remain in defence of the Kitilä crossroads, had been depleted to dangerously low levels. The attacking forces were then split into three detachments.

Firstly, Task Force Mehiläinen ('Bumble Bee'), led by the 13th Division commander Colonel Hannu Hannuksela himself, was to attack directly into the flank of the 18th Rifle Division. This meant bypassing the two northernmost Soviet formations of the division, the 208th and 316th Rifle regiments. Hannuksela hoped that this would leave these two Soviet regiments with only two options. Either they would have to launch a counter-attack of their own, which he believed his men were able to contain, or they would simply be forced to retreat along the shores of Lake Ladoga, which in turn would free up the rest of the 13th Division to aid in the attack.

Secondly, east of Hannuksela's troops was Task Force Lohikäärme ('Dragon'), commanded by Colonel Pietari Autti. This force was to start from the east side of Lake Pyhäjärvi and advance towards the section of the Uomaa road defended by the Soviet 34th Light Tank Brigade. The main task was to build on the success of Detachment Tykki ('Cannon'), which had earlier in December managed to sever the same road near Lake Lavajärvi.

A Finnish patrol returning to base in the Lavajärvi sector in January 1940. The Soviets were not at home in these silent forest expanses, where the *bielaja smjert* (white death) stalked their every footstep. In the end few Soviet troops dared to leave the roads or the protection of their heavy weapons. Those who did were most often never seen again. (SA-kuva)

Thirdly, the three-battalion-strong Detachment Tykki received orders to hold and reinforce their positions at the roadblock, thus denying the Soviets the easterly supply route. This would render both of the Soviet divisions reliant on the remaining southerly Pitkäranta road. The Finnish 12th Division took responsibility for the front beyond Uomaa village.

Early on the morning of 6 January, the Finnish units along the length of the line performed a feint against the Soviets in front of their positions. At the same time, task forces Mehiläinen and Lohikäärme sprang into action. Hannuksela's five battalions managed to gain control of the road bisecting the Soviet 18th Rifle Division. The same road was crossed further east by two battalions from Task Force Lohikäärme. What surprised the Finns was that the Soviet units did not panic; nor did they launch hasty counter-attacks or engage in fighting retreats. Instead, they just went to ground. This left the Finns with no other choice than to leave token forces to guard these *motti* while proceeding with the main attack.

GEORGE KONDRASHEV
BRIGADE COMMANDER, 18TH RIFLE DIVISION

(1900–1940)

George Fjodorovitch Kondrashev began his military career in the Red Army in 1919. During the Russian Civil War, he had time to go through cadet training at Petrograd (Leningrad) and took part in suppressing the Kronstadt Rebellion in 1921.

From 1925 to 1928, Kondrashev progressed from squad leader to company commander and eventually led a whole battalion for the Leningrad Military District. He was promoted to major in 1938, and made an aide to the commander of the 24th Rifle Division. On 27 January 1939 he was given the command of the 18th Rifle Division, and in November the same year, Kondrashev reached the rank of brigade commander.

His unit took part in the attack against Finland just north of Lake Ladoga. There, the whole division ended up being split, and the remaining individual cells surrounded in *motti*. On 28 February 1940, Kondrashev allegedly managed to escape the Lemetti *motti*, albeit lightly wounded. Having reached his own lines, he was arrested on 3 March, and condemned to death on 12 August. The sentence was carried out by firing squad on 29 August 1940. Some versions of Kondrashev's story have him escaping dressed as a regular infantryman, and being arrested in a Soviet military hospital, with his immediate execution carried out in the yard.

Consequently, the Finns managed to create one large *motti* at Lemetti, encircling the headquarters of the 18th Rifle Division, together with 3,800 of its men, 7 heavy guns and 78 tanks of different models. The rest of the division was still supplied through the southern road to Pitkäranta town, but by now its troops were engaging Finnish forces on three sides of their positions.

Based on the success of these attacks, IV Army Corps headquarters issued immediate orders to continue the offensive towards Koirinoja on the shores of Lake Ladoga. If this attack were successful, the 168th Rifle Division would be completely cut off from the rest of the Red Army.

First, Hannuksela had to tighten his grip around the large *motti* at Lemetti and repel any relief attempts by the rest of the 18th Rifle Division

(1893–1959)

PIETARI AUTTI
COLONEL, TASK FORCE
LOHIKÄÄRME (39TH REGIMENT)

Pietari Aleksanteri Autti was trained as a Jäger pioneer, and after the Civil War he was made commander of the Salmi Border Guards. In 1920, Autti took part in the unofficial Petsamo expedition. He was forced to resign for a period of a few years following this military misdemeanour. Autti returned to active service in 1931 as a district commander for the Civil Guard. He was promoted colonel in 1939.

Autti led the 39th Infantry Regiment, and Task Force Lohikäärme, for the duration of the Winter War. In the Continuation War, Autti was assigned the 8th Infantry Regiment of the 11th Division. For security reasons, each unit had received cover names before the start of the conflict. Autti's unit had the call sign 'Ukko'. One of the bestselling Finnish books of all time, Väinö Linna's *Unknown Soldier*, was based on the escapades of the 'Ukko' Regiment. Autti was made a Knight of the Mannerheim Cross on 1 March 1942. From March 1943 onwards, he commanded the 4th Division, taking part in the defensive victory at Tali–Ihantala.

After the war ended, Autti was interned for a short period in connection with the 'Weapons Cache' case. Autti was cleared of all charges, and returned to command the 3rd Division until his retirement and promotion to the rank of major-general in 1953.

from the west. Temperatures again plummeted to below -40°C as the Finns completed their encirclement and proceeded to Pukitsanmäki, a small hillock overlooking the railway and the Pitkäranta road. Due to the rapidity of their advance, the assaulting troops were not able to bring proper camping equipment. After around four dozen of the men had been seriously frostbitten, they were all pulled back to a better-prepared base. The cold weather also held back Autti's Task Force Lohikäärme.

By 9 January, Autti's troops were able to proceed to Koivuselkä hamlet, just east of Koirinoja, cutting the remaining Soviet road and railway supply routes to Pitkäranta town. The next day, the Finns finally reached Koirinoja village, thus preventing Bondarev's 168th Rifle Division from escaping to the south.

When the army commanders on both sides now looked at their maps, the situation must have appeared hopeless for the Soviet formations. The Red Army continued to defend the 11 remaining independent *motti* with great vigour and fanaticism. For instance, at the Uomaa *motti* the remnants of one of the Soviet companies refused to surrender, despite having suffered 83 of its 85 men either killed or wounded (Trotter, 1991).

The surrounded Red Army forces seemed content to bide their time, but would fight back fiercely if attacked. Although the Soviets had hundreds of artillery pieces and tanks, ammunition and petrol soon started to run low. However, even when immobilised the tanks could still provide formidable fire. Thanks to the large number of pack animals available for slaughter and the supply drops by air, there seemed little likelihood of starving the Soviets into submission.

ANDREI BONDAREV
COLONEL,
168TH RIFLE DIVISION

(1901–1961)

A Ukrainian national, Andrei Leontjevitch Bondarev joined the Red Army in 1921. After graduating from Kiova Military School in 1927, he held several ever-more senior positions within the Leningrad Front. Bondarev was promoted to the rank of colonel in 1938, and given the command of the 168th Rifle Division on 23 August 1939.

As part of the Soviet Fifteenth Army, his division took part in the battles in Ladoga Karelia. After a promising start, the unit was eventually surrounded and forced to hold firm in the Lemetti and Kitilä *motti*.

After the war, Bondarev remained in charge of the 168th Rifle Division. These same men stayed on the Finnish front and were eventually surrounded near Sortovala at the beginning of the Great Patriotic War.

Despite his lacklustre performances, Bondarev was promoted to take over Eighth Army and rose to the rank of major-general on 7 October 1941.

Graduating from the top Military Academy in 1942, he was promoted to lieutenant-general in 1943. During the Great Patriotic War, Bondarev earned the accolade of Hero of the Soviet Union.

In the post-war period, Bondarev first led the XXXVII Guards Rifle Corps, and then became adjutant to the First and Seventh Guards army commands from 1950 to 1955. He resigned from active service due to illness on 30 October 1955.

Next, a lull developed in the fighting while the Finns attempted and failed to strengthen their position along the Pitkäranta road. This left the 168th Rifle Division encircled within a 26km perimeter. This noose was slowly being tightened as the Soviets drew their troops inwards to gain better defensive positions. The superior firepower of the division enabled it to keep the Finns at bay, and although capitulation would have been the most likely eventual outcome, these 13,000 men would maintain discipline and resist until the end of the war.

By 16 December, Lieutenant-Colonel Frans U. Fagernäs' 64th Infantry Regiment had arrived from Suomussalmi. Hägglund gave their command over to Hannuksela, who immediately created a new Task Force Kilpa ('Race'). Fagernäs' new mission was to strike at the new enemy formations approaching Pitkäranta from the south-east.

Finnish soldiers building a dugout at Pyhäjärvi on 17 December 1939. The deep-set foundations allowed the men to use heavy timbers, making warm and safe dugouts that were impervious to everything except a direct hit from heavy artillery. (SA-kuva)

This Finnish machine-gun emplacement, located *c.*5km north of Lemetti and photographed on 21 February 1940, was positioned a mere 100m from the Soviet lines. (SA-kuva)

THE LEMETTI *MOTTI*

Instead of applying more pressure on the formidable 168th Rifle Division, the Finns were happy to contain the situation and concentrate their efforts on finishing off the neighbouring 18th Rifle Division at the two Lemetti *motti*. They had been individually helped in this task by its 316th and 208th Rifle regiments, whose troops had already abandoned their positions near Ruhtinaanmäki and Mitro and proceeded to withdraw into the fold of Kondrashev's division.

The village of Uomaa formed a strongpoint for the Red Army on the Kitilä–Käsnäselkä road. Colonel Tiainen, commander of the 12th Division, entrusted the newly formed Task Force Tiikeri ('Tiger') with taking Uomaa. Tiikeri was to be led by Major Yrjö A. Valkama and consisted of three full battalions, although only two would participate in the attack, as a detachment was sent to perform guerrilla activity further north against Soviet rear areas.

By 17 January, Tiikeri's two battalions had managed to cut off the road on both sides of the village. However, all attempts to capture Uomaa were repelled. Meanwhile, the rest of the 12th Division proceeded to take control

of the road from Uomaa up until the positions of the 13th Division's men at Lemetti. This soon created four small pockets of resistance around the key sections of the road and Lavajärvi hamlet.

The Soviet troops within the newly formed Uomaa and Siira crossroad *motti* managed to retain fighting capability until the end of the war. Despite heavy losses from both combat and freezing temperatures, they repelled all the Finnish efforts. The dogged defenders made clever use of their tanks and artillery pieces to repel attacks regardless of the direction from whence they came.

The 476 men encircled further west near Lake Saarijärvi were not so lucky. By the end of February they had all either been killed or captured, along with their eight howitzers and three tanks.

In early February, the 1,100 Soviet troops in the last of the *motti* near Lavajärvi hamlet finally received permission to attempt a breakout. They made preparations and scheduled their move for the evening of 15 February. Major Lovlev commanded the men in this desperate dash. The Finns did not have sufficient men to effectively contain the Soviets, who had displayed passivity to date. The heaviest Soviet losses were suffered by the rearguard company, which encountered encircling troops a few kilometres from the

Several Soviet soldiers surrender themselves. The Finns tried to encourage any enemy troops who wanted to stop fighting to put up their hands and ensure that their bayonets were pointing downwards. In this way, fatal misunderstandings could be avoided. (SA-kuva)

Kitilä and Ruhtinaanmäki 1940: formation of the *motti*, 17–22 January 1940

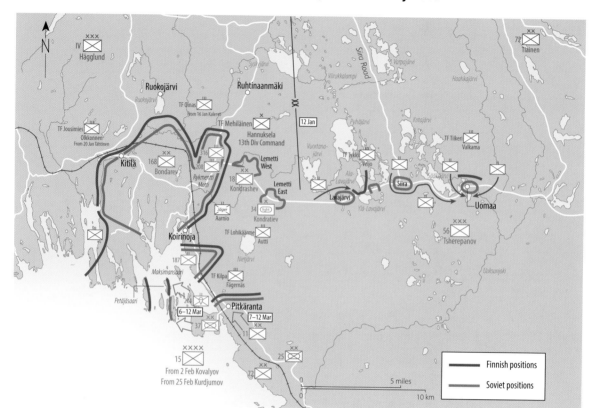

hamlet. In the ensuing battle, 40 of Lovlev's men died. The Finns, however, decided not to pursue the fleeing enemy into the night, allowing Lovlev to escort 810 men to the safety of their own lines.

Once responsibility for holding the road east towards Uomaa had been passed to the 12th Division, Task Force Mehiläinen could concentrate solely on the troops in the two Lemetti *motti*.

RIGHT
Major-General Woldemar Hägglund inspects destroyed Soviet BT and T-26 tanks at Mitro on 30 January 1940. (SA-kuva)

During the Winter War the Finns perfected the original Spanish Legion's design of a petrol bomb as an anti-tank weapon. The Finnish State Liquor Board went into overdrive, making over 450,000 half-litre glass bottles with ready mixes of waste alcohol, tar and gasoline. Towards the end of the war, more reliable ignition methods were also developed to replace the burning rag in the neck of the bottle. The name 'Molotov cocktail' was a further pun akin to 'Molotov's breadbaskets', which referred to the Soviet bombing of civilians. According to the Chair of the Council of People's Commissars, the Soviets were only dropping food on Finland, not bombs. Now the Finns repaid their armies by giving them back a drink – a cocktail. (SA-kuva)

The continued pressure from the Finns forced the 168th Rifle Division to reduce its perimeter in search of better defensive positions. On 22 January, all Finnish forces were ordered to cease attacks against the more easterly of the two *motti* at Lemetti. This was done in order to concentrate more troops in an attempt to crush the westerly Lemetti *motti* first.

The following day, one of the Finnish companies managed to occupy one of the enemy's fortified bases. This was to remain their only achievement until new plans were drawn up on 27 January by IV Army Corps commander Major-General Hägglund. The Finns lacked the kind of heavy firepower needed for direct assaults and to crush the fortified positions the Soviets had dug. As a result, most of the attacks in the 48 hours that followed were completed by small strike forces under the cover of darkness. These were largely unsuccessful, until, according to some accounts, a small detachment managed to infiltrate the Soviet lines and, by silently killing the gun crews, escaped back to their own side towing two heavy mortars. With the help of these new potent weapons the troops then managed to create a break and split the encircled troops into two smaller *motti*. The westernmost of the two, holding most of the enemy tanks, capitulated on 2 February. This enabled even more forces to be committed against the remaining half of the enemy. The Soviets fought valiantly, but had succumbed by 4 February. From this western Lemetti *motti* the Finns gained, amongst other plunder, 32 tanks and 6 field guns.

Task Force Oinas, now under the command of Major Reino I. Kalervo post 16 January, continued to apply its pressure from the north against the Soviet 316th and 208th Rifle regiments. Eventually, in early February, the Finns managed to cut off these regiments completely from their comrades in the 168th Rifle Division, creating the so-called *Rykmentti* ('Regiments') *Motti*.

From 9 February onwards, two Finnish battalions commenced a series of daily attacks aimed at destroying the *Rykmentti Motti*. Once again, the Soviet defenders used their tanks to great advantage and eventually the Finns had to cease all attacks due to heavy losses. While the Finns waited for reinforcements, the 168th Rifle Division launched a relief attempt. When the initial assault failed, the Soviets blamed the lack of ammunition available for the preliminary bombardments. After three days the Soviets had to admit failure, with significant losses. One battalion, for example, had now been reduced to 200 men from its original strength of 800 just two days previously.

Radio contact with the encircled troops was intermittent, but on 17 February they finally received a message granting permission for a breakthrough attempt of their own. On that very same evening, around 1,700 men tried to escape to the south and west. These men encountered Finnish troops predominantly belonging to Colonel Autti's task force, who

A Finnish soldier passing rows of dead Soviet troops after the destruction of the western Lemetti *motti* on 2 February 1940. (SA-kuva)

A Soviet tank officer who failed to escape from the western Lemetti *motti* on 2 February 1940. Interview by Pekka Tiilikainen, a radio broadcaster: 'The Russians tried to attack, but were bloodily beaten back. Some of the enemy were able to advance in the gloom right up to the machine-gun emplacement, but a merciless hail of bullets beat the Ivans back. The first attack was repulsed … and the cradle of Karelia drank up the blood of the enemy. The snowdrifts were painted red.' (SA-kuva)

proceeded to cut down the fleeing Soviets almost to a man. The last radio message from inside the *Rykmentti Motti* had announced: 'We do not need help' (Kilin and Raunio, 2010).

The Soviet forces escaping to the west had temporarily breached the encirclement, but were quickly herded up by Finnish reinforcements. The battles continued through the following night until no Soviet combatants remained at liberty. The 13th Division's headquarters received reports that 250 prisoners had been captured, while 1,500 lay dead on the battlefield. Captured equipment from this *motti* included 6 anti-aircraft guns, 66 heavy guns, 22 tanks and 250 other vehicles.

Believing that they would soon be reunited with rest of their division, the men in the eastern Lemetti *motti* had taken up positions on both sides of the road. As relief was late arriving, they had then dug in. After 21 January, this enclave remained relatively peaceful while the Finns concentrated their

forces on the destruction of the other two *motti* further to the west. Red Army records from the time indicate that around 240 men managed to integrate into this pocket after the destruction of the western Lemetti *motti*, and only 30 of them were fit for active duty. The experiences they recounted would surely not have helped morale within the pocket.

The eastern Lemetti *motti* contained the headquarters of Kondrashev's 18th Rifle Division as well as a good number of its troops. It seems that Kondrashev, the most senior officer among the encircled Soviets, had now started to crack under the pressure and had delegated the leadership of these 3,000 soldiers to his senior officers. The *motti* also housed the makeshift field hospital caring for 200 badly wounded troops, as well as strong armoured elements, although a lack of fuel was by now becoming a serious issue.

The war commanders at Stavka were very unhappy with the performance of 18th Rifle Division. They could not understand how such a potent force had been constricted into an area of roughly 8km². As a result, all the division's initial requests to be allowed to attempt a breakout were rebuffed. Meanwhile the Finns continued to increase pressure from all directions. On 23 February, the Soviet high command received another desperate message from inside the *motti*: 'We are dying, please pay our March wages to our families. Tell everybody that we died as heroes, we died but we did not

Destroyed Soviet tanks and other equipment at Tenamonmäki, inside the western Lemetti *motti*, on 3 February 1940. Mannerheim later commented: 'As our opponent generally attacked over the ice and open country, his losses were disproportionately high. The accuracy of our modest artillery made its superiority felt, despite the shortage of modern weapons and ammunition. Regarding the enemy's tactics, it was clear that [he] suffered from an obstinate adherence to the original operation plan without the ability to adapt it to the requirements of time and space.' (Mannerheim, 1954; photo SA-kuva)

Rykmentti motti and the 400 dead Soviets. 'When leaving for Finland, the Politruks had convinced one Russian soldier that this was a battle for liberation. Instead of meeting the happy faces of the people they had come to rescue, they found only dark forests, murderous fire from the Finns, and hunger and despair within their own ranks. There was no respite, the Finns were everywhere, unseen, on skis or firing from behind snowbanks and fir trees.' (SA-kuva)

surrender!' (Gordijenko, 2002). Finally, on 27 February, Kondrashev radioed the following: 'You keep urging us, like small children, but it hurts to be perishing when there is a big army nearby. Request immediate permission to withdraw. If permission is not granted, we will take it ourselves, or the men of the Red Army (the troops) will' (Kulkov, Rzheshevskii and Shukman, 2002).

By now, the Finns were already nearing the Soviet positions on the western side of the road, and Stavka finally agreed to the breakout option, even promising to send three large ski detachments to protect the division's planned route of escape to the east. The officers in the *motti*, however, did not accept the plans they had been given, and decided instead to attempt

Abandoned equipment of the Soviet 34th Light Tank Brigade at the Lemetti *Motti*. the tank in the forefront is a BT-7 Model 1935. (The Parola Armour Museum)

a bi-directional escape towards the south and east. They also decided to disobey direct orders and leave behind all the wounded who would slow them down. Furthermore, their own troops were to be kept in the dark about all these plans until the last possible moment.

The Finnish attack of the evening of 28 January had just commenced when the Soviets made their gambit and broke out. The regimental commissar, Razumov, gave this inspirational speech:

Brothers-in-arms, comrades of combat, we will depart for battle in one hour. In one hour, that which we have been waiting for these two long months finally happens. In one hour, we shall muster our last strength, and leave this lifeless place, which shall forever stand in the annals of war history as testimony of our division's steadfastness and determination. Tell the soldiers in the tents and dugouts that before we leave, we shall all bow to our dead comrades in this hostile land. We are surrounded by hallowed dead, expecting us to show courage, strength, obedience and above all absolute devotion to the bleeding flag of the 18th Division. Forward! (Gordijenko, 2002)

Colonel Ivan A. Smirnov was to take most of the able-bodied men and officers directly towards Lake Lavajärvi. The rush of Soviet forces pouring out of the usually quiet *motti* took the Finns completely by surprise. The Soviet push happened to bypass the headquarters of Colonel Matti Aarnio, the commander of the 4th Jäger Battalion. He quickly mustered every Finn in sight for action, including clerks, cooks, supply and medical personnel, while he himself radioed for help. A chaotic, point-blank firefight ensued. The Soviets finally managed to breakthrough, but in the aftermath the Finns counted over 400 enemy corpses between Aarnio's command tent and the outer defences.

Having escaped from the *motti*, Smirnov's body of men ran out of luck and ended up stumbling into Finnish positions on the shores of Lake Vuortanajärvi (a few kilometres due east). There his command was destroyed, with estimated losses of 850 dead and 660 missing. The Finns also believed Brigade Commander Stephen I. Kondratiev, commander of 34th Light Tank Brigade, to be among the dead. However, there seems to have been several cases of mistaken identity, as Soviet sources claim that Kondratiev made it back home badly wounded, where he either was executed or committed suicide. In contrast, the Finns believed that they had buried three senior Red Army commanders in the same shallow grave (the 'Three Generals' Grave'): Kondratiev, and the commanders of the 11th and 18th (Kondrashev) Rifle divisions.[10] Regardless of the truth of the matter, the eastern Lemetti *motti* rapidly became known as the 'general's *motti*' due to its vicinity to the purported burial site.

The second breakout group, led by Colonel Zinovi N. Alexejev, waited approximately one hour for the Finns to become distracted before making their own attempt. His command comprised around 900 wounded personnel, and only 327 fit men escorting them. Despite this handicap, the

10 11th Rifle Division led by Brigade Commander Pjotr P. Borisov was sent to relieve the 168th Division advancing along the coastal road through Pitkäranta. Borisov was killed while scouting ahead in tank at the Pitkäranta area on 5 February 1940.

Finnish officers examining the battle flag of the Soviet 34th Light Tank Brigade. It was recovered at the same time as the body of the unit's alleged commander. (SA-kuva)

detachment managed to leave without detection and make contact with one of the ski squadrons sent to meet them. Most of Alexejev's command made it back to safety.

The 18th Rifle Division's commander, Kondrashev, also made it back to the Soviet lines. Having been lightly wounded, he made his escape dressed in the uniform of a regular soldier. On 4 March, Kondrashev's identity was exposed in a hospital, and he was arrested. He was summarily executed in the yard outside.

Out of all the Soviet units engaged in the war, the 18th Rifle Division suffered the heaviest losses. Its casualties amounted to over 9,000 men, far exceeding those suffered during the Raate road battles.

In contrast, the troops in Bondarev's 168th Rifle Division continued to hold out within their perimeter. They had resorted to butchering their own

The word *motti* originally meant approximately 1m² of chopped logs. Lumberjacks were traditionally paid for each *motti* they managed to make. When working in the forests, the lumberjacks would leave the neatly stacked cubes of *motti* behind them at regular intervals to be collected later. During the Winter War, the word came to describe an encirclement of Soviet troops, which the Finns left to ripen with cold and hunger before later destroying it. (SA-kuva)

horses, and were heavily reliant upon supplies they received from airdrops, as well as on the few deliveries making it through across the frozen Lake Ladoga. For the Soviet troops carrying these supplies, it was a very risky business. They would mount machine guns onto the trucks leading the lines of horse-drawn carts. Screened by light tanks and armoured cars, they would then race towards the encircled division, as the Finns opened fire from the outlying islands and shoreline batteries. Counter bombardments from the Soviet forces on the mainland, in turn, forced the Finnish artillery to remain hidden, only daring to expose itself when shelling the most valuable targets.

The main responsibility for harassing these supply columns fell to the Finnish ski infantry. Night after night these guerrillas would perform their hit-and-run ambushes against the supply troops. On moonless nights, the same supply column could be hit twice every hour, until dawn's dim light would reveal the corpses littered on the ice plateau. Despite the Finnish efforts, enough supplies made it through for the 168th Rifle Division to maintain fighting order.

During January and early February, all the Soviet attempts to evict the Finns from their strongpoints on the smaller islands and to re-establish a permanent connection with their troops in Pitkäranta town had failed. These attempts cost the Red Army dearly, and on 5 February Brigade Commander Pjotr P. Borisov of the 11th Rifle Division paid a personal price for this failure: he died inside his command tank during an ambush on the Pitkäranta road. His body was the first to be laid in the so-called 'Three Generals' Grave'.

THE SOVIET FIFTEENTH ARMY

On 12 February, the Fifteenth Army was formed from the troops in the Pitkäranta area. Its command was given to Army Commander 2nd Class Michael Kovalyov, reporting directly to Stavka. On 25 February, after this new army had failed on numerous occasions to clear the Pitkäranta road of Finnish forces, Kovalyov was forced to step down in favour of his second-in-command, Army Commander 2nd Class Vladimir Kurdjumov. In order to help Kurdjumov carry out its directives, Stavka reinforced Fifteenth Army with the 144th and 119th Motorised divisions. However, the poor roads leading towards Pitkäranta meant that these units were going to be seriously delayed.

Despite this setback, Stavka overruled the new attack plans that Kurdjumov had put together. Instead, the Fifteenth Army would attack along the Pitkäranta road whilst performing a simultaneous direct attempt to liberate the 168th Rifle Division through the Finnish island fortifications.

The task of clearing the island was given to the 7,000-strong 37th Motorised Division. The attack began after a heavy preliminary bombardment on 6 March. Soon, the superior Soviet artillery and scores of light tanks were brought to bear. The 37th Motorised Division was making good progress by capturing the outlying positions, while the Finns were forced to retreat from island to island. Although the division's attack was hindered by Soviet planes accidentally hitting their own vanguard. The Finns were forced to concede the larger Petäjäsaari Island by the end of the first day. This now allowed the Soviets to concentrate their fire against the Finns on Maksimansaari Island.

(1895–1970)

VLADIMIR KURDJUMOV
ARMY COMMANDER
2ND CLASS, FIFTEENTH ARMY

Vladimir Nikolajavitch Kurdjumov first saw combat as a battalion commander on the Western Front in 1915. He served as a brigade commander and divisional chief of staff in the Russian Civil War.

During the Winter War, Kurdjumov first worked as an adjutant to the Southern Group of the Eighth Army, and then to Michael Kovalyov, the commander of Fifteenth Army. When Kovalyov was removed from his duties by Stavka, the top job was handed to Kurdjumov on 25 February 1940.

In June 1940, Kurdjumov received the rank of lieutenant-general. From 1941 onwards, he acted as commander of the Eastern Urals, Northern Caucasus and Siberian military districts. After the war, Kurdjumov became an inspector general and also served as a commander of the Western Siberian Military District. He resigned from active service on 9 March 1957 for health reasons.

(1892–1946)

ANTERO SVENSSON
COLONEL, 12TH DIVISION

In the pre-Winter War years, Antero Johannes Svensson was commander of the Karelian Guards Regiment. He was reassigned to lead the 2nd Brigade during the Extraordinary Autumn Manoeuvres of 1939. On 1 February 1940, Colonel Svensson was appointed to command the 12th Division on the hard-pressed Kollaa front.

During the Interim Peace, Svensson served as the commander of the Savo-Karelia Military District. From there he took over his pre-assigned wartime post at the head of the 7th Division on 17 June 1941.

Svensson's 7th Division was to attack on the north side of Ladoga. On 16 August 1941, he was made a Knight of the Mannerheim Cross, following the capture of Sortovala.

While temporarily holding the position of acting commander of VI Army Corps, Svensson was promoted major-general. He then returned to lead the 7th Division until 1 August 1943. Svensson was then given command of V Army Corps until it stood down on 5 December 1944.

Following an hour-long preparatory bombardment and strikes from ground-attack planes, Maksimansaari Island was attacked from three directions. The encircled Finns resisted desperately, causing significant losses to the Soviets. The fighting was so bloody that when the island was captured later that night, only 12 men out of all those who surrendered were spared as the Soviets vented their frustrations on these prisoners of war.

Despite both sides losing around 500 men during the attack, this was hailed as an important strategic victory by the Soviets, and was a great boost to the morale of their troops. A significant factor in their success was air power, which delivered more than 80 tonnes of bombs, while the Soviet artillery fired over 11,600 shells.

Over the next few days, the last of the islands were cleared and a more durable supply road with the 168th Rifle Division was established over the ice. Meanwhile, the Finns had withdrawn most of their forces to better defensive positions on the mainland. These positions held until the end of the war on 13 March. By this time, losses among the 168th Rifle Division had risen to 5,493 men, comprising 1,583 dead, 3,613 wounded and 297 missing. The sick and frostbitten accounted for a further 1,249 casualties. On 9 March, in the light of the 56th Army Corps' lack of overall success, Ivan N. Tsherepanov chose to take his own life with a pistol.

HOLDING KOLLAA

In December 1939, the Finns had barely managed to halt the Soviet Eighth Army's advance along the road and railway next to the narrow Kollaa River. The Soviets hoped to crush the Finnish defences and push through to the Loimola crossroads a mere 10km behind these lines. From Loimola, the Eighth Army could then choose from several roads to threaten the rear of the Finnish lines on the Karelian Isthmus. It was thus imperative that the Finns hold at Kollaa.

From 12 January onwards, parts of Colonel Tiainen's 12th Division had to be diverted south to help to keep the Uomaa *motti* and the Käsnäselkä road enclosed. This left even fewer Finns defending the precarious Kollaa front. Towards the end of that month, Mannerheim realised how depleted the forces there had become, he ordered the entire 23rd Division to the sector, (in order to bolster the lines held by the remaining four battalions). However, when the Soviet offensive on the Karelian Isthmus began, only the 69th Infantry Regiment could be spared for this front, while the rest of the 23rd Division was diverted south. At the end of the month, Tiainen was

Kollaa Kestää 1940: Kollaa holds against the Soviet attack, 7 March 1940

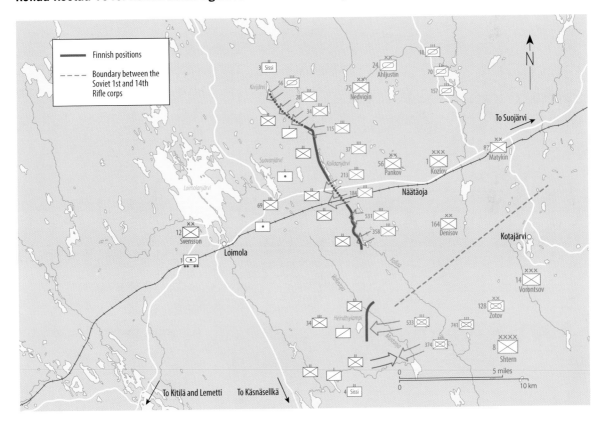

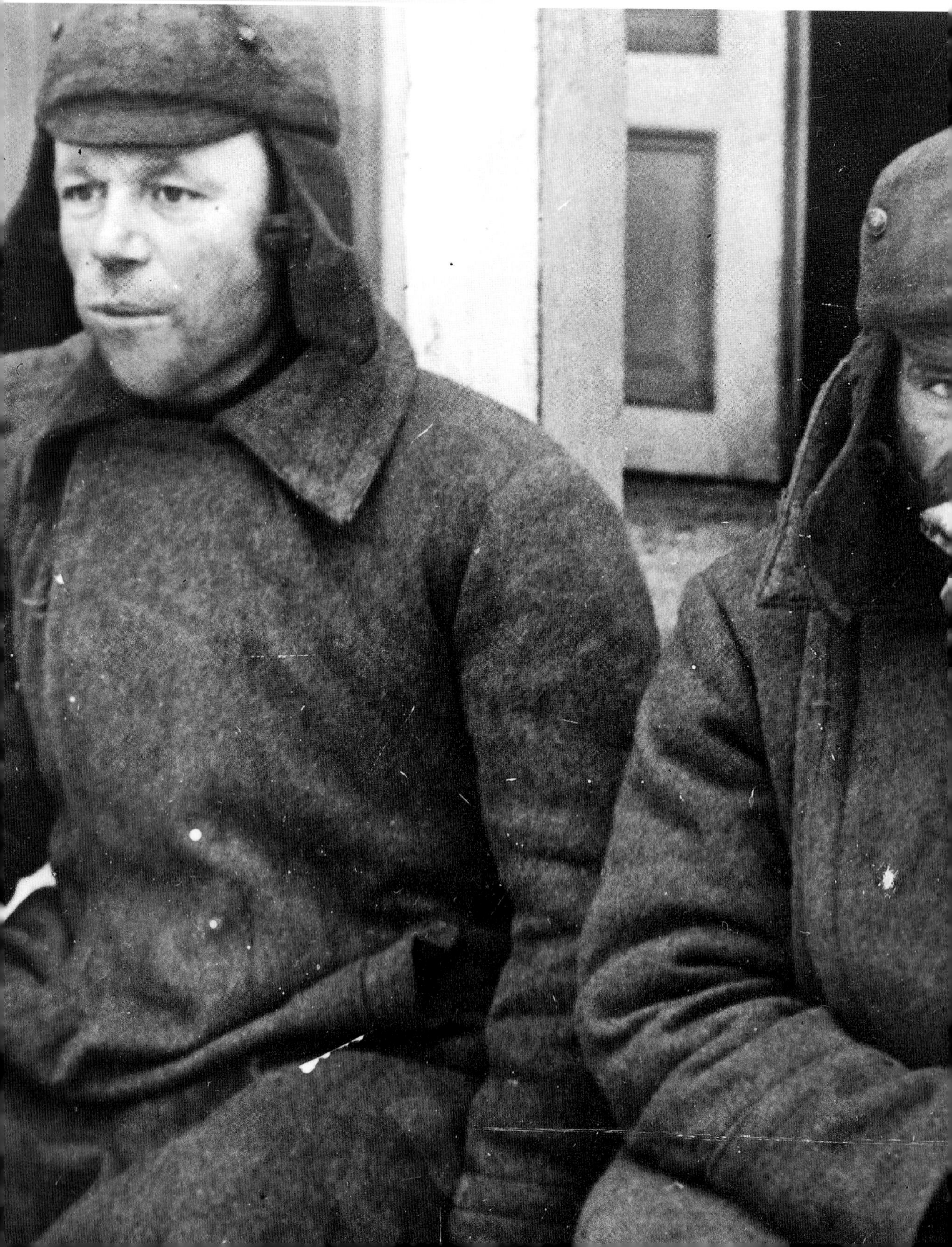

Ravenous Soviet troops would sometimes surrender just to get something to eat, a fact that Finnish propaganda tried to exploit to the full. In an interview, one Soviet soldier, who had been captured at Raate road, stated: 'I remembered being told that we were again on a mission of liberating our worker friends from capitalism, but I can feel in my own skin how we were welcomed by those we had come to free. What can we possibly offer you Finns that you don't already have? Even though I am a prisoner, I have looked around and have seen a few things that have convinced me that the Finnish worker is better dressed than the Russian communist official.' (Eagle and Paananen, 1973; photo SA-kuva)

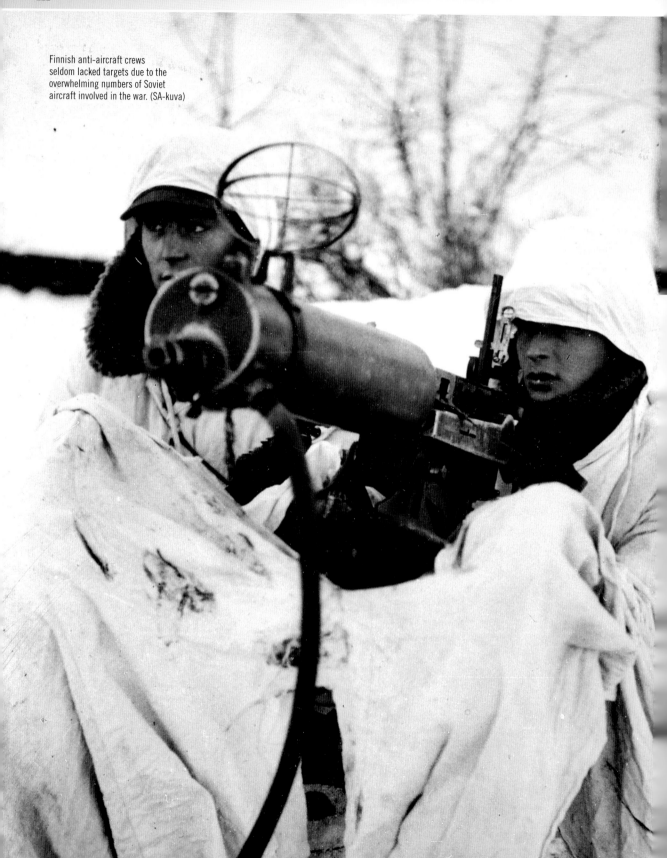

Finnish anti-aircraft crews seldom lacked targets due to the overwhelming numbers of Soviet aircraft involved in the war. (SA-kuva)

hospitalised due to his heart condition, and command of the 12th Division was given over to Colonel Antero Svensson.

Towards the end of February, Stavka decided to prioritise the conquest of Kollaa. The formation of Fifteenth Army on the Pitkäranta road had now freed more elements of Eighth Army to focus on this front. Although two of Eighth Army's divisions were operating further north near Ilomantsi and Aittojoki villages, this still left Gregory Shtern with six full divisions to carry out the offensive towards the crossroads at Loimola.

The Soviet plan was to attack in a three-division-wide front along the Kollaa River. Shtern reasoned that this would prevent the Finns from encircling and attacking the flanks of his formations. It was also decided that the defenders should first be ground down by relentless artillery bombardment. The commander of the 1st Rifle Corps, Dmitry T. Kozlov, was to be in charge of the three attacking divisions. The 24th Mechanised Cavalry Division, led by Brigade Commander P. N. Ahljustin, was to remain in reserve, ready to exploit any opening that Kozlov could create.

South of the 1st Rifle Corps, the two-division-strong 14th Rifle Corps was led by Division Commander V. G. Vorontsov. His plan was to first send the 128th Motorised Division on a flanking sweep through the wilderness about 10km south of the Finnish defences; followed shortly afterwards by the 87th Rifle Division as the second wave of this attack.

The Finns had 18,903 men, armed with 212 machine guns, 18 mortars and 60 guns, available for the defence of Kollaa. The Soviet Eighth Army had now assembled 74,199 men for the attack. Their armament included 806 artillery pieces, 400 grenade launchers and 262 tanks. With their overwhelming strength, the Soviets were expecting rapid victory.

On 2 March, the Soviet preliminary bombardment and air-strike missions began. The Finns estimated later that some 30,000 to 40,000 shells hit them, while only 1,000 had been fired back by their own limited artillery. By 10:00, all four Soviet divisions had begun their advance.

The attack of the northernmost unit, 75th Rifle Division, led by Brigade Commander Simon I. Nedvigin, was stopped early on by barbed-wire obstacles. All their subsequent attempts to find a way around these barricades were thwarted by fierce counter-attacks.

The unit occupying the central position, the 56th Rifle Division led by Colonel G. P. Pankov, attacked along the road with all of its regiments. Its drive finally stalled just short of the Finnish defensive positions.

South of the 56th, Brigade Commander Sergei Denisov's 164th Rifle Division failed to advance more than a few hundred metres from its jumping-off point due to deep snow. The poorly trained men could not operate the skis they

At the headquarters of the 34th Infantry Regiment, at Loimola on 31 December 1939, Colonel Tiainen of the 12th Division (right) and his subordinate Lieutenant-Colonel Teittinen of the 34th Infantry Regiment. (left) examine captured 7.62mm Degtjarev DP-27s. (SA-kuva)

were issued with and broke all their snowshoes almost immediately. Potholing in the waist-deep snow while carrying weapons was simply impossible.

Meanwhile, the 24th Mechanised Cavalry Division sent one of its regiments to help the 75th Rifle Division on the northern flank. Realising that none of their comrades were now likely to breach the Finnish lines, the rest of the unit had started to prepare for the following day's frontal assault instead.

On the army's southern flank, the 128th Motorised Division, led by Brigade Commander A. S. Zotov, fared a little better. After crossing the Kollaa River, Zotov's three regiments managed to advance for the best part of 2km, reaching the eastern edge of the small Lake Heinätsylampi.

After a disappointing day, Eighth Army's leadership was furious, especially with the 56th Rifle Division, which despite the preliminary bombardment had not achieved anything of significance. It was made clear that similar failures in future would have personal consequences for those in command.

Unfortunately for the Soviets, the second day of attacks did not go much better. The determined efforts of the 56th Rifle Division saw them break through the barbed-wire obstacles at a few points. This was achieved with massive losses and for little gain, as the Finns killed everybody who made it all the way to the breach.

The 128th Motorised Division did manage to lumber forward a further 2km, but was now forced to start diverting troops north to help the 164th Rifle Division, which was still struggling to make any progress at all.

Following a few days of recovery, the operation continued in full force on 7 March. Eighth Army's plans remained largely unchanged, except that this time everybody felt an enormous pressure to succeed.

The 128th Motorised Division, south of Lake Heinätsylampi, was ordered to turn directly northwards in an attempt to fold the Finnish lines in on themselves. The original second wave of the attack from this direction by the 87th Rifle Division was cancelled, and these troops were readied to relieve the 56th Rifle Division in the army's centre.

After a preliminary bombardment lasting a few hours, the forward elements of the 56th Rifle Division managed to cross the Kollaa River. Once over, they had to repel several counter-attacks by the Finns while establishing their own bridgehead a couple of hundred metres from the back. At the same time, Denisov's 164th Rifle Division was again thwarted by the deep snow as the ski-less troops managed to wade forward only 200m. The southerly 128th Motorised Division was able to plough on a further 500m through the wilderness.

Regardless of the demands and threats made by Eighth Army's leadership, very little progress was made to exploit the achievements of the 56th Rifle Division over the following days. The next night, Finnish forces managed to push back the troops at the bridgehead and regain the main defensive line.

Politruk Klimov noted in his diary:

> Red Army regulations state: during peacetime, no exercises will be held when the temperature goes below -15°C. This instruction many seem to have taken to heart, and truth be told, our men do not start their attacks and reconnaissance missions with the same enthusiasm they did before the temperatures fell. (Gordijenko, 2002)[11]

Despite the arrival of Finnish reinforcements and an armoured train on 10 March, the Soviets finally took permanent control of the defences along the river.

---

11   Temperatures at Kollaa plummeted to below -40C at times

The Kollaa River front photographed in the summer of 1942, showing the effects of the continuous Soviet shelling. One soldier wrote in a letter back home: 'Not much is happening here. It's the same every day. Aircraft are flying at treetop level firing at us, but we are deep down in our trenches. Some of the men are shooting, some are sleeping, some are going to the sauna, and some are making jokes and brewing coffee. The trees around our dugouts are all being broken off by the enemy artillery but we don't pay much attention to that. We are short of ammunition and have now figured out that it does not pay to fire before you see the Russians' beards shaking.' (Eagle and Paananen, 1973; photo SA-kuva)

The advance of the 128th Motorised Division in the south had been stopped by a Finnish counter-attack. This caused confusion among the Soviets, who then opened fire on their own units. Despite these setbacks, the division managed to crawl forward some 600m during the day.

On the northern flank, the 75th Rifle Division conquered the hill that had been their original objective. The Finnish attempts to retake this vantage point failed, and by that night the Soviets had broken through the defences, progressing a kilometre inland.

By now, the 56th Rifle Division had lost its ability to continue fighting and needed to be relieved at the front by Brigade Commander Philip. N. Matykin's 87th Rifle Division. The Finns attempted to disrupt these manoeuvres with as much fire as they could muster. Despite this, the 87th Rifle Division was ready to start its attack on the morning of 12 March. By the end of the day, the Soviets had progressed a further 300m along the road.

On their left flank, half of the forces of the 164th Rifle Division, the 358th Regiment, managed to make nearly 700m progress, while the division's 531st Regiment again failed to move at all. A northern flanking move by the 24th Mechanised Cavalry Division around Lake Loimolanjärvi did not reach its objectives, nor did the 75th Rifle Division advancing alongside it. The southernmost 128th Motorised Division also failed to fulfill its mission.

Regardless of these failings, the Finns were finally forced to abandon almost all of the prepared positions along Kollaa River. New defences were being planned further back and the 12th Division was already starting to prepare for withdrawal, when Svensson, the division commander, decided against any such further retreats. Instead he insisted on attempting combined counter-attacks by all his forces to regain the river front. These counter-plans were never executed. The surprised and relieved men ended up being saved by the beginning of a ceasefire agreement.

A Finnish messenger runs through the shelling to deliver vital messages at the eastern end of the Kollaa front. (SA-kuva)

Despite the overwhelming odds in favour of the Red Army, and the progress the Soviets had made on the previous day, the battle had not ended in victory for either party. Although the Finnish defences had clearly started to crack, both sides still retained most of their fighting ability. It is difficult to guess how much longer the Finns would have held out, or what untold damage they might have ended up inflicting on the Red Army, had the ceasefire not been called.

The uneasy truce had been negotiated in secret in Sweden, and in order to gain a better bargaining position, Finland's line had to hold. At Kollaa, Mannerheim's wishes had come true and the Finns had held up long and strongly enough to influence the peace.

On the front lines at the Kollaanjoki River, a Finnish sniper and spotter work in tandem. At Kollaa these marksmen proved extremely effective and played a part in the miraculous defensive victory. (SA-kuva)

CHAPTER 10
THE KARELIAN ISTHMUS, 1940

In December, after ordering Soviet troops into defensive positions, Stavka concentrated on reassessing its failed invasion plans. It came to the conclusion that currently there were insufficient numbers of men available to exploit any breakthrough achieved by the front-line divisions. Accordingly, Stavka decided that the number of troops along the front should be increased to total 1.3 million. Most of the reinforcements were to be deployed on the narrow Karelian Isthmus, where the hammer would soon fall. Stavka chose to appoint Army Commander Simon K. Timoshenko to lead these forces, naming his new combined command North-Western Front.

Under Timoshenko, the Soviets concentrated 30 divisions. These were split into the following commands. The Seventh Army, on the western side of the isthmus, led by Army Commander Cyril Meretskov, held 14 divisions. A further

A Finnish machine gun mounted on a sledge, ready to mow down the enemy. The sledge provided a highly manoeuvrable yet stable firing platform. As a result, transporting this heavy weapon around was much easier during the winter months than it had been carrying it in the previous autumn's exercises. The Finnish model of a Maxim included an opening on the top into which snow could be rammed in order to cool the weapon, an innovation that many of the Soviets came to envy. (SA-kuva)

SIMON TIMOSHENKO
ARMY COMMANDER, NORTH WESTERN FRONT

Timoshenko started his military career in 1915 in the Imperial Army as a regular soldier. By 1925, he had been made commander of all the cavalry corps. Following this, he held several military district commands until, in January 1940, he was made responsible for the troops fighting against the Finns on the Karelian Isthmus as the commander of the North-Western Front army group. For breaching the Mannerheim Line, Timoshenko was made a marshal of the Soviet Union and awarded the Hero of Soviet Union.

In May 1940, Timoshenko replaced Voroshilov as the People's Commissar for Defence. Under his tutelage, the army was greatly modernised; tank production especially was dramatically increased. He held this position until Stalin took over personally when Operation *Barbarossa* began. Timoshenko remained a member of Stavka and held the command of the Western Front. In September he took over the South-Western Front and in July 1942 transferred to head the Stalingrad Front. From there he returned, a mere three months later, to the South-Western Front. In 1943, Timoshenko was given the task of coordinating the different fronts as Stavka's representative.

After the war, Timoshenko held several military district commands and from April 1961 onwards was a member of the Defence Ministry's Chief Inspectors. Timoshenko was buried in the Kremlin Wall.

nine divisions on the eastern side were formed into the new Thirteenth Army, under Corps Commander Vladimir Grendahl. The remaining seven divisions were held back in reserve directly under Timoshenko's own control, ready to exploit any success achieved by Meretskov or Grendahl.

To help control the troops in his fourteen divisions, Meretskov's Seventh Army was further grouped into the 10th, 19th, 34th, and 50th Rifle corps. Grendahl's Thirteenth Army grouped its nine divisions under three Rifle corps: 3rd, 15th and 23rd. This smaller force alone had nearly as many men and much materiel as the whole of the Red Army had possessed during the initial attack on the Karelian Isthmus less than two months earlier.

Timoshenko's new template for war was to be as effective as it was monstrous:

> In frontal attack no enemy or combination of enemies can hope to compare with us. By making a succession of direct attacks we shall compel him to lose blood, in other word to lose something he has less of than we have. Of course we shall have enormous losses too, but in war one has to count not one's own losses but those of the enemy. Even if we lose more men than the enemy, we must view it dispassionately. (Chew, 2008)

In contrast, the Finnish forces on the Karelian Isthmus were worn out. Even during the relative quiet of January 1940, Soviet artillery had shelled their positions on a daily basis. The men were forced to remain alert throughout and after these bombardments in order to repel any possible enemy attacks starting in their wake. During night-time, the tired defenders had to repair the dugouts and assault obstacles from the day's punishing barrages.

Lieutenant-General Hugo Österman directed the Finnish Army of the Isthmus. His troops were grouped into two formations. In the west

around Viipuri was II Army Corps, under Lieutenant-General Harald Öhquist. His corps contained the following divisions: 1st Division (Major-General Taavetti Laatikainen), 2nd Division (Colonel Eino Koskimies),[12] 3rd Division (Colonel Paavo Paalu, in the hard-pressed Summa sector) and 4th Division (Colonel Auno Kaila). Colonel Isakson's 5th Division, which had withstood the brunt of the Soviet attacks in December, now formed Mannerheim's strategic reserve to the south of Viipuri.

The eastern half of the isthmus was held by III Army Corps under Major-General Heinrichs. In the heavily contested Taipale sector, the 10th Division had been renamed the 7th, and from 9 January was led by Colonel Einar Wihma. Colonel Bertel Winell's 8th Division was located at Kiviniemi. Also deployed in the area was Colonel Niilo Hersalo's 21st Division, comprising reservists and serving as Mannerheim's strategic reserve. In the wake of the recent reorganisations, troops available for use as reinforcements were very thin on the ground.[13]

A Vickers-Armstrong G-ton tank armed with a 37mm Bofors cannon. Most of the these tanks had arrived to Finland with empty turrets and had to be fitted with weapons locally. This tank was soon to take part in the ill-fated battle of Honkaniemi. (SA-kuva)

12 In order to confuse the Soviets, Koskimies' 11th Division had been renamed the 2nd Division on 1 January 1940.
13 It is worth noting that none of the Finnish troops in the area had been rotated out; instead, many of the divisions had been given new designation numbers during January.

Karelian Isthmus January–February 1940: defending the Mannerheim Line

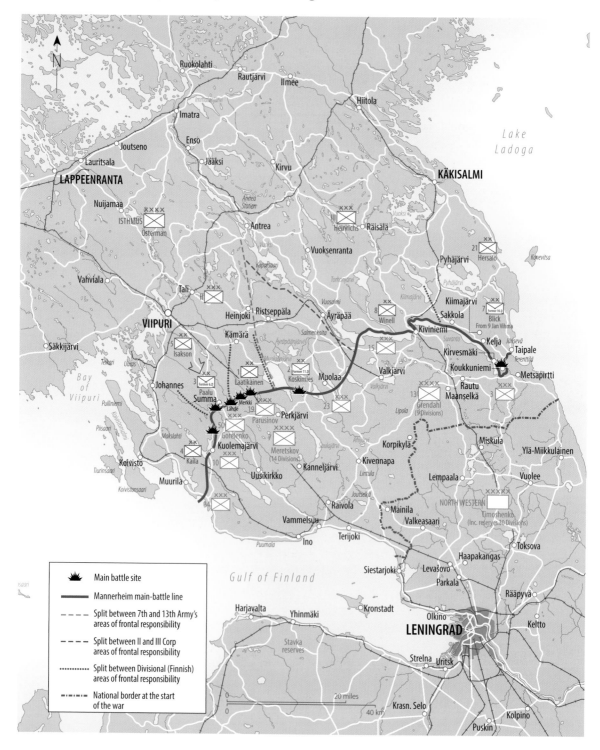

Legend:

- ✹ Main battle site
- ▬▬▬ Mannerheim main-battle line
- – – – Split between 7th and 13th Army's areas of frontal responsibility
- ▬ ▬ ▬ Split between II and III Corp areas of frontal responsibility
- ·········· Split between Divisional (Finnish) areas of frontal responsibility
- –·–·–· National border at the start of the war

0   20 miles
0   40 km

On the isthmus, the Finns still hung on to the so-called Main Defensive or Mannerheim Line. Behind it lay the poorly prepared Interim Line. The Finns only had time to complete some of the emplacements and facilities on this defensive line, and along the length of it troops would rarely be provided with places to rest and sleep. The last and final obstacle for the Soviets was the so-called Rear Line or T-Line, which ran from Viipuri to Kuparsaari and from there to Taipale. The fortifications for the T-Line were still woefully inadequate.

The disparity of eight defensive divisions against 30 attacking ones soon started to tilt the scales in the Red Army's favour.

(1892–1975)

HUGO ÖSTERMAN
LIEUTENANT-GENERAL.
ARMY OF THE ISTHMUS

Österman, a former Jäger, took part in the Finnish Civil War with the rank of major. After the conflict, Österman led the 3rd Division from 1925. He subsequently became inspector of infantry in 1928. In 1933, Österman was made commander of the armed forces, and promoted lieutenant-general on 16 May 1935.

When the Winter War began, Österman took command of the Army of the Isthmus. This was the command centre between Mannerheim's headquarters and the army corps operating on the Karelian Isthmus. He asked to be relieved from his position during the defensive battles of 1940, and was succeeded by the commander of III Army Corps, Erik Heinrichs.

Österman then held several senior inspectorial positions until February 1944. At this point he was sent to German Army headquarters as Mannerheim's personal envoy.

When Finland switched back to its peacetime formations in November 1944, Österman took over the position of chief inspector of infantry. He resigned at his own request on 1946.

Lieutenant Sarvanto holding the insignia from one of his kills on 8 January 1940. Sarvanto became the first Finnish fighter ace by shooting down six enemy bombers in less than five minutes, a feat considered a world record at the time. (SA-kuva)

A Finnish dog patrol practises locating enemy troops in winter conditions. The dogs were extremely useful both as guards and for tracing the scent of enemy desants in the rear of the lines. (SA-kuva)

THE SUMMA AND LÄHDE SECTORS

The Finnish 3rd Division (the former 6th Division, from Mannerheim's central reserves) under Colonel Paalu was now responsible for the defence of the Summa sector. There the Soviets started battalion-strength preparatory attacks across the length of the front from Summa village to Lake Muolaanjärvi to the east. These attacks were intended to wear down the defenders, and as such, they were highly successful.

The following extract from the memoirs of II Army Corps' Lieutenant-General Öhquist records the events of January and February in this sector:

(1890–1965)

 ERIK HEINRICHS
LIEUTENANT–GENERAL,
ARMY OF THE ISTHMUS

After the Civil War, former Jäger Erik Heinrichs held several senior positions at army central command, and in different regiments and divisions. In 1921 he transferred to France, where he completed the special communications training for divisional and army corps commanders, and graduated from the French Military Academy.

In October 1939 Major-General Heinrichs, who had been the inspector of infantry, took over command of III Army Corps on the eastern Karelian Isthmus. On 19 February 1940, Mannerheim promoted Heinrichs to lieutenant-general and appointed him to lead the Army of the Isthmus.

After the Winter War, Heinrichs first assumed overall command of the Finnish Army, and then transferred in May 1940 to become Mannerheim's chief of staff.

During the 1941 summer offensive, Heinrichs led the 100,000-strong Karelian Army. He was promoted to full general in October 1941. In January 1942, he returned to army headquarters as chief of staff.

Heinrichs was to be one of only two people ever to receive the Knight of the 1st Class Mannerheim Cross (the other being Mannerheim himself, although he felt it somewhat strange to receive a commendation carrying his own name). Both also received the 2nd Class cross at the same time.

In January 1945, Mannerheim made Heinrichs his successor as the commander-in-chief of the Finnish armed forces. This position was to be a short assignment: following the political upheaval from the 'Weapons Cache' case, he resigned that same summer. After the incident, Heinrichs worked as a military expert and writer.

16.01. 3rd Division requests more pioneers to fix the concrete fortifications at Summa and Lähde. These are being demolished by enemy bombardment each day and have to be repaired each night anew.

21.01. Heavy artillery bombardment and occasional probing attacks on the 3rd Division's sector throughout the night. Russian infantry that now assaults in small groups are well trained and valiant ...

Similar kinds of attacks at Taipale all over yesterday ...

Yesterday and today our troops (1st, 3rd and 4th divisions) have after a long hiatus again managed to destroy some assaulting tanks, a total of three.

23.01. The Russian patrol that had advanced to Suursaari Island on Muolaanjärvi is still being dealt with; so far, the enemy has left behind 19 dead and a prisoner.

28.01. 3rd Division has again been targeted by heavy artillery strikes; a few of the dugouts have been destroyed and 8 men have lost their lives.

01.02. Morning is misty, -11°C, it finally started to clear around 13:00

hours, during the evening -23°C and northern lights in the sky ...

Since early morning, we have been able to hear a continuous thunder from the south-east, as we did during the worst of the December offensive. 11:50 hours, 3rd Division informs that the artillery barrage against Summa is heavier than ever before. When I take into account the increased patrol actions of the previous night, I think an all-out infantry attack is soon to be expected. (Halsti, 1957)

After the relative calm of January, the Soviet assaults were focused on the Summa and Lähde sectors, where, by 1 February, they had managed to reach and capture a section of the Finnish trenches. Despite being forced to withdraw for the night, the Soviets were able to return the following day, further eroding the confidence of the defenders. Each day the Soviet forces renewed their attacks, chipping away at the defences and gaining a bunker here or a dugout there. Despite the numerous counter-attacks launched by the Finns, some sites remained in permanent Soviet control.

A passage from Öhquist's memoirs from 8 February records the worsening situation across the front:

The situation with available artillery shells ... has now become so bad, that I have again had to restrict their use to the absolute minimum that is absolutely required for holding our own ... we had to again strip all batteries to scrape together munitions for the 3rd Division, our stores are beginning to empty.

However, by 10 February, 3rd Division's commander Paalu had come back to believe that things were once again under control, having withstood all of the previous Soviet attacks on his sector. Unfortunately, it turned out to be only the calm before the storm.

Finland's political leaders had desperately been trying to start up peace talks with the Soviet Union since early January. Foreign Minister

PAAVO PAALU
COLONEL, 3RD DIVISION

Paalu was trained as a Jäger in Germany in 1916, and received his baptism of fire in World War I.

In the Winter War, he served as the commander of the 6th Division (later renamed 3rd Division) on the Karelian Isthmus. During the last month of the war, he was forced to take **(1895–1971)** recuperative rest, but returned within a matter of days to lead Task Force Paalu, a special force assisting in the defence of Viipuri Bay.

During the assault phase of the Continuation War, Major-General Paalu led the 1st Division and remained at the disposal of the Maaselkä Group in the trench warfare phase. On 2 November 1943, he was transferred to lead the 18th Division on the Karelian Isthmus. After the Soviets achieved a breakthrough in his unit's sector, Paalu was transferred to headquarters for special assignment by the commander-in-chief. The reasons for the transfer were differences in opinion between him and the commander of IV Army Corps, Taavetti Laatikainen.

Paalu resigned in 1945, and worked as an insurance inspector until 1963.

Finnish soldiers transporting a wounded comrade on a sleigh. Coming to the front, the men would haul in ammunition, foodstuffs and other supplies. On their return journey, these *pulkka* sleighs would often carry wounded men. (SA-kuva)

Väinö Tanner spent considerable time in Stockholm, where together with the intermediary efforts of the Soviet Ambassador to Sweden, Alexandra Kollontai, they tried to hammer out a peace agreement. Although Kollontai seems to have been a key player in discouraging Sweden from taking a more active part in the war, she at least offered a channel through which Finland could communicate with Stalin. The latter's patience with the unyielding Finns was wearing very thin by now, as his missive, sent a few weeks later, clearly indicates: 'Either you, Messrs Finnish bourgeois, make concessions, or we will impose a government under Kuusinen on you which will disembowel you' (Kulkov, Rzheshevskii and Shukman, 2002).[14]

A preliminary Soviet bombardment began on the morning of Sunday 11 February. Having received a ration of 100ml of vodka per man, the infantry divisions and armour started their advance at noon (Edwards, 2006). While the Finns managed to repel all the attacks by the 19th Rifle Corps in the east of the isthmus, Gorelenko's 50th Rifle Corps fared somewhat better. His two westernmost divisions achieved little, apart from tying in the weakening defenders. Nevertheless, the Soviet heroes of the day were to be found in Brigade Commander Philip Aljabushev's 123rd Rifle Division, which managed to push through Paalu's 3rd Division lines just east of Lake Summa in the Lähde sector.

By 13:00 the Soviets had captured the Poppius bunker and all the strongpoints east of it. By 19:00, their attack had breached the Mannerheim Line and reached the Interim Line at Lähde. This defensive line was established as a first rallying point in case the Mannerheim Line was

14 Otto Wille Kuusinen was the head of the puppet Finnish Democratic Republic (or Terijoki Government) Stalin had set up for Finland.

overrun. It lacked dugouts and shelters for the men to rest in, and in many places even rudimentary firing positions or fortifications were still missing.

The Finnish counter-attack launched during the following night lacked the arms and men needed, and thus was destined to be unsuccessful. Immediately after this, the 1st Battalion of the 8th Infantry Regiment led by Captain Lahja A. Oksanen was sent to reinforce the breach. Meanwhile, the rest of the 3rd Division managed to repel and throw back the Soviet attacks at other locations along its front.

As the Finnish high command became aware of the breakthrough later that night, they immediately engaged the reserve troops of Colonel Isakson's 5th Division. The first of Isakson's regiments moved into position that same night, while the rest of his men would arrive at the front during the following day. In the meantime, the

PHILIP GORELENKO
DIVISION COMMANDER,
50TH RIFLE CORPS

(1888–1956)

Philip Danilovitch Gorelenko joined the Red Guards in 1917 as a guerrilla commander, and a year later he was officially sworn into the Red Army. During the Russian Civil War, Gorelenko served as a brigade and division commander.

He graduated from the Military Academy in 1934. In August 1939, Gorelenko was given command of the 50th Rifle Corps. When his men finally breached the Mannerheim Line in February 1940, Gorelenko was made a Hero of the Soviet Union.

During the Interim Peace, Gorelenko was first the acting commander of the Leningrad Military District. Upon the reinstatement of the former general ranks on 4 June 1940, Gorelenko was made a lieutenant-general. From January 1941 onwards, he led Seventh Army on the Finnish front.

Throughout the Great Patriotic War, Gorelenko commanded Thirty-Second Army on the Maaselkä front against the Finnish II Army Corps. In one of the final battles of the war, Gorelenko's troops suffered a resounding defeat in the Ilomantsi area.

Soviets sent reinforcements of their own to widen the opening they had created.

A Finnish counter-attack planned for 13 February never got going, due to the distractions of Soviet activity along the front. Most of the troops were simply needed elsewhere, or by oversight had been placed too far from the front to act quickly enough. Two brave battalions from Colonel Väinö Polttina's 14th Infantry Regiment (5th Division) did manage to push back the enemy at first, but a renewed Soviet push, spearheaded by tanks, drove the Finns back to the questionable safety of the Interim Line. In the process, Polttina was mortally wounded. Worse still, during the Finnish counter-attack, Soviet artillery had already started their preliminary bombardment of the Interim Line and deeper Finnish positions. As the defenders recovered from the failure of their own counter-attack, Soviet armoured forces rolled straight through them. Just east of the Lähde road, the Soviets created a 100m-wide gap in the Interim Line. Now that they had breached these final defensive positions, the Red Army was in touching distance of the crossroads at Lähde village, which would open up passage in every direction throughout the isthmus.

During the following day, the Soviets continued to widen the breach. Fortunately for the Finns, the Red Army infantry was slow to take full

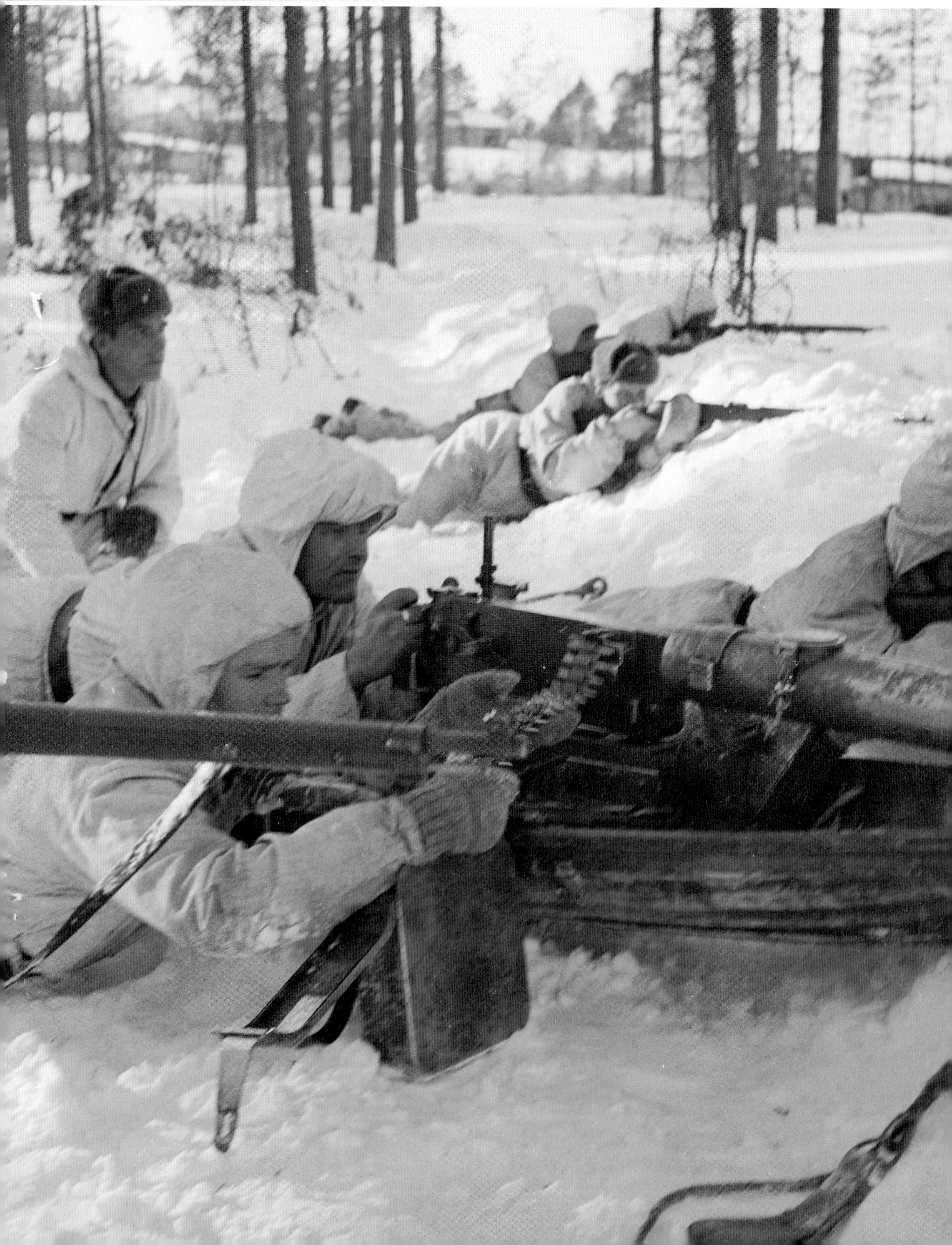

HARALD ÖHQUIST
LIEUTENANT-GENERAL, II ARMY CORPS

(1891–1971)

As a Jäger, Öhquist fought in World War I on the Eastern Front at the Misse and Aa rivers, as well as the Bay of Riga. He did not return to Finland before February 1918, when the Civil War was already raging. The newly promoted Major Öhquist commanded the 9th Jäger Battalion in the battles for Viipuri.

During the years of peace, he led the Karelian Guards Regiment, and after being promoted to the rank of colonel in 1925, Öhquist commanded the 2nd Division garrisoned in Viipuri.

At the outbreak of the Winter War, Öhquist was the commander-in-chief of the peacetime army, and as was originally planned, he immediately transferred to take over II Army Corps on the Karelian Isthmus.

Öhquist operated as a liaison officer for Hitler's headquarters during the Continuation War. From March 1942 to February 1944 he led the Isthmus Army (IV Army Corps).

Mannerheim relieved Öhquist of this duty, making him chief inspector of military training. Lieutenant-General Taavetti Laatikainen was to command IV Army Corps during the fateful defensive victories that summer. In November 1944, Öhquist was reassigned to the reserves. He resigned from the military in 1951, and worked as the chief of Helsinki's Civil Protection Department until 1959.

advantage of the progress made by the rapidly advancing tanks. The latter had meanwhile proceeded eastwards towards Lähde, capturing all the equipment of the Finnish 2nd Heavy Artillery Battery in the process. For the time being, the rest of the Finnish lines were managing to hold. This enabled Österman and Öhquist to remedy earlier poor troop deployments, and pool all the available reinforcements to stem this breach. Had the 5th Division been closer at hand from the beginning, its infantry could have attempted to push back the Soviet attack before it took hold. Now without ammunition for the artillery and with woefully few anti-tank weapons, their chances looked slim.

In the wake of the penetration of the Main Defensive Line, Soviet Brigade Commander Minjuk boasted in the *Ogonek* newspaper on 25 February 1941: 'The breakthrough against the Mannerheim Line holds the highest place in all the history books for bravery, military ability and examples of war tactics. The difficult terrain, forests, swamps and lakes all added to the strength of the Finnish Main Defensive Line, and made it stronger than any other European fortress. The Red Army was the first one in history that could have made such a brave breakthrough on this kind of fortress. The honour belongs to the Red Army from now on.' (SA-kuva)

THE FALL OF THE MANNERHEIM LINE

While the Soviet tanks rampaged in the rear of the Finnish defences, the rest of the 123rd Rifle Division continued to pour through the gap at Lähde. During the day, they succeeded in extending the tear in the Mannerheim Line to roughly 6km in width.

Elsewhere, the Finns still fought for control of their defensive positions, although due west Brigade Commander Panteleimon A. Zaitsev's 90th Rifle Division now managed to make some progress. During the afternoon of 13 February, his troops were engaged in fierce combat in the Merkki sector. By the end of the day, the Main Defensive Line had been irretrievably breached to a depth and width of several kilometres.

That night, Seventh Army Commander Meretskov noted that the strategic installations of the Mannerheim Line had finally been overwhelmed. He then proceeded to give orders for the 50th and 19th Rifle corps to concentrate their efforts on exploiting this opportunity.

Öhquist now gave permission for Isakson's 5th Division to start withdrawing eastward, if it became absolutely necessary. Control of practically all the troops in the breach area was handed to the newly arrived Lieutenant-Colonel Ernst Ruben Lagus. The following morning, his decimated command included the remains of the 14th Regiment, one infantry battalion and two companies with additional reinforcements soon arriving in the form of the 4th and 5th Independent battalions and two companies' worth of Civil Guard troops, consisting primarily of volunteer schoolboys from the city of Viipuri. This had all the hallmarks of a last ditch effort to save the front.

The decision to throw in such a junior officer as Lagus to take command of all the troops was not only strange but also caused resentment among the more senior officers present. He simply did not have the resources, nor the knowledge of the troops and the area needed to complete his mission. Worse still, Lagus was suddenly recalled a few days later, disrupting the chain of command even further.

The area east of the breach was still controlled by Lieutenant-Colonel Antti Kääriäinen and his reinforced 3rd Brigade (1st Division, with its 1st and 2nd Brigades continuing to hold the main line

In his order of the day, dated 14 March 1940, Mannerheim stated: 'Soldiers! I have fought on many battlefields, but I have never seen warriors like you. I am as proud of you as of my own children, equally proud of the man from the northern tundra as of the sons of the Ostrobothnian plains, the forests of Karelia, the gay countryside of Savo.' (SA-kuva)

east towards Muolaanjärvi Lake). During the day, he was given permission to withdraw from contact with Zaitsev's 90th Rifle Division in the Merkki sector and to perform an orderly retreat towards the north-east. The Soviets did not follow the disengaging Finns and instead concentrated on consolidating their victory.

On 14 February, Commander-in-Chief Mannerheim arrived personally to assess the situation on the front line. A conference with his top commanders concluded that although Finnish forces still held the Main Defensive Line everywhere else except in the area controlled by 5th Division, all the troops along the isthmus now needed to perform a tactical retreat to the Interim Line. At the meeting, it was also decided to keep hold of the strategically important Koivisto (Beryozovye) Islands in the Gulf of Finland. Mannerheim later wrote in his memoirs: 'The fact that our efforts seeking a peace agreement were still underway made me want to further emphasise that ... it was absolutely critical that the positions in depth at the Interim Line would now be kept.'

Thus, while the Soviets continued their attacks on 15 February, the defenders received the order to begin disengaging. By now, practically all the battalions were at less than half their normal fighting strength. The withdrawal went well, as most enemy units chose to let the Finns make their escape freely and without hindrance.

By 17 February, the Finns had made it to their designated positions along the temporary Interim Line. Over the past three days of fighting, II Army Corps had lost 6,406 men; of these, 1,531 were dead, 4,430 wounded and 445 missing. To help strengthen the holding positions at the Interim Line, Mannerheim also released the reserve 23rd Division.

In spite of the plans made to hold the Koivisto Islands in the Gulf of Finland, the regiment responsible for their defence had been given leave to break contact with the enemy on 21 February. The men scuttled all their heavy equipment and then escaped by skiing over the frozen Viipuri Bay to its west bank. The islands north of these positions, along with those closer to the city of Viipuri, were to be held at all costs. At the same time, other Finnish forces performed tactical withdrawals along the isthmus. The centrally positioned 2nd Division fell back to the pre-war concrete bunkers and dugouts in the Äyräpää sector.

Finnish cavalry on their way to the front. The front-line horse handlers taught their animals to take cover from incoming enemy fire. Olavi Rintamäki handed over a horse called Sävy to the defence authorities at the beginning of the Continuation War. He recalled: 'Sävy survived the war and eventually was returned home ... I was visiting my old home and left Sävy outside. From the window I could see how Sävy suddenly fell off her feet and flattened herself against the ground. Why did she do that? I quickly found out that they were blowing up bedrock at the nearby road construction site. Every time there was an explosion, Sävy would hit the dirt, just like they did at the front.' (Rislakki, 1977; photo The Finnish Museum of Photography)

Vickers tanks at their base at Poltinaho Barracks, Hämeenlinna, winter 1940. During the Winter War the Finnish armoured forces were small and remained largely unused. In isolated instances, Finnish tanks were trialled as moving machine-gun emplacements. The unreliability of the machines and poor supply conditions made this tactic impractical. Seeing some of their own tanks was, however, always a great boost to the Finns' morale. (The Parola Armour Museum)

The Soviets maintained their pressure, and attacks against the Interim Line commenced immediately after the Finns had manned it. The transport elements supporting Colonel Gunnar Heinrichs'[15] 23rd Division were late getting the troops into position, and when the men finally arrived, they found that their dugouts were already under attack. However, by 22 February, this newly arrived division was finally able to relieve the exhausted 5th Division in this part of the front.

While these attacks were being launched, Österman decided to step down as Army of the Isthmus commander. In his 1966 memoir, he explained that he and Mannerheim could not agree on sector strategy; moreover, Mannerheim wanted to take a more hands-on role in leading the forces in the area, and so Österman felt that he should stand aside and allow a more flexible leader to take on the role (Österman, 1966). Heinrichs, commander of III Army Corps, was promoted to head the Army of the Isthmus, while Paavo Talvela took over from Heinrichs.

Mannerheim also decided to form a new I Army Corps on the isthmus, drawing in the 1st and 2nd divisions (currently part of II Army Corps) from the western side of the isthmus. Major-General Laatikainen was chosen to command the new corps. However, due to a shortage of officers within his units, Laatikainen was unable to take over full front-line responsibility, on the left flank of II Army Corps, until 26 February.

15   Brother of Lieutenant-General Erik Heinrichs, III Army Corps commander.

Karelian Isthmus, end of February 1940: fall to Interim Line

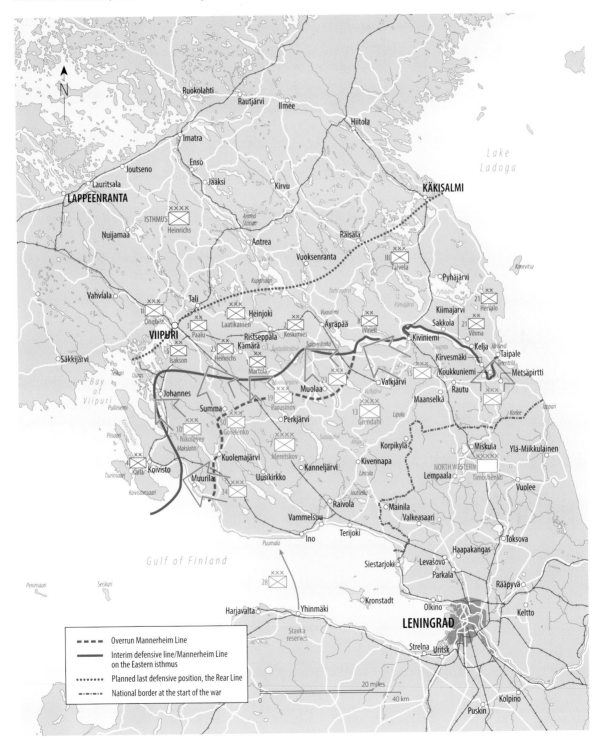

N

Ruokolahti
Rautjärvi
Ilmee
Hiitola
Imatra
Imatranjärvi
Joutseno
Enso
Jääksi
Kirvu
Lauritsala
LAPPEENRANTA
KÄKISALMI
Lake Ladoga
Konevitsa
ISTHMUS
XXXX
Heinrichs
Nuijamaa
Antrea Statian
Antrea
Räisälä
Pyhäjärvi
Vahviala
Vuoksenranta
III
Talvela
Pyhäjärvi
Kuparsaari
Torficanjärvi
Kiimajärvi
Kiimajärvi
XX
21
Hersalo
Tali
Vuoksi
Vuosalmi
Kiimajärvi
Sakkola
XXX
II
Öhqtüst.
XXX
Heinjoki
XX
Äyräpää
8
XX
Winell
Kiiminiemi
XX
21
Vihma
VIIPURI
Paalu
Laatikainen
Koskimies
Knyopdänjärvi
Salmenkaita
Suvanto
Kelja
Järisevä
Taipale
Terenttilä
Säkkijärvi
Teikari
Isakson
23
Heinrichs
Kämärä
Martola
1
XX
Muolaa
XX
23
Salmenkaita
XXX
15
Koukkuniemi
Kirvesmäki
Metsäpirtti
Uuras
Pullniemi
Johannes
Summa
19
Parusinov
Muolaa
Valkjärvi
Valkjärvi
Maanselkä
Rautu
XXX
3
Korlee
Tappari
Bay of Viipuri
Piisaari
Makslahti
Nikoläyev
10
XXX
Gorelenko
50
XXX
Perkjärvi
13
Grendahl
Lipola
Satagörvi
Korpikylä
Miskula
XXXXX
Ylä-Miikkulainen
Tiurinsaari
Kaila
Koivisto
4
XX
Kuolemajärvi
Meretskov
XXX
Kanneljärvi
Kivennapa
Lintula
NORTH WESTERN
Lempaala
Timoshenko
Vuolee
Koivistonsaari
Muurila
34
XXX
Uusikirkko
Joutselkä
Raivola
Mainila
Valkeasaari
Haapakangas
Toksova
Vammelsuu
Terijoki
Puumala
Ino
Gulf of Finland
Siestarjoki
Levašovo
Parkala
Rääpyvä
Peninsaari
Seiskari
28
XXX
Yhinmäki
Kronstadt
Olkino
Keltto
Harjavalta
Stavka reserves
LENINGRAD
Strelna
Uritsk
Kolpino
Puskin

- - - - - Overrun Mannerheim Line
——— Interim defensive line/Mannerheim Line on the Eastern isthmus
· · · · · Planned last defensive position, the Rear Line
—·—·— National border at the start of the war

0   20 miles
0   40 km

Soviet soldiers examining a Finnish Vickers tank destroyed during the battle of Honkaniemi on 26 February 1940. In a farcical attempt, the Finnish Tank Battalion sent forth 15 of its Vickers tanks. Due to enemy action and technical problems, only one of the tanks was able to return from the battle. Despite having destroyed nine Soviet tanks, the Finns suffered a resounding defeat and the nation's armoured forces were unable to continue the war. (The Parola Armour Museum)

Öhquist continued as commander of II Army Corps. It seems that Mannerheim chose the more junior Heinrichs for the role of army commander for reasons of personal chemistry. During an earlier telephone conversation with Talvela, Mannerheim even considered replacing Öhquist altogether. It appears that previous orders allowing his units to retreat, and subsequent comments he made undermining his commander-in-chief, had damaged Öhquist's reputation with Mannerheim.

THE TAIPALE SECTOR

Heinrich's previous sector of command – in the east of the Karelian Isthmus – had been under constant Soviet attack since the beginning of the war. Although fresh troops had been sent to replace some of the dead and the wounded, each day demanded more and more *sisu* (determination, or resilience) from those men still standing. Soon the worn-down defenders were to face concentrated attacks from the Soviet 3rd and 15th Rifle corps.

In the Taipale sector, Colonel Vihma had taken over the command of the newly assigned 7th Division on 9 January 1940, the third change in the unit's leadership since the beginning of the war; many of its men, by contrast, had been involved in the fighting from the outset. In addition to the division's field artillery regiment, one heavy artillery battery and two batteries from the eastern isthmus were now sent to reinforce the 7th. These guns were, in the end, to play a very decisive role.

Vihma's men faced the men of the 3rd Rifle Corps from Grendahl's Thirteenth Army. The initial Soviet objectives were to advance 5km through the Finnish defences to reach the road network on a line running through Kelja, Korpikylä and Järisevä. Grendahl had assigned the 49th and 150th Rifle divisions to execute this task. These units were further reinforced by the 101st Rifle Regiment reinforced, along with the independent 97th Ski Battalion and an independent tank battalion. In addition to the divisions' own artillery formations, the attacking forces could call upon the help of six full artillery batteries.

Advancing on the tracks made by the men in front considerably decreased the effort for the men further back. During the Winter War the weather conditions were ideal for skiing. Once made, these tracks would hold their shape and use for months, unless they ended up being covered by fresh snowfalls. Another benefit of this single-track system was that the Soviets could not know how many Finns had passed by, nor when. (The Finnish Museum of Photography)

EINAR VIHMA
COLONEL, 7TH DIVISION

Born with the name 'Wichmann', Einar August Vihma joined the Jäger training in October 1915. He was sent back to Finland in 1916 to help with further recruitment for the unit. He escaped only narrowly when a group of would-be Jägers were arrested; after this, Einar returned to continue his training in Germany, reaching

(1893–1944)

the rank of Hilfsgruppenführer.

Together with the men of Kuopio Civil Guard, he took part in many battles of the Finnish Civil War. In 1918, Einar was made a company commander and promoted to the rank of lieutenant.

After the war, Einar was made captain in 1919, major in 1922, lieutenant-colonel in 1927 and finally a full colonel in 1933. He served as the director of the Cadet School from 1933 to 1936. That year he changed his name to the more Finnish sounding 'Vihma' and was made the commander of the Finnish White Guard battalion stationed in Helsinki.

At the start of the Winter War, Vihma's unit was incorporated into the newly established 1st Brigade as its 1st Battalion. At the same time, Vihma took charge of the whole brigade with the objective of delaying the Soviet attack on the western side of the isthmus.

Towards the end of December, Vihma was transferred to lead the 10th Division in the eastern Isthmus. On 9 January 1940, when he assumed command, the unit's call sign was changed to the 7th Division. Vihma led this unit until the end of the war.

During the Interim Peace, Vihma was the commander of the Helsinki Military District. On the outbreak of the Continuation War, Vihma took over the 12th Division, and, from 18 December 1941 onwards, the 6th Division as well. Vihma was made a Knight of the Mannerheim Cross on 12 October 1941.

Vihma's 6th Division achieved legendary fame in the battle of Tali–Ihantala. There his forces arrived just in the nick of time to save the last of the Finnish defences from collapsing.

Major-General Vihma was killed in action on 5 August 1944. He was the last of the Jäger and the only Finnish general to die in combat. His untimely death put an end to brewing courts martial over his extremely harsh disciplinary actions, and Vihma received a burial befitting a hero of the nation. As Mannerheim later put it: 'The last of the units transferred in from eastern Karelia was the 6th Division, commanded by the brave Major-General Vihma, who fell as a hero in these battles, having arrived just in time in order to stabilise the defences at Ihantala.'

On the morning of 8 February, the Soviet preliminary bombardment began in the Taipale sector. After roughly an hour, two battalions from the 49th Rifle Division launched a wide-fronted assault, resulting in the capture of two bases at Terenttilä hamlet. The immediate Finnish counter-attack did not manage to recapture these positions. During the following night, an additional battalion renewed the attempt. Their initial assault was also fruitless, during which the Finnish commander suffered frostbite to his feet forcing one of his juniors to take over. A third and final desperate effort returned the positions at Terenttilä to Finnish hands.

After a short lull, the Soviets renewed their heavy bombardment on 11 February. Around noon, the main attack went in. However, at the end of another very heavy day's fighting, the Finns were still in control of their main defensive lines. A surprise counter-attack launched near Suvanto forced the Red Army to relinquish its newly captured positions in such a hurry that its troops left behind all their heavy weapons and equipment. This victory came at a hefty price for the Finns: the units that had taken part in the fighting had suffered such heavy losses that they had to be rotated out under the cover of the following night. For the next few days, the front line waved back and forth. Everytime the Finns managed to retake the positions during the night that the Soviets had captured the previous day.

By 17 February, Thirteenth Army headquarters issued orders its 49th and 150th Rifle divisions orders to cease future assaults and instead to concentrate on wearing the Finns down with artillery bombardments. The Soviets needed time to reorganise their troops, as by now many of their battalions had lost almost all value as fighting formations.

By 18 February Grendahl felt that sufficient cohesion had been restored to his forces, and ordered another all-out assault against the Finnish positions. Around Kirvesmäki, the 150th Rifle Division, led following recent changes in leadership, gained rapid victories. There on the south-eastern corner of III Army Corps' area of responsibility, they poured out of their bridgehead at Koukkuniemi, routing the Finnish 1st Battalion (61st Regiment, 21st Division) and taking control of strongholds at the southern end of the Kirvesmäki sector, as well as

SERGEI KNJAZKOV
COLONEL,
150TH RIFLE DIVISION

(1896–1976)

Sergei Aleksejevitch Knjazkov started his military career in the Imperial Army in 1915. He completed the Ensign School in 1917, and a year later volunteered for the Revolutionary Red Army. During the Russian Revolution, Knjazkov served as a company commander.

From 1923 to 1937, Knjazkov served as a battalion and regiment commander, and was promoted colonel in 1936. Until the beginning of the Winter War, he was posted as an aide to the 4th Division's commander.

On 19 August 1939, Knjazkov was made commander of the 150th Rifle Division. Under his command, the unit took part in the attacks against the Mannerheim Line in the Taipale sector.

Knjazkov was relieved of his command on 12 February 1940 as a result of the division's poor performance. He was replaced by Brigade Commander Alexander Pastrevich. Pastrevich himself had been relieved from the command of the 138th Rifle Division previously, but by now the Soviets were running very short on suitable high ranking officers.

After his dismissal, Knjazkov became the director of the Kalin Infantry Academy. During the Great Patriotic War, he acted as a divisional and army corps commander on many fronts. Knjazkov was made a major-general in 1943 and lieutenant-general in 1949. He retired from active service in 1962.

the three westernmost strongholds in the Terenttilä sector. After capturing this part of the Main Defensive Line, they failed to press home their advantage. Rather, the Soviet troops hunkered down, fearing a Finnish counter-attack. Meanwhile, the Finnish 1st Battalion had been ordered to retreat to the Interim Line. Somehow, its troops became disoriented, and ended up running into heavy enemy fire in open terrain at Kirvesmäki. The battalion lost 86 dead and 58 wounded.

On 19 February, the Finns strengthened their positions along the Interim Line at Kirvesmäki. Meanwhile, the Soviet 49th Rifle Division managed to push the Finns out of the strongholds of the Main Defensive Line at Terenttilä.

During the following night, the retreating Finns finally managed to stop the advancing enemy near a large gravel pit, with the Finns taking up positions on its rim. Once these troops had been reinforced with a second battalion, they managed to retake all the lost strongholds. Subsequently, these exhausted men had to be sent to the rear for rest and recovery. For a while during this transfer, only the Finnish artillery kept the Soviets from overrunning the nearly empty trenches.

Referring to the events of these past days, Mannerheim sent the men at Taipale the following message:

> I have witnessed with admiration the tenacity, the willingness for self-sacrifice and the courage that especially the men of the 7th Division in the Taipale sector have shown in repelling the enemy assaults. I expect that going forward, the 7th division will continue to heroically hold its positions, and even if the enemy somewhere temporarily breaks through, will throw it back with a counter-attack.

The Soviet assault continued on 22 February. This time the deeper Finnish positions at Kirvesmäki held, while the Main Defensive Line was breached at Terenttilä, where once again the Finns were forced to retreat to the gravel pit. Talvela's III Army Corps launched a counter-attack with the remnants of all of its six battalions in the area. In the following two days of fierce fighting, the Finns managed to recapture two of the strongholds at Terenttilä and set up a new defensive line running along the rim of the gravel pit.

At this point, III Army Corps finally managed to regroup, and established more permanent positions. These defences were to hold until the end of the war. The Soviets continued to use their artillery and to assault these positions, but by now their focus had moved to exploiting the breach around Lähde in the west of the isthmus.

In March, the Finns completed their final strategic retreat into well-prepared positions on the Rear Line, about half a kilometre away. The war ended before this easternmost section of the defensive line was placed under any serious pressure.

It is interesting to note the effect that Soviet artillery fire had on the Finnish III Army Corps forces on the isthmus. In a post-war exchange between Army Commissar 2nd Class Zaporozhets and Stalin, the former explained why the Soviet infantry often fired so few rounds: 'When we counted the Finnish casualties, it turned out that 95 per cent had been killed by shells. That was normal in fact, because artillery performed well' (Kulkov, Rzheshevskii and Shukman, 2002). In general it was the overwhelming superiority in artillery that enabled the Red Army to make any progress at all. Even after heavy bombardments, the Finns continued to fight to the bitter end.

Following the successful penetration of the Mannerheim Line at Lähde, the Taipale sector was now of secondary importance to the Red Army. After the breaching of the Main Defensive Line on 17 February, all available units had been ordered into relentless pursuit in order to prevent the Finns from digging new defensive positions in front of the city of Viipuri, on the western side of the isthmus. Seventh Army headquarters now ordered a task force consisting of two tank brigades and two infantry battalions to take Viipuri and the surrounding area. At this time, Viipuri was a bustling regional centre and by Finnish standards a large conurbation with a peacetime population of nearly 80,000. The vast majority of these people were soon forced to become refugees in western Finland. The Soviet headquarters believed that the Finnish forces had by now suffered a total collapse; but the ensuing days of fierce fighting would prove them wrong.

The Finnish I and II Army corps had been given permission to retreat to the still incomplete Rear Line positions by 27 February. This line ran from the southern side of the city of Viipuri to Lake Vuoksi, where it met III Army Corps' front-line sector, proceeding along the Vuoksi River to Taipale. This strategic retreat proved to be an intuitive move by the Finns. Unknown to them, the Soviets were planning to start their main offensive the following day. The Finns began their retreat just as the Soviets finalised their assault preparations.

Such was the force of the new Soviet attack that it managed to overrun the Interim Line along its whole length. During the delaying actions and over the first few days of the battle, the Finnish II Army Corps suffered over 5,000 casualties. Their objective from now on was to hold the city of Viipuri, an anchor point for the last remaining line of defence. Meanwhile, an emboldened Stavka issued orders for the Red Army to break through this last Rear Line by 3 March at the latest.

The Rear Line was intended as the final defensive fortification along the Isthmus. If this last stand was to fail too many crossroads would fall into Soviet hands and their onslaught would become impossible to contain. Öhquist's II Army Corps formed its troops so that the 4th Division (under the command of Colonel Johan Arajuuri from 1 March) took responsibility for the coastal defences west of the city across Viipuri Bay, while the 3rd and 5th divisions were now tasked with securing the city's main approaches. Immediately east of them, the 1st and 3rd divisions of Laatikainen's I Army Corps took position east of the Tali crossroads, a battleground which would find lasting fame four years hence.

The main Soviet battle plan for Viipuri was simple: to conquer it with relatively light infantry and pioneer formations supported by artillery and tanks. The bulk from Meretskov's Seventh Army was to skirt the city from the east. The conquest of the outlying islands and crossing the frozen bay west of Viipuri was handed to the 10th and 28th Rifle corps (drafted mainly from Stavka's reserves and deployed on the Seventh Army's left flank at the beginning of March). As the Taipale sector had proven so resilient, Grendahl now directed the focus of 13th Army to breaking the Rear Line on the central Isthmus

Horses played a vital role in the Finnish Army, supplying front-line troops and enabling the rapid transport of troops and equipment. Virtually all army units employed horses, and during the Winter War some 90,627 animals served the nation. Despite the greatly increased degree of mechanisation, 45,426 horses continued to serve between 1941 and 1944. The horses suffered high casualty rates compared to the men handling them. The horse-driven supply columns were also favourite targets for enemy airplanes and artillery. During the Winter War, the casualty rate for horses was 16.6 per cent and during the Continuation War 12.8 per cent. (Rislakki, 1977; photo SA-kuva)

THE CENTRAL ISTHMUS: ÄYRÄPÄÄ

In the centre of the isthmus, on Seventh Army's right flank, Grendahl's Thirteenth Army divided its forces against Talvela's divisions. Grendahl planned to use the 19th (transferred to the Thirteenth Army on 2 March) and 23rd Rifle Corps to push north and secure the train station in the village of Antrea. Meanwhile, further east, the 15th Rifle Corps was to cross the Vuoksi River near Äyräpää village.

The Finnish retreat in the western isthmus to the Rear Line had forced III Army Corps to stretch their frontal responsibility along the Mannerheim Line on the Vuoksi River. This left the 2nd Division, led by Colonel Eino Koskimies, as the main defensive force in the Äyräpää–Vuosalmi sector. Lieutenant-Colonel Matti Laurila's 23rd Infantry Regiment protected Äyräpää village, which stretched across the river into Vuosalmi on the northern shore. East of these troops, the 8th Division, in III Army Corps' sector, still held the original defences on the shores of the Vuoksi.

On 29 February, Grendahl was able to confirm that he exercised complete control of the Finnish Interim Line west of Äyräpää. While the

A Finnish soldier demonstrating how to use a captured Soviet gun shield. The shortcomings of items such as this, and the tank-sledge (where a tank would push or drag along a steel container full of infantry), were soon revealed. Such equipment simply was too heavy to assault with, and in the case of the Soviets at least, gave the men a reason to hunker down and stay safe, rather than pressing on the attack. (SA-kuva)

23rd Rifle Corps would proceed straight towards the Finnish Rear Line, Grendahl now gave orders for the 25th Rifle Corps to capture the village of Äyräpää. Destroying this critical strongpoint would allow the Soviets to start rolling up the Rear Line from this end.

The Soviet 17th Motorised and 4th Rifle divisions were to first destroy the defences at Äyräpää village on the south side of the Vuoksi River and then proceed straight across to the Finnish rear. Koskimies' 2nd Division was to receive the combined attack of the Soviet 97th Rifle and 17th Motorised divisions just east of Äyräpää, while Laurila's 23rd Infantry Regiment was left to deal with the Soviet 4th Rifle Division in the village proper.

The first Soviet attempt to take Äyräpää began on 1 March. This attack was repelled, but the following day a renewed effort finally achieved

✚ MATTI LAURILA
COLONEL, 23RD REGIMENT

(1895–1983)

Laurila's family was nationalistic to the core. Matti's father led the Civil Guard in Lapua, and both he and Matti's brother Ilmari perished during the Civil War fighting for the Whites. After their deaths, Matti inherited his father's command and continued to lead the unit of Guards to Tampere. Laurila's actions during the war gained legendary fame, earning him the call sign 'Lapuan Lumiaura' or 'Lapua's snowplow'. During the Mäntäsälä Rebellion, Matti Laurila together with the editor of *Ilkka* magazine, Artturi Leinonen, were instrumental in preventing a new civil war. Both were influential former members of the Lapua Movement, and now surprisingly sided with the elected president and government. This and some of their more proactive measures prevented thousands of armed militants from leaving the Etelä–Pohjanmaa district to revolt against the legal government.

Due to his pro-governmental actions, Laurila was allowed to retain control of the Etelä–Pohjanmaa Civil Guard district, and at the beginning of the Winter War he took command of the 23rd Infantry Regiment. His unit was to take part in the fierce battles at Taipale and Vuosalmi. After the war, Laurila was promoted to the rank of colonel.

Upon the outbreak of the Continuation War, Laurila was made the commander of the 16th Infantry Regiment from 19th Division. Laurila's men proved to be excellent tank destroyers, but due to a clash of personality with his superior, Matti decided to apply for transfer. Laurila ended up as the commander of the 22nd Infantry Regiment in Colonel Ilmari Karhu's 5th Division.

At the battle of the Tuulos River, Laurila again proved his worth, as his men were to deeply breach the enemy lines, capturing many artillery pieces and severing Soviet supply routes.

From 1942 to 1944, Laurila worked as the commander of Vaasa Military District. He resigned from service once the armistice was signed. After the war, Laurila worked in the insurance business.

(1892–1975)

EINO KOSKIMIES
COLONEL, 2ND DIVISION

Koskimies trained as a Jäger, and was wounded at the battle of Kalevankangas on 28 March 1918. Following the Finnish Civil War, he held several positions including that of battalion commander. He was made commander of the Tampere Regiment in 1928, and promoted colonel the following year. From 1933 onwards, he was in charge of the Kymi Military District.

At the outbreak of the Winter War, Koskimies was given command of the 11th Division, which was to be renamed the 2nd Division at the beginning of 1940. He led the unit into battle at Lake Muolaanjärvi, Äyräpää, Kuparsaari, Sintola and Vuosalmi.

Once the Continuation War had begun, Koskimies took over command of the 5th Division. Soon afterwards, he was to transfer to army headquarters and from there onwards to the command of Group Hanko.

Colonel Koskimies resigned after the wars and began working for the company Wärtsilä Oy as an inspector in its insurance division. He retired from this position in 1967.

(1893–1973)

PHILIP PARUSINOV
ARMY COMMANDER
2ND CLASS, THIRTEENTH ARMY

Enlisted in 1914, Philip Alexeyevich Parusinov officially joined the Red Army in 1918. Prior to the Winter War, his last post had been to command the Twelfth Army of the Kiev Military District.

From January 1940 onwards, Parusinov became the commander of the 19th Rifle Corps on the Viipuri front. After Grendhal's Thirteenth Army had failed to reach its objectives, Parusinov was promoted to replace him on 3 March. Parusinov received the Order of Lenin for his participation in the breakthrough of the Mannerheim Line.

After the Winter War, Parusinov was promoted lieutenant-general and became the deputy commander of Twelfth Army of the Southern Front. From March 1941 until 1943, he acted as commander of Twenty-Fifth Army. Several senior army roles in the eastern provinces followed. He resigned from active service in 1956.

a breakthrough in the Finnish lines at the village. Later that same day, a Finnish battalion managed to recapture the positions it had earlier lost. So far, the 97th Rifle Division had not yet exchanged fire with the Finns, as it wheeled its troops into position on the eastern flank.

At this point, Stavka expressed its dissatisfaction with the slow progress of Thirteenth Army's troops by replacing Grendahl as commander. The formation's new leader was to be Army Commander 2nd Class Philip A. Parusinov, who immediately issued new orders for an assault. However, despite these new orders, and an hour-long preliminary bombardment, the Soviet attacks on 3 March also failed.

In an April 1940 debriefing on the Winter War, Grendahl gave the following critique to Stalin of the Soviet infantry:

I must say that the Russian infantrymen, the Red Army infantrymen, are good soldiers. They performed a great many heroic feats on the Finnish front. But we must admit at the same time that their combat training was extremely poor … In this regard, we must admit that the training of the Finnish soldiers, their technical and tactical training, was of a higher order. One Finnish solder with an automatic rifle operates as a squad and knows how to manoeuvre. (Kulkov, Rzheshevskii and Shukman, 2002)

Towards the end of February 1940, the Finnish forces in the central isthmus suffered two remarkable defeats. Although the events themselves had little impact on the overall course of the war, they had far reaching consequences within the armed forces themselves.

The first event was the battle of Honkaniemi, the only occasion when the Finnish Tank Battalion played a part in the war. The battle was an utter fiasco for the Finns, and highlighted key changes needed within the nation's armoured forces.

On 25 February, the Tank Battalion sent 15 Vickers 6-ton tanks from the 4th Tank Company into battle. Their mission was to coordinate with and support the infantry, in order to regain lost sections of the Interim Line near Viipuri. Only eight of the tanks made it to the staging area; seven had been immobilised by water contamination of their fuel. Out of these eight, two had engine problems and could not join the attack. On their way forward, out of the six battle ready tanks, one got stuck in a ditch, which left only five. The attack planned for the next morning had to be postponed as the Finnish artillery accidentally shelled their own infantry, who had been preparing to support the Vickers. Eventually the troops were reorganised, and after ten minutes of preliminary bombardment, a belated command to advance was finally given.

Soviet tanks and *tankodesantniki* (tank riders) attacking over a frozen lake. These specially trained men were taught to ride the tanks into combat, a rapid deployment tactic which was also an effective counter-measure to Finnish close range anti-tank weaponry and infantry tactics. (Soviet War Photography)

An anti-tank infantryman prepares to tackle the oncoming Soviet armour at close quarters, during the Continuation War at Sirkiänsaari Island. His weaponry includes grenades and a satchel charge. (SA-kuva)

The Finns managed to cross the battlefield with relatively little damage, until they drew closer to the forest edge. From there some 20 Soviet T-28 tanks opened fire. Eight Soviet tanks were destroyed, while the Finns lost four. The last of the Vickers then withdrew.

There were now only seven Vickers remaining in somewhat working order out of the original 15 and of these, four were badly damaged. Although in total eight Soviet tanks had been destroyed, the Finns failed to accomplish their objective and the Tank Battalion never managed to recover for remainder of the war. Whilst the destruction of enemy armour had demonstrated promising skills, this event again highlighted the neglect this branch of service had received prior to the war. During the Continuation War, Finnish tank crews would redeem themselves and gain international fame for the impressive kill ratios they would achieve.

⬧⬧

The second formative incident took place at Vuosalmi, where a unit consisting of men conscripted solely from the village of Nurmo were ordered to recapture a dominating hill feature.

By 06:00 on 4 March, the Soviet artillery had already commenced its bombardment. During the day, one of the two Finnish commanders in the village was killed. Despite this, his men held their positions around the station. Unfortunately, the second defending battalion had to retreat from their vantage points on the church hill, and by the evening, this had fallen into enemy hands. This high ground provided the Soviets with a commanding view over the large Vasikkasaari Island on the river.

The retaking of this hill was very important to the Finns, and so the 8th Light Detachment from the neighbouring 8th Division was tasked with assaulting the hill that same night. These men did not reach the area before 05:30 in the morning, so the plans for the attack were altered to a fateful daytime assault. In order to improve unit cohesion, this detachment consisted solely of men from the village of Nurmo. Whilst making a dash across exposed, open terrain, the Soviet fire from the hill cut them all down to a man. In this incident, the village of Nurmo lost nearly all of its adult males. Forty of the villagers lay dead in the snow, while 30 were badly wounded. Only 19 were ever able to return to their stricken homes. After this fiasco, the Finns changed their overall doctrine for raising units, separating men from the same villages and homes among different units.

The church hill was never recaptured. With the benefit of the elevated firing positions, the Soviets soon managed to advance onto Vasikkasaari Island halfway across the river.

NIILO HERSALO
COLONEL, 21ST DIVISION

Niilo Hersalo began serving his country by establishing and training Civil Guard units in the areas around Lahti and Lappeenranta. After the Civil War, Hersalo was one of the two officers to be sent to the Weimar Republic for a private general staff officers' course. He was promoted to colonel in 1935.

(1895–1979)

In the Winter War, Hersalo led the 21st Division. It was initially held as a reserve under the commander-in-chief. His unit was subsequently deployed to support III Army Corps in January 1940.

During the Interim Peace, Hersalo assumed the command of Satakunta Military District, and when the war again broke out, he led the 15th Division raised from his district. Hersalo was promoted major-general in April 1942.

Hersalo retired from the armed forces at his own request in 1946.

The remaining Finnish troops south of the river at Äyräpää had to retreat on 4 March. From the vantage point of the opposing shore, they proceeded to repel another enemy assault on the smaller Vitsaari Island. More artillery was diverted to the area, increasing the defensive firepower to four batteries – an impressive total of 48 artillery pieces, at least by Finnish standards

VUOSALMI

Following the fall of Äyräpää village on the south side of Vuoksi, three Soviet divisions were ordered to capture Vasikkasaari Island in the

Two Finnish infantrymen on patrol, pulling their heavy machine gun along the ice near Someri Island on Viipuri Bay, on 21 February 1942. (SA-kuva)

centre of the river. Preceded by an hour-long bombardment, they pushed forward at noon on 4 March. Somehow, rather miraculously, at the end of the day the island was still largely in Finnish hands.

The following day, the Soviet 50th Rifle Division (25th Rifle Corps) managed finally to conquer the island. Its troops even tried to continue push forward to the northern bank of the river. All this was achieved at a high price: the regiments of the 50th Rifle Division suffered heavy losses, even to the point where one of them had been reduced to just a single battalion.

On 6 March, under the cover of darkness, the Finns again tried to recapture Vasikkasaari Island, with two battalions. The Soviets followed this failed attempt with a counter-attack along a 2km-long stretch of the river. This time, the Red Army managed to gain a shallow foothold across the river at Vuosalmi, just north of Vasikkasaari Island, but in turn they were pushed back during 24 hours of fighting. By the next morning, all positions were again securely in Finnish hands, and the Soviets regrouped on the island.

Following the Soviet successes, responsibility for the breached sector of the line was handed to Colonel Niilo Hersalo's 21st Division, from II Army

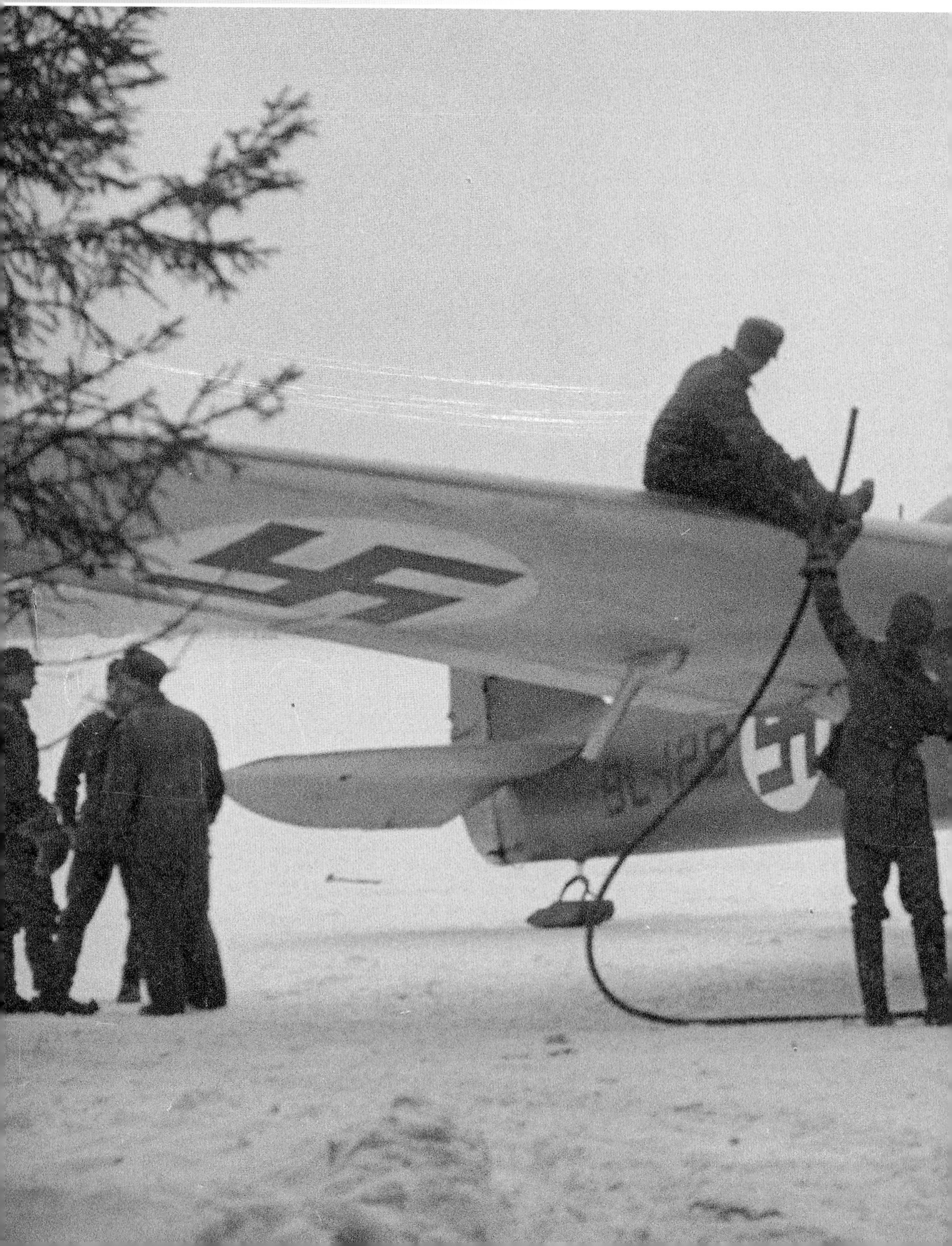

A Bristol Blenheim bomber from the 46th Flight Squadron being refuelled at Tikkakoski airfield in the winter of 1940. (SA-kuva)

Corps. Most of his forces were already engaged in the area, and only one regiment of reinforcements was able to join the fray in the Äyräpää area. It took days for the Finns to complete the reorganisation of their lines, while Hersalo's troops continued to repel daily assaults.

Although the 50th Rifle Division had managed to gain a small bridgehead on the northern bank, its battalions had effectively been halved in strength; some units were forced into reserve duties away the front lines.

During the afternoon of 11 March, Soviet forces finally managed to reach the road near the northern edge of their bridgehead. The planned counter-attack by the Finns lost some of its impetus, as by this stage the enemy had gained the remaining high ground, forcing some of their troops to be diverted to deal with this new threat.

The next day, the delayed Finnish attack was stopped in its tracks by enemy fire. When a second attempt also failed, Hersalo decided to withdraw the majority of his men a kilometre or so, to the deeper defensive positions. Following this, on 12 March, Talvela decided to withdraw the rest of his III Army Corps troops in the area to the supporting Interim Line. The manoeuvre was never completed: the armistice was declared a day later.

Considering that Parusinov's Thirteenth Army had five full divisions at its disposal, its performance left a lot to be desired. Parusinov, to be fair, had only been in command for ten days, so much of the blame must lie with Grendahl. The Finns were effective at containing the smaller bridgeheads gained by the Soviets, who paid a heavy price for the limited terrain they captured. When the firing finally ceased in the Vuosalmi sector, thousands or Russian soldiers and around a hundred Finns stood up from their foxholes. Many of the Soviets asked, 'Where are the rest of the Finns?' (Brantberg, 1998).

THE WESTERN ISTHMUS

In the west of the isthmus, the objective of Meretskov's Seventh Army was the capture of the city of Viipuri, followed by a drive towards Finland's capital along the coast. Viipuri held great symbolic meaning for both sides in the conflict, and was of critical strategic importance in protecting Viipuri Bay and transport links through the Karelian Isthmus. The Soviet high command wanted to avoid becoming bogged down in street-to-street fighting, and so decided to use the majority of its forces to encircle the city from the north-east. Also, the frozen-solid Viipuri Bay allowed the Soviets to send forces to bypass and surround the city from the east. These forces would soon cut the Hamina road leading west from Viipuri, with Finnish forces stretched to breaking point in their attempts to contain this breach. Meanwhile,

Karelian Isthmus February 1940: the Rear Line March

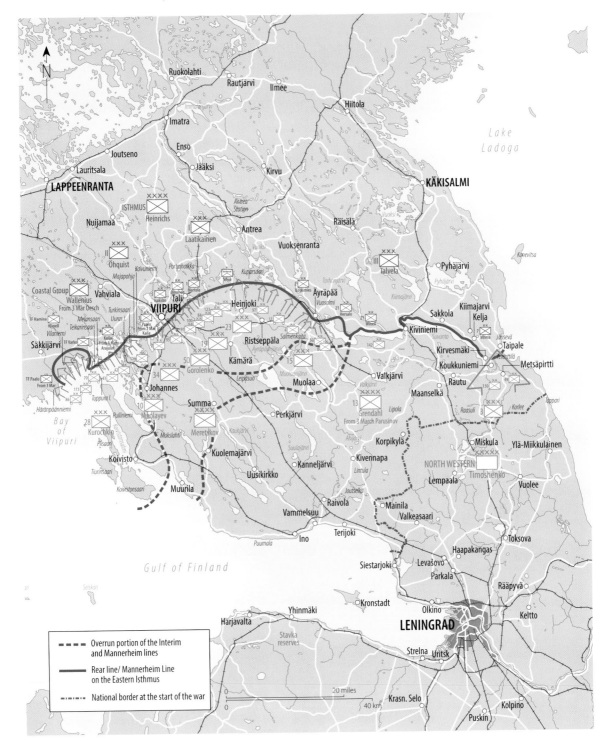

Overrun portion of the Interim
and Mannerheim lines

Rear line/ Mannerheim Line
on the Eastern Isthmus

National border at the start of the war

20 miles

40 km

(1892–1978)

LENNART OESCH
LIEUTENANT-GENERAL, COASTAL GROUP

Karl Lennart Oesch's military career had begun on the 1915 *Pfadfinder* course. He commanded an infantry battalion during the Finnish Civil War. From 1923 to 1926, Oesch furthered his military education in France. Upon his return, he headed the newly created Academy for General Staff. In 1929 Oesch took over command of the 1st Division, and then a year later the influential position of chief of the general staff. A decade later, when war broke out once again, he was still in this role.

For the better part of the Winter War, Oesch acted as Mannerheim's closest confidant in the role of chief of the general staff. In the last weeks of the war, Mannerheim sent Oesch to take command of the Coastal Group on Viipuri Bay. There the Soviets had bypassed the Main Defensive Line and used the frozen gulf to land strong formations to the north-west of the city. If they could not be contained, the road to the capital Helsinki would be open.

During the Interim Peace, Oesch was given command of II Army Corps. This unit ended up in the Karelian Isthmus, and changed its name to IV Army Corps for the Continuation War. There Oesch was forced to wait while Mannerheim held his troops in check. When he was finally given permission to attack, his force drove the Soviets to the outskirts of Leningrad.

Later in the war, Oesch rose to command the Finnish forces on the Karelian Isthmus. For his role in controlling nearly two-thirds of Finland's armed forces and repelling the Soviets at Tali–Ihantala, Oesch was made a Knight of the Mannerheim Cross on 26 June 1944.

After the war, Oesch again served as the chief of the general staff until September 1945. In 1946 a military court heavily influenced by the Soviet Union convicted Oesch of military crimes. Although the initial prison sentence was later commuted to a much less severe one, his military career was over.

Oesch was released from prison in 1948, and concentrated on researching and writing military history.

Finnish politicians laboured day and night to resolve the conflict peacefully, before all of Finland was occupied. The Finnish military knew that every setback and delay inflicted on the Red Army would improve their nation's negotiating position.

The narrow Viipuri Bay, with its many small islands, had always acted as an effective barrier on the western flank of the city. The three larger islands of Tuppura, Teikarsaari and Melansaari were well defended. Whilst the seas were still open, this had deterred the Soviets from attempting any landings; their troops and vessels would have been subject to Finnish artillery crossfire, whilst their own supporting artillery and tanks would have been left far behind.

In February, the factor that had been the bane of the Red Army – the unusually cold winter – actually proved beneficial for it. The bay around the city had frozen over so thickly that even tanks could cross it safely. Stavka wanted to exploit this unforeseen opportunity immediately.

Towards the end of February, the overall command of the Viipuri area defences was handed over to Major-General Martti Wallenius, who led the newly formed Coastal Group. The shoreline to the west was left in the hands of the Finnish Navy's coastal troops, while Wallenius' left flank was anchored with the remaining forces of the Finnish II Army Corps. By 1 March, the Soviets had forced all the defenders to retreat from the two large peninsulae extending into the bay south of Viipuri.

Between these two peninsulae was the large island of Uuras. It was heavily manned by the Finnish 11th Infantry Regiment. The Finnish plan was to keep

THE KARELIAN ISTHMUS, 1940

Soviet soldiers manning a water-cooled M1910 Maxim-Sokolov machine gun on the Viipuri front. With the Sokolov base and shield, the weight of the weapon rose to a staggering 74kg. In addition, a considerable amount of bullets was needed to maintain the firing rate of 550 rounds per minute. (Ukrainian State Archives)

firm hold of the line of islands formed by Tuppura, Teikarsaari, Uuras and Turkinsaari and extending to the port of Viipuri, which was under the control of the 3rd Infantry Division. It was made clear that permission to retreat from any of the islands could only be granted directly by the Coastal Group. Wallenius' men were to face the combined attacks of the 28th and 10th Rifle corps. Between the two corps, three whole divisions, the 86th Motorised Rifle Division and 70th and 43rd Rifle divisions) were sent to cross the bay.

When the first Soviet attack was launched, Finnish forces on the

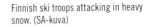

Finnish ski troops attacking in heavy snow. (SA-kuva)

westernmost island, Tuppura, held their ground. The 800-strong defenders faced the 169th Motorised Rifle Regiment, which had been further strengthened with two Soviet infantry ski battalions. As the island lay only a short distance from the Pulliniemi Peninsula, the Soviets soon managed to occupy the smaller islands just north of the Finnish main defences. Despite this, the Finns succeeded in repelling another infantry assault by nightfall. On the evening of 2 March, the Finns found their

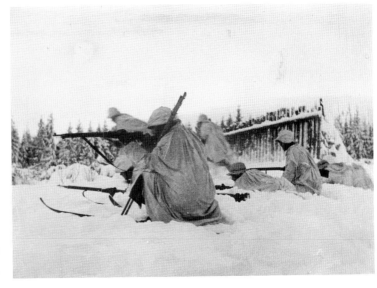

position untenable. Their artillery had expended all its shells, and so the remaining defenders made their escape under cover of darkness. Around 650 of the Finns made it across the bay to safety.

The Finnish troops positioned on the next link in the defensive chain, Teikarsaari Island, also repelled the initial probing attempts and all the subsequent attacks until 2 March. The following night, they chose to retreat to the final defensive lines on the Vilaniemi Peninsula on the west side of the bay. This was not what the sector commander Wallenius wanted, and he continued to insist that the last positions on Teikarsaari should be held at all costs. However, this command came too late, as by then the Finns had already withdrawn.

Meanwhile, to the west of these troops, Soviet forces surprised the Finns by skiing over to the Häränpääniemi Peninsula, lying some 30km to the west of Viipuri. There the Soviet troops drove back the coastal defenders along a stretch of land a couple of kilometres long. At noon, the Finnish 18th Independent Battalion rushed to the peninsula and launched a counter-attack. More troops were sent to the breach and the peninsula was back in Finnish hands by the morning of 3 March.

These setbacks now drove the Finns to reorganise their troop configurations in this sector. By the end of the day, positions on the planned defensive line running along the outlying islands were abandoned, and only Turkinsaari Island, which was nearest to the city of Viipuri, was to be kept defended. Coastal Group Commander Wallenius still felt some misgivings about this, and argued that at least Teikarsaari Island should be recaptured. However, before he could enact any plans to do so, II Army Corps commander Öhquist used the disorganised state of the Coastal Group as an excuse to have Wallenius removed from command, allocating him to the reserves. As Wallenius had only taken over the Coastal Group three days prior to this, any failures in communications and poor coordination of artillery support could not solely have been his fault.

The critical objective of protecting the road to Helsinki now fell to Lieutenant-General Lennart Oesch, Mannerheim's trusted second-in-command, who had so far been working as the Chief of the General Staff at Mikkeli headquarters. Oesch soon decided to follow the plans Wallenius had put forward, and so early on the morning of 4 March, a reinforced

A young messenger boy gives a lift to a senior soldier. (The Finnish Museum of Photography)

battalion led by Captain Alfons Järvi launched an attack towards the north end of Teikarsaari Island. Their advance was halted by enemy fire, and by 09:00 the troops had returned to Vilaniemi Peninsula.

Shortly afterwards, the forward elements of the two Soviet divisions launched an attack, creating a bridgehead on the Häränpääniemi Peninsula. The Finnish defenders quickly rerouted three additional battalions to the area for a combined counter-attack on the night of 5 March. By lunchtime the following day, it was clear that the Finns were unable to displace the forces of the 86th Motorised Rifle Division. To

IVAN NIKOLAYEV
BRIGADE COMMANDER, 10TH RIFLE CORPS

(1890–1944)

Ivan Federovitch Nikolayev began his career in the tsar's army in 1912. He made the rank of ensign in 1915 and was promoted to captain during World War I. He joined the Red Army in 1918, and acted as a regimental commander during the Russian Civil War.

Nikolayev took over command of the 10th Rifle Corps on 19 February 1940. Prior to this, he had already acted as the deputy commander of the 19th Rifle Corps since 1937.

From September 1941, Nikolayev went on to command Forty-Second Army under the Leningrad Front in the Great Patriotic War. In 1944, when Lieutenant-General Nikolayev had taken over command of the Seventieth Army, he was promptly forced to resign due to health reasons. He died a few months later from a heart attack, on 29 March 1944.

make matters worse for them, some Soviet troops had penetrated deeper between the two peninsulae, reaching an undefended bay by the Vilajoki River. Luckily, the supply troops stationed in the area reacted quickly and halted the enemy attempts to secure the shoreline.

When the Soviets refocused their attack towards the Vilaniemi Peninsula on the night of 5 March, the Finnish defenders panicked and ran away. From there the Soviet forces attempted to swing back east, towards the rear of the troops at Viipuri, but were forced to a halt on the Karjaniemi Peninsula. The previous day, the Finnish 9th Infantry Regiment had been withdrawn from the defences of Viipuri and sent to strengthen this area. These men were ordered to recapture the area around the Vilaniemi Peninsula. Meanwhile, the Soviet 86th Motorised Rifle Division and 70th Rifle Division at the bridgehead received further reinforcements in preparation for their planned attacks the following day.

The Finnish counter-attack for Vilaniemi Peninsula started at 03:00 on 6 March. Two battalions from the 9th Infantry Regiment made good progress initially, but soon the Soviets responded with renewed attacks of their own. Further Finnish efforts by the 24th Independent Battalion into the Soviet flank from Vilajoki direction also failed. Fighting continued until the following night, when the Finns finally had to retreat. All attempts to turn the Soviet flanks the following day were repelled; both sides suffered heavy losses.

A soldier staring at the ruins of his former home in Karelia, most likely sharing the sentiments of a Finnish historian Wolf Halsti, who served as the quartermaster of the 5th Division on the Karelian Isthmus. He made the following comments on the woeful state of armaments in his diary, following a particularly poor series of attacks: 'The tactical situation in and of itself if not hopeless! Only the means to deal with it are lacking! If only we had some heavy weapons! … What a pleasure it would be to form a battalion out of politicians and bureaucrats and then order them to make such an attack, without the tanks and artillery their stupidity has deprived us of today.'

Although the Finns had so far managed to contain the breach in the Vilaniemi area by retaining hold of the peninsulae on both sides, the Soviets reached an important strategic milestone when the 378th Motorised Rifle Regiment cut the Hamina–Viipuri road. However, despite their vastly superior numbers, for the time being they were unable to further exploit this foothold.

Much political manoeuvring was taking place at the same time as these military movements to the west of Viipuri. On 6 March, after Viipuri had effectively been cut off from the Finnish capital Helsinki, the Soviets finally sent summons for a delegation to visit Moscow. Prime Minister Risto Ryti promptly accepted, departing for Moscow the following day with Juho Paasikivi (Minister without Portfolio), Cabinet Secretary Rudolf Walden and Official of the Diet Väinö Voionmaa. The Soviets had already made it clear that there could be neither truce nor ceasefire while these talks lasted, nor until their demands were fully met. So while the Finnish politicians laboured to bring the war to an end, the front lines would just have to hold a while longer. The Finnish delegation were well aware that the longer their countrymen held the Soviets at bay, the more likely a Western intervention became, and the better the terms they could hope to reach with Stalin. Before their departure, Army of the Isthmus commander Heinrichs submitted a dire assessment of the situation facing Finnish forces:[16]

16 At the time, Commander-in-Chief Mannerheim was sick with flu and suffering from exhaustion.

It is my duty to report that the present state of the Army is such that continued military operations can lead to nothing but further debilitation and fresh losses of territory ... Lieutenant-General Oesch, the commander of the Coastal Group, has emphasised to me the scant numbers and the moral exhaustion of his forces, and does not seem to believe he can succeed with them. Lieutenant-General Öhquist, commander of II Army Corps, has expressed the opinion that if no surprises take place, his present front may last a week, but no longer, due to expenditure of personnel, particularly officers. Major-General Talvela, of III Army Corps, expresses his view by saying that everything is hanging by a thread.

Finland's Foreign Minister Tanner responded to this report with his own advice: 'We must make haste before the collapse occurs. After that our views would not be asked' (Edwards, 2006).

Now it was the Soviets' turn to stall. Knowing that the war was practically won, they added more demands and used every passing minute as an effective tool with which to pressure the Finns. This tactic was bound to work, as Ryti well knew how many young Finnish men were dying while the delegation negotiated. It took a full 12 hours for the cables to reach President Kallio in Helsinki and then be returned with his comments to the delegates. From the Finnish soldiers' point of view, this was all taking too long.

On 9 March, the Soviet Seventh Army headquarters reinforced the troops in the Vilaniemi area, and gave instructions for them to press on. The 173rd Motorised Rifle and 70th Rifle divisions were to attack from Vilaniemi, while the 86th Motorised Rifle Division guarded the bridgehead's left flank on the Häränpääniemi Peninsula. That same day, the Hamina–Viipuri road was permanently severed. On 10 March, Soviet forces were able to advance northwards beyond the road. The Finnish command structures on this front had grown ever more confusing, as new sectors and areas of responsibility were created on an almost daily basis. Partially due to these rapid changes, no significant counter-attacks were organised, but nor was much more terrain lost to the Soviets during this period.

Only on the western flank did Captain Fredrick W. Saarela's 2nd Battalion (40th Infantry Regiment) have to retreat to the southern edge of Lake Petrusjärvi, where his troops were reinforced by the arrival of a second battalion. The following day, 11 March, to the east of these men, the commander of the 20th Battalion fell in combat, triggering the retreat of all his troops. Two more Soviet battalions had also joined the attack, forcing the Finns to disengage from their positions along the road. This soon led to some elements fleeing in terror.

PAUL KUROCHKIN
BRIGADE COMMANDER,
28TH RIFLE CORPS

Pavel Aleksejevitch Kurochkin started his military career as a private during the Russian Civil War. In 1918, he took part in the occupation of the tsar's Winter Palace in Petrograd (Leningrad). Kurochkin progressed rapidly through the ranks during the conflict, and rose to command a whole cavalry brigade.

(1900–89)

In 1923, he underwent formal military training, graduating from the top cavalry academy. In 1932, Kurochkin completed the War Academy course. He took over the position of Senior Master Lecturer of Cavalry at the War Academy in 1934. His last command before hostilities with Finland broke out in 1939 was that of chief of staff in the Kiova Military District.

During the Winter War, Kurochkin commanded the 28th Rifle Corps. His troops took part in the battle for Viipuri Bay on its western side. On 4 June 1940, the same day that the old military ranks returned in the Red Army, Kurochkin was made a lieutenant-general.

During the Great Patriotic War, Kurochkin held several roles. Amongst these was a short period in 1944 as the commander of the Belarusian Front. He was made a full army general in 1949, and became a professor at the Frunze Military Academy in 1961.

The Finnish battalions further east towards Viipuri lost contact with their commanders in this sector. Major Lasse G. Varko, the commander of 7th Independent Battalion, quickly started to rally the troops in the area into a single group, organically forming Group Varko. In addition to his own men, it contained the 5th Bicycle Battalion, the 1st Battalion from the 1st Brigade (1st Division, on loan to Coastal Group), the 4th Light Detachment and the 1st Battalion from the 11th Infantry Regiment. Varko's rapid action stopped the Soviets from advancing further east along the road, and rallied the panicked Finns.

By 11 March, the troops of the 28th Rifle Corps, led by Brigade Commander Paul A. Kurochkin, had more or less reached the 9 March objectives set by Seventh Army headquarters – one of the few, perhaps even the first, instance during the war when a Soviet-instructed timescale was adhered to. From the Finnish point of view, the situation had barely been contained. Had the war continued beyond 13 March, it is difficult to say whether the defences could have held any longer or not.

In contrast, on the eastern side of the bay the 10th Rifle Corps, led by the recently appointed Brigade Commander Ivan Nikolayev, could not quite replicate his comrade's success. Nikolayev's objectives were focused on taking Uuraansaari Island, and then establishing positions beyond the Hamina–Viipuri road by 11 March. Colonel Vladimir Kirpichnikov's 43rd Rifle Division was to attack along Uuraansaari Island. The 42nd Rifle Division led by Colonel Ivan S. Lazarenko was to capture Turkinsaari Island, while Colonel Christopher N. Alaverdov's 113th Rifle Division would attack directly across the bay on the eastern flank.

On Uuraansaari, since the beginning of March, the Finnish 4th Division had managed to hold their ground and defend their positions, despite repeated Soviet attempts to take it. The main defence of the island was carried out by the 11th and 12th Infantry regiments. The

Marksmanship training whilst wearing a gas mask. Despite all the fears, the Soviets never used gas during the war. (SA-kuva)

68th Infantry Regiment reinforced the coast, with an additional battalion acting as reserve. Some of these men were later diverted to help counter the Soviet landing at Vilaniemi.

The battles for the islets forward of Uuraansaari Island began on 7 March. Now slowly and relentlessly, the Soviets managed to push their way onto all of the larger islands in the bay. On Uuraansaari, the defending Finnish units were forced first to retreat towards the centre of the island and then, by 9 March, abandon it altogether. On their left flank, Ravansaari Island was abandoned on 8 March, and during the following day the islands of Hapenensaari, Turkinsaari and Piispansaari were also lost. Only in the easternmost part of the sector at Majapohja did Lieutenant-Colonel Aaro Rautiainen's 12th Infantry Regiment manage to halt the enemy on the ice just in front of the Finnish positions.

A Finnish anti-tank gun in position, ready to meet the advancing Soviet armour. (SA-kuva)

The Soviet 113th Rifle Division renewed its assault on 10 March, forcing Rautiainen's men to retreat from Majapohja towards the Koivuniemi Peninsula. By the evening, the Finns were withdrawing all along the front into their final designated defensive positions on the coast.

The Soviets had worn out their forces in these bloody battles to take the islands. Despite their best efforts and the use of three whole divisions, they only had a shallow bridgehead upon the shoreline. When the war ended, the 10th Rifle Corps was still well short of all its objectives

THE BATTLE FOR VIIPURI

Lieutenant-General Öhquist, the commander of the Finnish II Army Corps, was responsible for Viipuri and the area of front line up to about 10km east of the city, ending at the station at Repola village. From there, the front was the responsibility of the 1st Division of I Army Corps. Towards the end of February, the Finnish high command placed its reserve, Colonel Paalu's 3rd Division, at Öhquist's disposal.

Paalu was ordered to hold the city of Viipuri, as well as the outlying stretches of coastline. Paalu's forces were split so that the 7th Infantry Regiment, led by Colonel Kaarlo Heiskanen, held the actual city, while Major Eero Laaksonen's 8th Infantry Regiment controlled the peninsula leading into the western areas of the city. The 9th Infantry Regiment (a Swedish-speaking unit) led by Lieutenant-Colonel Emil Hagelberg was left further back to act as a reserve and to guard the rear, should the Soviets try to circle in over the frozen bay from the west. On 2 March, Colonel Kaila, the former commander of the 4th Division, had transferred in to take command of the 3rd Division, while Paalu was tasked with defending against the Soviet 86th Motorised Rifle Division in the Häränpääniemi sector.

By this point, Colonel Isakson's 5th Division had already deployed to positions immediately north-east of the city. There, the front was split between the 15th and 67th Infantry regiments, while the 14th Infantry Regiment acted as the divisional reserve.

The easternmost edge of the sector around Repola was defended by Colonel Woldermar Oinonen's 23rd Division. The area around Tali station was held by the 13th Infantry Regiment. The 62nd Infantry Regiment formed a second concentration around the church at Tali. The 68th Infantry Regiment formed the division's reserve, and was located a few kilometres north at Portinhoikka village.

While the Soviet 28th and 10th Rifle corps were pushing across Viipuri Bay, the 34th and 50th Rifle corps had been ordered to circle and sack

Viipuri from the north-east, taking control of the city and the western coast by 2 March at the latest.

The 34th Rifle Corps was to avoid having larger elements of its command becoming bogged down in the city. Instead, it was to clear it with light formations, winning decisive victories and applying pressure on the coastal sections, while surrounding the city from the north-east. Meanwhile, Gorelenko's 50th Rifle Corps was to advance in the direction of Repola. These massive forces went on to initially achieve very little, and were reprimanded by Seventh Army headquarters for poorly organised attacks and the resultant slow forward progress. According to Meretskov, the troops lacked the required tenacity.

On 2 March, the initial Soviet attacks managed to create a small breach in the positions of Captain Könönen's 3rd Battalion from Major Laaksonen's 8th Infantry Regiment on the southern edge of the city of Viipuri. The division's reserves were immediately used to launch a counter-attack, but despite their valiant efforts the main battle line was lost. Meanwhile, the rest of Laaksonen's battalions managed to repel all of the Soviet attacks against their positions. In the 7th Infantry Regiment's sector, the situation remained so peaceful that one of its regiments was freed to reinforce the Finns fighting further west along the bay.

The Soviets started the next series of preliminary bombardments against all the defended positions on 7 March. Again, the 3rd Battalion was to prove a weak link in the Finnish defences: they retreated, before finally rallying to defend the railway line. There, Könönen quickly launched a counter-attack to try to regain the lost positions. This also failed. Thankfully for the Finns, the 1st Battalion still held its ground, thus preventing the Red Army from sweeping into the city. This gave time for the 8th Infantry Regiment to send in more troops to help Könönen launch a concentrated counter-attack. When his effort failed, the whole battalion was withdrawn from the front and replaced with Captain Viisterä's Light Detachment.

According to the intelligence passed to Seventh Army headquarters, the Finns were now holding onto Viipuri with the last of their forces. On 9 March, Meretskov gave orders for the 34th Rifle Corps to continue its attack against the city, while setting objectives for the main elements deep behind Viipuri. These objectives were to be secured no later than 14 March.

So far, the 34th and 50th Rifle corps had already suffered heavy losses. Now they were to prepare for a new main offensive that was due to start on 11 March. Their combined power included seven full divisions, although one of these was to be responsible for tying down the Finnish combatants in Viipuri.

For two consecutive days the Soviets threw all their artillery and armour against the Finnish lines, but to no avail. Despite their overwhelming numbers, they were unable to break the determined defenders and had to pay dearly for every step forward. The Finns fought to the last man, knowing that there was no one left behind them and no place safe to retreat to. Every possible obstacle was thrown in front of the Red Army; some lowland areas were even purposefully flooded in order to hinder the enemy's advance.

When the ceasefire began, the embittered Meretskov gave orders for the 34th Rifle Corps to continue its attack against Viipuri. While the rest of the Soviet armies were to stand down and obey the rules of armistice, the 34th was told keep fighting until the city was in Soviet hands.

On the Finnish side of the lines, Öhquist had repeatedly requested permission to retreat from Viipuri city into better defensive positions. Mannerheim had personally ordered him to desist from preparing for any such retreat, and instead hold to the last man. Öhquist, who had been keen to withdraw many times earlier, was unaware of the political talks for peace and of the advantage that solid Finnish resistance gave to his side's negotiators. He was rightly very worried that his troops in Viipuri would become surrounded and crushed. The enemy had already reached positions north of the city, both along the bay in the west and near Tali east of the city. Consequently, on 12 March, Heinrichs finally relented and gave permission to start withdrawing the troops within the city into deeper positions. Öhquist immediately instructed the 3rd Division to leave one infantry regiment to hold the front line while the rest of its forces would group together on the north side of the city.

Before the Soviets could complete the capture of the city, the Finnish delegation in Moscow finally capitulated to Stalin's terms, where in the end, according to Prime Minister Ryti, 'not even a single comma had been up for negotiation'. This prompted President Kallio to curse: 'Let the hand wither that is forced to sign such a paper' (Edwards, 2006).

In accordance with the terms of the Moscow Peace Treaty, the fighting stopped at 11:00 Finnish time (12:00 Moscow time) on 13 March. The majority of the relieved II Army Corps began an immediate retreat towards the newly agreed border. The 3rd Division remained in Viipuri; they were to stand guard and perform the lowering of the national flag, then withdraw by 06:00 on 15 March. The fall of Viipuri would surely have been inevitable, as the Soviets had now amassed 13 divisions between Viipuri Bay and the village of Repola. It was remarkable that the three Finnish defending divisions had managed to hold their ground through to the end of the Winter War.

On most fronts, peace had come just in the nick of time. Now the heavy price of this peace was just starting to dawn on the exhausted Finnish population. Bitterness and resentment would remain. One Soviet soldier asked a comrade with Finnish roots: 'Tell me honestly, what kind of a character do the Finns possess? … They say the Finns are mean.' His comrade replied: 'They are not mean, they just really hold a grudge. They remember who has done them harm in the past. God forgives, the Finns do not.' This statement would prove to be somewhat prophetic, as less that a year later the two nations would again find themselves at war

A lone sentry gazing east, image taken in January 1940 from Kuhavuori heights at Sortavala.

CHAPER 11
AN INTERIM PEACE

As the terms of the Moscow Peace Treaty were being settled, Molotov had remarked: 'Since blood has been shed against the Soviet government's wishes and without Russia being to blame, the territorial concessions Finland offered must be greater than those proposed by Russia in Moscow in October and November of 1939 [i.e. before the war started]' (Eagle and Paananen, 1973). In all, the territorial losses that resulted for Finland following the Winter War amounted to 10 per cent of the country's total pre-war surface area. Nearly 12 per cent of the population had to be resettled from ceded lands. Despite this heavy cost, most Finns thought that retaining independence was more important than the loss of territory.

The USSR was to receive the whole Karelian Isthmus, including the city of Viipuri, along with practically all of the outlying islands. In

The Finnish flag still flying at the top of Viipuri Castle on 7 March 1940. By now the city was burning, and its defences had nearly been breached. (SA-kuva)

addition, the Finns had to relinquish the north-western shoreline of Lake Ladoga; this included the towns of Käkisalmi and Sortavala. Further to the north, the village of Suojärvi, where Paavo Talvela had won Finland's first major victories, had to be surrendered. The Salla and Kuusamo areas were also lost, as was the strategically important isthmus of Kalastajasaarento at Petsamo, while the southernmost point of Finland, Hankoniemi, was to be leased out as a Soviet naval base. To consolidate the Soviet Navy's grip on the Gulf of Finland, Suursaari and several other larger islands were also handed over to the USSR.

Continuing Finnish freedom came with a high human cost. The number of civilian and military casualties totalled 24,918 dead and 43,557 wounded, of whom 9,562 were to remain permanently disabled. The total losses for the Soviet Union have never been published, but the best estimates put them at well over 200,000 killed and a much larger number of wounded (Condon, 1972).

The later-day Soviet Premier Nikita Khrushchev made a claim in his 1970s memoirs that the total number of Soviet lives lost in the Winter War exceeded 1 million. He also noted that around 1,000 airplanes and 2,300 tanks had been destroyed. Khrushchev also commented that, although the Red Army had employed their superior numbers well and had carefully chosen the timing and place of each attack, 'even in these most favourable conditions, it was only after great difficulty and enormous losses that we were finally able to win. A victory at such a cost was actually a moral defeat.' Khrushchev also recalled how greatly the Finns had been underestimated by the Soviets at the start of the war: 'All we had to do was raise our voice a little bit and the Finns would obey. If that didn't work, we could fire one shot and the Finns would put up their hands and surrender. Or so we thought … The Finns turned out to be good warriors. We soon realised we had bitten off more than we could chew' (Khrushchev, 1971).

When the truce was announced, flags flew at half-mast all over Finland. The Foreign Minister Väinö Tanner summed up the mixture of relief and resentment that many felt: 'Peace has been restored, but what kind of peace? Henceforth our country will continue to live as a mutilated nation' (Eagle and Paananen, 1973).

Once the Soviet demands for peace had been accepted, hundreds of thousands of civilians had to leave the ceded territories. Practically no one wanted to stay and live under Bolshevik rule. The Soviets only gave these refugees ten days to leave with all their worldly possessions. Without considerable help from Sweden, there simply would not have been sufficient means of transport to move these people, never mind their goods and animals.

A mother and baby being forcibly evacuated from their homes in March 1940. (SA-kuva)

Ceded Finland

N

Hammerfest

Kalastajasaarento

Barents Sea

Petsamo

Murmansk

Tromsö

Nautsi

Inarijärvi   *Luttojoki*

Narvik

Kantalahti

Ponoy

Kiruna

Pelkosenniemi

Salla

White Sea

SWEDEN

Kemijärvi

Rovaniemi

Kuusamo

Tornio
Kemi

Perenka

Vienan Kemi

Boden
Luleå

Juntusranta

Sorokka

Oulu

Suomussalmi

Raate

Kuhmo

Kem

Kajaani

Repola

SOVIET UNION

Gulf of Bothnia

Karhumäki

Umeå

FINLAND

Lieksa

Kuopio

Ilomantsi

Äglajärvi

Porajärvi

Vaasa

Korpiselkä

Tolvajärvi

Suojärvi

Petroskoi
Lake Onega

Pieksämäki

Kollaa

Kitilä

Sortavala

Svir

Mikkeli

Käkisalmi

Lake Ladoga

Gulf of Bothnia

Pori

Tampere

Ihantala

Tali

Taipale

Lahti

VIIPURI

Summa

Mainila

Turku

Terijoki

LENINGRAD

Åland

HELSINKI

Suursaari

Gulf of Finland

Hanko

TALLIN

STOCKHOLM

Baltic Sea

Hiiumaa

ESTONIA

Saaremaa

0   100 miles
0   200 km

Land ceded to the Soviet Union

Rented naval base

The 420,000 refugees that suddenly streamed out of the lands lost to the USSR created a major internal socio-economic problem in Finland. In order to preserve communities, Finns took pride in relocating people from the same village into the same vicinity. These settlers where then compensated for all lost property and possessions by the Finnish government; as a result, 30 per cent of all privately owned forests and 63 per cent of arable land in Finland were redistributed to them.

Mannerheim remained in his position as commander-in-chief. Wartime rationing, censorship and limitations on travel continued, while further commercial restrictions were introduced. Despite the unusually cold winter, which had ruined most of the fruit trees and berry bushes, there was generally enough food to go around. When the harvest of the following summer turned out poorer than usual, rationing was further tightened.

In the spring of 1940, the international conflict spread, limiting the use of the seas in the south. Now Petsamo harbour on the Barents Sea was the only available safe commercial naval route. Even from this Nordic port, all traffic was subject to the continued goodwill of the warring nations.

Children being forced to move out of their homes in Karelia after the lands were ceded to the Soviet Union. (SA-kuva)

The veterans of the Winter War often formed 'Brothers in Arms' associations. To counter this movement, in May 1940 the far left established the Finland–Soviet Union Peace and Friendship Society. According to its own enrolment register, the society's membership had swollen to 35,000 by the end of the year. The unofficial goal of the organisation was to fight a propaganda war and incite civil unrest within Finland, which would force further armed intervention by the Soviet Union.

Although Finland was now at peace, the flames of global war were beginning to fan higher. This growing tension meant that Finnish politicians had ample reason to learn from the mistakes of the pre-war era and now gave more focus and resources to the armed forces. During this unsettled time, Finland tried desperately to remain neutral and not be drawn into yet another conflict. This position became increasingly more difficult, and the Finns did their best to form an alliance with the rest of the Nordic countries. It was their hope that the support of the Swedish Army in particular would help to quell the threat of any further invasions. However, both the Soviets and the Germans objected strongly to these plans, and under pressure from them the talks faltered. Shortly afterwards, Hitler occupied Norway and Denmark, while Stalin made preparations for another attack aimed at annexing the rest of Finland.

During 1940, Finland tried to seek political and defensive allies in the West. At each stage the Finnish delegates were given kind words and praise for their nation's efforts in retaining its independence, but no promises of concrete help. Towards the end of the year, Hitler, who had his own plans for the USSR, suddenly changed Germany's national policy towards Finland: grain and weapons purchases became possible, and talks of future cooperation began.

Half a year later, Finland had found a new comrade in arms in the German nation, a country which promised to help them in case the Soviets attacked once more. This help was timely, as in the summer of 1941 war between Finland and the Soviet Union was renewed.

BIBLIOGRAPHY

Amis, Martin, *Koba the Dread* (Random House, 2013)

Antila, Olavi, *Voittojen Tiellä* (Raision Painopojat, 1993)

Anttala, Esa, *Talvisota: Sataviisi Taistelujen Päivää* (Karisto, 1975)

Brantberg, Robert, *Sotakenraalit* (Revontuli, 1998)

——, *Mannerheim* (Revontuli, 2003)

——, *Käärmeenpesä* (Revontuli, 2007)

——, *Suuret Suomalaiset Sotasankarit* (Revontuli, 2007)

——, *Kaukopartioritari* (Revontuli, 2009)

——, *Sotasankarit* (Revontuli, 2009)

——, *Motti-Matti* (Revontuli, 2012)

——, *Mannerheimin Sodat* (Readme.fi, 2014)

Bull, Steven, *World War II Winter and Mountain Warfare Tactics* (Osprey Publishing, 2013)

Carell, Paul, *Hitler Moves East 1941–1943* (Bantam Books, 1966)

Chew, Allen F., *The White Death* (KiwE Publishing, 2008)

Churchill, Winston S., *The Second World War: Their Finest Hour* (Houghton Mifflin Company, 1948–53)

Citrine, Sir Walter, *My Finnish Diary* (Penguin, 1940)

Clemens, Jonathan, *Mannerheim: President, Soldier, Spy* (Haus, 2012)

Condon, Richard W., *The Winter War: Russia against Finland* (Ballantine Books, 1972)

Daninen, Tatiana, *The Memories of the Russian Military Paramedic Michael Novikov of the Finnish War* (self-published, 2014)

Eagle, Eloise and Lauri Paananen, *The Winter War: The Russo-Finnish Conflict, 1939–40* (Sidgwick & Jackson, 1973)

Edwards, Robert, *White Death: Russia's War on Finland 1939–40* (Weidenfeld & Nicolson, 2006)

——, *The Winter War: Russia's Invasion of Finland, 1939–40* (Pegasus Book, 2009)

Eilola, Jari, Matti Rautiainen and Heikki Roiko-Jokela, *Talvisota: Matkalla Ajassa* (WSOY, 2002)

Elliston, Herbert B., *Finland Fights* (George G. Harrap & Co., 1940)

Enkengerg, Ilkka, *Talvisota Päivä Päivältä* (Readme.fi, 2013)

Erfurth, Waldemar, *The Last Finnish War and the German Liaison Officer with the Finnish Armed Forces* (US Army European Theatre Historical Interrogations, n.d.)

——, *The Last Finnish War* (University Publications of America, 1979)

Feiling, Keith, *The Life of Neville Chamberlain* (Macmillan, 1970)

Geust, Carl-Fredrik, *Talvisota ilmassa: The Winter War in the Air* (Apali, 2011)

Gordijenko, Anatoli (trans. Eero Balk), *Kuoleman Divisioona* (Gummerus, 2002)

Gripenberg, Georg A., *Finland and the Great Powers: Memoirs of a Diplomat* (University of Nebraska Press, 1965)

Haataja, Lauri, *Kun Kansa Kokosi Itsensä* (Tammi, 1989)

Haavikko, Paavo, *Päämaja: Suomen Hovi* (Fälth & Hässler, 1999)

Halsti, Wolf H., *Suomen Sota 1939–1945*, 3 vols (Otava, 1957)

Hammerton, Sir John, *The War Illustrated*, Vols. I and II (Amalgamated Press, 1940)

Hast, Mauri, *Pappapataljoona* (Väylä, 2011)

Hietanen, Silvo (ed.), *Kansakunta Sodassa 1: Sodasta Sotaan* (Valtion painatuskeskus, 1989)

Holmila, Antero, *Talvisota Muiden Silmin: Maailman Lehdistö ja Suomen Taistelu* (Atena, 2009)

Irincheev, Bair, *War of the White Death* (Pen and Sword, 2011)

——, *Talvisota Venäläisin Silmin* (Minerva, 2012)

Ilmavalvontakäsikirja (Suojeluskuntain Yliesikunta, 1937)

Jaatinen, Pekka, *Uhrivalkeat* (WS Bookwell Oy, 2005)

Jakobson, Max, *Diplomaattien Talvisota* (WSOY, 2002)

Jagerskiold, Stig, *Mannerheim: Marshal of Finland* (University of Minnesota, 1987)

Jäntti, Lauri, *Kannaksen Suurtaisteluissa Kesälle 1944* (WSOY, 1956)

Järvinen, Yrjö A., *Suomalainen ja Venäläinen Taktiikka Talvisodassa* (WSOY, 1948)

Jermo, Aake, *Siiranmäen Miehet* (Otava, 1977)

Käkelä, Erkki, *Marskin Panssarintuhoojat: Suomen Panssarintorjunnan Kehitys ja Panssariyhtymän Panssarintorjuntayksiköiden Historia* (WSOY, 2000)

Käkönen Uljas A., *Sotilasasiamiehenä Moskovassa 1939* (Otava, 1966)

——, *Miehityksen Varalta* (Otava, 1970)

Karhunen, Joppe, *Talvisodan Taivas* (Apali Oy, 2009)

Karjalainen, Mikko, *Jatkosodan Taistelut* (Gummerus, 2002)

Karttakeskus, Karjala, *Sotahistorian Tiekartta: Taistelupaikat ja Rintamalinjat 1939–1944* (Karttakeskus, 2013)

Khrushchev, Nikita S., *Khrushchev Remembers* (trans. E. Crankshaw) Bantam Books, 1971)

Kilin, Juri and Ari Raunio, *Talvisodan Taisteluja* (Karttakeskus, 2010)

Kivakka, Niilo, *Kymmenen Yhtä Vastaan: Kuhmon Taistelut 1939–40* (WSOY, 1977)

Kivimäki, Ville, *Murtuneet Mielet* (WSOY, 2013)

Korhonen, Arvi, *Viisi sodan vuotta* (WSOY, 1958)

Koskimaa, Matti, *Suomen Kohtalon Ratkaisut* (Docendo, 2013)

Krivesheev, G. F. (ed.), *Soviet Casualties and Combat Losses in the Twentieth Century* (Greenhill Books, 1997)

Kulju, Mika, *Raatteen Tie* (Ajatus, 2007)

——, *Kenraalin Viisi Sotaa* (Gummerus, 2011)

Kulkov, Evgenii Nikolaevich, Oleg Aleksandrovich Rzheshevskii and Harold Shukman (eds.), *Stalin and the Soviet-Finnish War, 1939–1940* (Routledge, 2002)

Laaksonen, Lasse, *Todellisuus ja Harhat: Kannaksen Taistelut ja Suomalaisten Joukkojen Tila Talvisodan Lopussa 1940* (Ajatus, 2005)

Laine, Antti, *Suomen Historian Pikkujättiläinen* (WSOY, 2003)

Lehväslaiho, Reino, *Panssarisotaa* (Werner Söderström Oy, 1958)

Lenin, Vladimir I., *Letters from Afar* (International Publishers, 1932)

Leskinen, Jari, *Jatkosodan Pikkujättiläinen* (WSOY, 2005)

—— and Antti Juutilainen, *Talvisodan pikkujättiläinen* (WSOY, 1999)

Liikanen, Simo, *Panssarinmurskaajat* (Gummerus, 2014)

Lunde, Henrik O., *Finland's War of Choice: The Troubled German-Finnish Coalition in World War II* (Casemate Publishers, 2011)

Luukkanen, Eino, *Hävittäjälentäjänä Kahdessa Sodassa* (Werner Söderstöm Oy, 1955)

Mannerheim, Carl G. (trans. E. Lewenhaupt), *The Memoirs of Marshal Mannerheim* (E.P. Dutton & Company, 1954)

——and Sakari Virkkunen, *Suomen Marsalkan Muistelmat* (Suuri suomalainen kirjakerho, 1995)

Manninen, Ohto, *Talvisodan Salatut Taustat* (Kirjaneuvos, 1994)

Martikainen, Tyyne, *Talvisodan Evakot ja Siviilisotavangit* (TM-kirjat, 2008)

Meinander, Henrik, *Suomen Historia: Linjat, Rakenteet, Käännekohdat* (WSOY, 2006)

Merikallio, Väinö, *Jääkäriprikaati Hyökkää* (Otava, 1954)

Merridale, Catherine, *Ivan's War: Inside The Red Army, 1939–45* (Faber and Faber, 2005)

Mononen, Väinö, *Tuonelan Tulenliekit* (Edico, 2011)

Nevakivi, Jukka, *Tuntematon Talvisota:Suomi 1939-1940* (Helsingin Yliopiston Poliittisen Historian Laitos – Helsingin Yliopiston Paino, 1989)

Nevalainen, Petri, *Kollaanjoen Taistelut* (Paasilinna, 2013)

Öhquist, Harald, *Talvisota Minun Näkökulmastani* (WSOY, 1949)

Oksanen, Tauno, *Kahden Sodan Aloittaja* (Myllylahti, 2013)

Österman, Hugo, *Neljännesvuosisata Elämästäni* (WSOY, 1966)

Pajala, Lasse, *Kaikilla Rintamilla* (Otava, 2009)

Pajari, Risto, *Talvisota Ilmassa* (WSOY, 1971)

Palaste, Onni, *Kaukopartio* (WSOY, 2003)

Palmunen, Rainer (ed.), *Kun Suomi Taisteli* (Valitut Palat/ Otava, 1989)

——, *Tuntematon Sota* (Valitut Palat, 1991)

Palolampi, Erkki, *Kollaa Kestää* (WSOY, 1940)

'Party Piece Uncovered', *The Telegraph* (6 September 2001)

Peitsara, Tapio, *Suomen ja Venäjän Talvisota 1939–40* (Otava, 1941)

Pesonen, Pertti and Keijo Immonen, *Talvisota* (Gummerus, 1998)

Peuranheimo, Orvo, Jouko Pirinen and Kalervo Killinen, *Laivat Puuta, mihehtet Rautaa: Moottoritorpedoveneiden Taistelut Suomenlahdella, 1941–1944* (WSOY, 1956)

Piipponen, Jukka, *Illu: Lentomestari Ilmari Juutilaisen Elämä* (Koala, 2014)

Pohjonen, Juha, *Tuntematon Lauri Törni* (Otava, 2013)

Porvali, Seppo, *Talvisodan Ritarit* (Revontuli, 2013)

Rajala, Pertti, *Talvisota* (Avain, 2014)

Raunio, Ari and Juri Kilin, *Sotatoimet: Suomen Sotien 1939–45 Kulku Kartoin* (Genimap, 2004)

——, *Hyökkäystaisteluja 1941* (Otava, 2007)

——, *Talvisodan Taisteluja* (Karttakeskus, 2010)

——, *Jatkosota: Torjuntataisteluja 1942–1944* (Print Best, 2013)

Raunio, Jukka, *Lentäjän Näkökulma II* (Jukka Raunio, 1993)

Rautkallio, Hannu, *Mannerheim vai Stalin* (Otava, 2014)

Ries, Tomas, *Cold Will: The Defence of Finland* (Brassey's, 1988)

Rislakki, Veikko, *Hevosten Sotasavotta* (Suomen Hippos ry, 1977)

Saarinen, Ahti, *Jäätukikohdan Talvisota Hollolan Pyhäniemessä: Ilmasotaa Turun Artukaisissa ja Littoisissa, Naantalissa,*

Säkylän Pyhäjärvellä, Tampereen Härmälässä, Utin Haukkajärvellä ja Valkealan Vuohijärvellä (Ahti Saarinen ja 5 hullua miestä, 2011)

Sakaida, Henry, *Heroes of the Soviet Union 1941–45* (Osprey Publishing, 2004)

Sander, Gordon F. (trans. Arto Häilä), *Taistelu Suomesta 1939–1940* (WSOY, 2010)

——, *The 100 Day Winter War* (Kansas University Press, 2013)

Sarjanen, Petri, *Valkoinen Kuolema* (Revontuli, 1998)

Sariola, Mauri, *Marsking Ritarit* (Weiling Göös, 1968)

——, *Näin Tekivät Ritarit* (Weiling Göös, 1969)

Screen, John E. O., *Mannerheim: The Finnish Years* (Hurst, 2014)

Siilasvuo, Ensio et al., *Talvisota: Kronikka* (Gummerus, 1989)

Siilasvuo, Hjalmar J., *Kuhmo Talvisodassa* (Otava, 1944)

Sinerma, Martti, Sampo Ahto and Teuvo Rönkkönen, *Kun Suomi Taisteli* (Valitut Palat, 1989)

Sivonen, Pauli, *Miltä Sota Tuntui* (Gummerus, 2008)

Suomen meterorologinen Vuosikirja 1939 (The Meteorology Yearbook of Finland 1939), vols. I and II (Ilmatieteellinen Keskuslaitos, 1953)

Tala, Henrik, *Talvisodan Ranskalaiset Ratkaisijat: Ranskan apu Suomelle 1939–1940* (Minerva, 2014)

Talvela, Heikki, *Seis!– Tulikomento!* (Alea-Kirja, 1990)

——, *Heikki Talvela at World War* (interviewer: V. Nenye) (Tuusula, 2 January 2014)

Talvela, Paavo, *Sotilaan Elämä* (Gummerus. 1976)

——, Paavo, *Paavo Talvela Muistelmat II* (Gummerus, 1977)

Talvisodan Historia: Suomi Joutuu Talvisotaan, Vols. I and II (WSOY, 1978)

Talvisota Kronikka (Gummerus, 1989)

Tanner, Väinö, *Olin Ulkoministerinä Talvisodan Aikana* (Albert Bonniers Förlag, 1950)

Thomas, Nigel, *World War II Soviet Armed Forces (1) 1939–41* (Osprey Publishing, 2010)

Topi, Törmä, *Siiranmäki Vuosalmi 2. D:n taistelukertomus 9.6–18.7.1944* (WSOY, 1954)

Trotter, William R., *A Frozen Hell: The Russo-Finnish Winter War of 1939–1940* (Algonquin Books of Chapel Hill, 1991)

Troy, Thomas F., *In and Out of Stalin's GRU: A Tatar's Escape from Red Army Intelligence* (Praeger, 1984)

Tuomikoski, Pekka, *Talvisota: Väestönsiirrot* (AtlasArt, 2010)

——, Finljandija: *Puna-Armeijan Suomi-Opas 1939* (Minerva, 2013)

Tuompo, Wiljo E. and Karikoski, Väinö A. M., *Kunnia Isanmaa Suomen ja Neuvostoliiton Sota 1939–40* (Kivi, 1942)

Uitto, Antero and Carl-Fredrik Geust, *Mannerheim-Linja: Talvisodan Legenda* (Ajatus Kirjat, 2006)

Ulkuniemi, Martti, *Tykistö Taistelussa* (WSOY, 1952)

Valkonen Markku, *Ateljeena Sotatanner* (Otava, 1989)

Van Dyke, Carl, *The Soviet Invasion of Finland 1939–40* (Frank Cass, 1997)

Vehviläinen, Olli, *Finland in the Second World War: Between Germany and Russia* (Palgrave Publishers, 2002)

Venna, Yrjö, Eini Karhulahti and Reino A. Halonen, *Pittää Lähtii!* (Sortavala-seura, 2012)

Vihavainen, Timo, *Marssi Helsinkiin: Suomen Talvisota Neuvostolehdistössä* (Tammi, 1990)

——, *Talvisota, Suomi ja Venäjä: XII Suomalais-Neuvostoliittolainen Historiantutkijoiden Symposiumi; Moskova 24.–27.10.1989* (Suomen historiallinen seura, 1991)

Viljanen, Jussi, *Suomalaisen Sotilaan Historia: Ristriretkistä Rauhanturvaamiseen* (Karttakeskus Oy, 2011)

Voronov, Nicholas, *Na Sluzhbe Voyennoy* (Voyenizdat, 1963)

Warner, Oliver, *Marshal Mannerheim and the Finns* (Weidenfeld & Nicolson, 1967)

Woodman, Richard, *Arctic Convoys* (John Murray, 1994)

Wuorinen, John H., *Finland and World War II, 1939–1944* (Ronald Press Company, 1948)

Ylikangas, Heikki, *Tulkintani Talvisodasta* (WSOY, 2001)

——, *Romahtaako Rintama?* (Otava, 2013)

Zetterberg, Seppo and Allan Tiitta, *Suomi Kautta Aikojen* (Otava, 1992)

Ziemke, Earl F., *The German Northern Theatre of Operations 1940–1945*, Pamphlet No. 20-271 (US Department of the Army, 1959)

Websites

'Mad Jack' Churchill: A Rare Breed of Warrior [website] <http://warfarehistorynetwork.com/daily/wwii/mad-jack-churchill-a-rare-breed-of-warrior>, accessed April 2015

Talvisota 1939–1940 [website] <http://www.iltalehti.fi/talvisota/2009120410608432_ts.shtml>, accessed April 2015

APPENDIX

Notes on sizes of population centres and lakes: The terms city and town, village, etc. Have been liberally used to describe the relative size of the locations at the time of the events, rather than any accurate legal status.

ENGLISH (FINNISH)	RUSSIAN	DESCRIPTION
Aittojoki (river)	Айттойоки	River running through the namesake village from north to south.
Aittojoki (village)	Айттойоки	Small village 10km west of Suojärvi where Group Talvela's advance was finally stopped. Present day town of New-Vegarus.
Alasjärvi Lake	Аласенъярви	Lake on the north side of Saunajärvi Lake towards Kuhmo village.
Ala-Vuokki (Peninsula)	Ала-Вуокки	Protruding peninsula in the Vuokkijärvi Lake south of the Raate road
Äglajärvi Lake	Ягляярви	Lake and village in nothern Karelia, site of a major Finnish victory by Group Talvela in December 1939.
Äglajärvi village	Ягляярви	Village located halfway between Tolvajärvi and Suojärvi in nothern Karelia.
Äyräpää village	Эюряпяя	Village on the southern shore of Vuoksi River opposite Vuosalmi village.
Barents Sea (Barentsinmeri)	Баренцево море	The sea linking the White Sea to the Arctic and Atlantic oceans.
Bay of Viborg (Viipurinlahti)	Выборгский залив	Northeastern end of the Gulf of Finland.
Finland (Suomi)	Финля́ндия	Democratic nation independent since 6 December 1917
Gulf of Bothnia (Pohjanlahti)	Ботнический залив	The sea separating Finland and Sweden, continues south as the Baltic Sea and to South East as Gulf of Finland.
Gulf of Finland (Suomenlahti)	Финский залив	Eastern arm of the Baltic Sea separating Finland from Estonia and ending in the Bay of Viipuri bythe Karelian Ishtmus.
Haahkajärvi Lake	Озеро Хахкаярви	Small lake about 8 kilometresnorth of Uomaa village.
Hamina town	Хамина	Important Finnish port on the south coast west ofViipuri.
Hapenensaari Island	-	Island with a population of 57, just north of Uuras Island on the Bay of Viipuri
Häränpäänniemi peninsula	Мыс Бычья Голова	Peninsula where the Soviets landed just north west of the city of Viipuri.
Haukila hamlet	-	Very small settlement east of Suomussalmi on theroad to Raate. Around 3km east of the original Finnish roadblock.
Haukiperä Lake	Хаукиперя	Part of Kiantajärvi Lake.
Heinätsylampi Lake	-	Small shallow lake 3–5km south of themain Finnish defences at Kollaa.
Helsinki City	Хельсинки	Capital city of Finland.
Hirvasjärvi Lake	Хирвас-ярви	North-eastern part of Tolvajärvi lake.

ENGLISH (FINNISH)	RUSSIAN	DESCRIPTION
Honkaniemi	Хонканиеми (since 1948 Лебедевка)	Segment of the Interim Line near Viipuri where the Finnish Armoured Corps had its only battle.
Hulkonniemi Peninsula	Хулконниеми	Peninsula on the Kiantajärvi Lake with a ferrycrossing east to Suomussalmi village.
Hyövynvaara	-	Location just north of the Palovaara crossroads, where Task Force Šarov abondoned much of its heavy equipment.
Ilomantsi town	Иломантси	Small town in northern Karelia.
Jänisjärvi Lake	Янисъярви	Large lake north of Ladoga.
Joensuu town	Йоэнсуу	Large town in northern Karelia.
Joutsijärvi Lake	Озеро Йоутсиярви	Lake 20km east of Kemijärvi town where theSoviet 122nd Division was finally halted.
Juntusranta village	Юнтусранта	Village at the north-eastern corner of KiantajärviLake, roughly 65km by road from Suomussalmi.
Kaarnajoki (settlement)	Карнайоки	Small settlement near Sakkola village on theeastern Karelian Isthmus. Location of the famous 'Angel of Taipale' artillery battery.
Kajaani town	Каяани	Large town in central Finland located on the eastside of Oulunjärvi Lake.
Käkimäki	-	Small hill just north-east of Kylänmäki roughly 5km north-west of Suomussalmi.
Käkisalmi	Приозерск (since 1948)	Large town on the western shores of Lake Ladoga.
Kalatanlampi Lake	-	Small shallow lake north of Rupisuo and west of Vegarusjärvi lake.
Kälkänen Lake	Озеро Кялкянен	Lake to the north of the main encirclements at Kuhmo.
Kannuslampi area	-	Small pond-like lakes approximately 1km northeast of Suomussalmi.
Karelian Isthmus (Karjalankannas)	Карельский перешеек	An Isthmus separating the Gulf of Finlandand Lake Ladoga. The southern edge of the Isthmusis guarded by Leningrad and the northern edge by the cities of Viipuri and Käkisalmi.
Karjaniemi Peninsula	-	Peninsula east of Vilaniemi where a flanking Russian attack east towards Viipuri was halted.
Kelja Village	Келье	Village between Sakkola and Taipale along the banks of Vuoksi River.
Kemijärvi town	Кемиярви	Town in central Lapland.
Kesseli	Кессе линкюля	Small settlement 7–8km north of the main *motti* at Kuhmo sector.
Kiantajärvi Lake	Озеро Киантаярви	Large lake with total area of 191 square kilometres at Suomussalmi. In the north the lake splits into two with its longest branch being 45km long.
Kilpelänkangas	-	Heavily contested flat area between the hills Löytövaara and Riihivaara.
Kirvesmäki	-	Northern end of the koukkuniemi peninsula at Taipale.
Kitilä Village	Китеия	Important village controlling rail and road crossing slocated at the the northern corner of Lake Ladoga.

ENGLISH (FINNISH)	RUSSIAN	DESCRIPTION
Kitinen River	-	River flowing into the large Kemijoki River near pelkosenniemi town. Ferry crossing was located onthe Kitinen River side before the two waterwaysjoined.
Kivijärvi Lake	Кивиярви	Small lake roughly 10km north ofSuomussalmi on the road to Palovaara.
Kiviniemi rapids	Лосево (since 1948)	River crossing over the rapids where Vuoksi Riverand Lake Suvanto (Lake Sukhodolskoye) join onthe Karelian Isthmus.
Kiviniemi village	Лосево (since 1948)	Small village with a road and railway bridge overthe narrow part and rapids from Vuoksi to Suvanto.
Kivisalmi Peninsula	-	Narrows between lakes Taivaljärvi and Tolvajärviwhere Group Talvela finally stopped the Russianonslaught.
Klemetti	-	Location of one of the *motti* during the Kuhmobattle on the east-west road.
Koirinoja	Койрихоя	Small village on the northern shore of Lake Ladoga.
Koivisto Islands	Остров Большой Берёзовый	Largest and most southernly of the islands on the Bay of Viipuri.
Koivu Lake	-	Small lake on the river Kollaa just south of the railroad to Loimola.
Koivuniemi Peninsula	Берёзовый мыс	Eastern end of Majapohja Peninsula closest point to Viipuri across the bay from the west.
Koivuselkä hamlet	Койвуселка	Small settlement along the road to Kitiläapproximately 1km east of Koirinoja.
Kokkojärvi Lake	Озеро Коккоярви	Lake where the roads to the southeast towards Raate and north-east towards Puras join.
Kollaa	Колле	Famous battleground where the road and railroad to Loimola crossed the River Kollaa.
Kollaa River	Колласйоки	Narrow river stemming from Kollaanjärvi Lake and flowing south into Tulemajärvi Lake, location of the Finnish last ditch effort to stop the Soviet 56th Army Corps.
Korpiselkä village	Корписелька	Important crossroads and village about 30km south of Ilomantsi and 20km west of Tolvajärvi.
Kotajärvi Lake	Оз. Котаярви	Lake north-west of Uomaa village.
Kotisaari Island	-	Island on the central part of Tolvajärvi lake.
Koukkuniemi Peninsula	Коуккуниеми	Most southernly point of the Taipale area on the bend of Vuoksi River on the eastern edge of theKarelian Isthmus.
Kuhmo town	Кухмо	Town near the Soviet border in central Finland.
Kuivasjärvi Lake	Озеро Куйвасъярви	The easternmost bay of Lake Kiantajärvi, only connected by the very narrow Kuivassalmi Isthmus.
Kuivassalmi Peninsula	-	Very narrow isthumus between the Haukiperä partof the Kiantajärvi and the easternmost bay of Lake Kuivassalmi.

ENGLISH (FINNISH)	RUSSIAN	DESCRIPTION
Kuomasjärvi Lake	Озеро Куоманъярви	Lake just north of Kuivasjärvi. In the narrow area between these two lakes the Finns set a small rearguard that ended up holding off the whole 44th Division.
Kuusamo town	Куусамо	Eastern town near the southern edge of Lapland, located roughly on the same latitude as Tornio on the west coast.
Kylänmäki	Кюлянмяки	Settlement around a small hill just north of Hulkonniemi peninsula on the road towards Palovaara.
Ladoga Lake (Laatokka)	Ладога	Largest lake in Europe, the northern half belonged to the Finns until the region was lost in the War.
Ladoga-Karelia (Laatokan Karjala)	Ладожская Карелия	Karelia regions lying to north of Lake Ladoga
Lähde Sector	-	Key sector on the eastern side of Summa. Munasuowas located on the south-east corner of this sector.
Lahti City	Лахти	Small city where the authors are from, approximately 100km due north from Helsinki.
Lappeenranta town	Лаппеэнранта	Town 60km north-west from Viipuri.
Lavajärvi Lake	Ала- & Иля-Лаваярви	Lake that consist of two parts; Ylä- (upper) andAla- (lower) Lavajärvi lakes. The road from Uomaa to Kitilä runs betwen them.
Lemetti	Леметти	Small settlement on the road from Uomaa to Kitilä. Site of very famous motti encirclement battles.
Leningrad (St. Petersburg)	Ленингра́д	Former capital of the Tsarist Russia, St Petersburgwas renamed Leningrad in 1924 and again back to the original name in 1991.
Lieksa	Лиекса	Town roughly halfway between Kuhmo andIlomantsi near Finland's eastern border.
Loimola village	Лоймола	Important crossroads and village on the southern tip of Lake Loimolanjärvi, roughly 10km along the road due west from River Kollaa.
Lonkka hamlet	Лонка	Small Russian village next to the Finnish border. Roughly 10km on the road east from Juntusranta.
Loso Motti	Лосо	Easternmost of the major *motti* during the Kuhmo encirclement battles.
Löytövaara hill	Гора Лёютёвара	Key hill overlooking the Kilpelänkangas area between lakes Kylmänjärvi and Löytöjärvi.
Luelahti Motti	-	One of the larger central *motti*, located around the north-western bay of Saunajärvi Lake during the Kuhmo encirclement battles.
Mainila village	Майнило	Soviet border village which was shelled by the Red Army to create an incident excusing the invasion of Finland.
Majapohja Peninsula	Маяпохья	Western end of Koivuniemi Peninsula located east across the bay from the city of Viipuri.
Maksimansaari Island	Остров Маскимансари	Key island on the north-eastern corner of the Lake Ladoga.
Mäntyvaara	-	Small hill north of lake Kälkänen.

ENGLISH (FINNISH)	RUSSIAN	DESCRIPTION
Märkäjärvi village	Озеро Мяркяярви	Village located halfway between Joutsijärvi and village of Salla lost in the Winter War. Due to the large amount of Sallan refugees relocating to the area renamed Salla after the wars.
Miljoonalinnake Fort	Миллионер	Famous fortification/bunker SJ5 (or SummajärviBunker 5) on the Mannerheim Line on the Summa Sector near Summajärvi Lake.
Mitro hamlet	Митро	Small settlement on the southern edge of Ruhtinaanmäki, north of Lemetti.
Möhkö village	-	Village in the central region of Group Talvela's area of responsibility, and the location where the southern thrust of the 155th Division was halted. Now a border village in eastern Finland.
Moitavaara hill	-	Small hill 5km east of Joutsijärvi.
Moscow City	Москва́	Capital city of Soviet Union.
Munasuo (Marsh)	-	Heavily contested segment of the Mannerheim Linerunning through a marshy area in the southeasterncorner of Lähde sector due east of Summa.
Muolaanjärvi Lake	Глубо́кое	Large lake lying centraly on the Karelian Ishtmus.(since 1948)
Mustajoki River	Йоки-Муста	Narrow river running west east across the road to Perenka approximately 10km north of Palovaara crossroads.
Mustaoja Stream	-	Small stream running along the Mannerheim Line south-west of Summa sector where the 'Idiot'sNudge' took place. Also a southern part of Valkeaoja stream near west of Kollaa River.
Näätäoja	Няятяоя	Area 5 kilometres west of the River Kollaa along the railway.
Nurmo village	-	Small village in western Finland that tragically lostmost of its male population in a single failed attack during the Winter War.
Oraviselkä Lake	Залив Орависелькя	Western part of Kiantajärvi Lake, separated from Suomussalmi by Hulkonniemi Peninsula.
Oulu City	Оулу	City located at the mouth of River Oulu on the Gulfof Bothnia.
Palovaara (Crossroads)	Паловара	Crossroads leading north towards Perenka, East towards Juntusranta and South towards Suomussalmi.
Patrusjärvi Lake	-	Long and narrow lake that Vilajoki flows fromaround 30km west from Viipuri above Vilaniemi.
Pelkosenniemi village	Пелкосенниеми	Heavily contested village in Lapland around 40km north of town of Kemijärvi.
Peranka village	Перенка	Village holding key crossroads around 60km north of Suomussalmi.
Petäjäsaari Island	-	Small island southwest of Maksimansaari Island,about 5km north-west of Pitkäranta on theLake Ladoga.
Petsamo (Area)	Печенга	Valuable Finnish mining district and arctic harbourtown, lost partially in the Moscow Peace Treaty in 1940, and then completely and permanently in theParis Peace Treaty of 1947. Currently the most north-western point of Russian Federation.

ENGLISH (FINNISH)	RUSSIAN	DESCRIPTION
Pihlajalampi Lake	Озеро Пихлаялампи	Small lake just east of Suomussalmi along the road to Raate.
Piispajärvi Lake (village)	Писпаярви Piispajärvi	Lake and village lie about 5km south of Perenka village. Task Force Susitaival turned back the 662nd Regiment here.
Piispansaari Island	Остров Подберёзовый	One of the islands on the Bay of Viipuri.
Pitkäranta Town	Питкяра́нта	Town on the noth-eastern shores of Lake Ladoga.
Poppius Fort	Поппиус	Famous fortification/bunker of the MannerheimLine also known as SJ4 or Summajärvi Bunker 4.
Pukitsanmäki Hill	-	Small hill on the southeastern edge of Koirinojaoverlooking the railroad and road to Pitkärantatown.
Puraksenjoki River	-	River running north to south parallel to the borderand crossed by the Raate road, roughly halway between the village of Raate and Kokkojärvi lake.
Raate road (Raatteentie)	Раатской дороге	Road running east from Suomussalmi towards the Soviet border through the village of Raate on theborder.
Raate village	Раате	Small Finnish settlement that was at the time the closest settlement to the border with Soviet Union east of Suomussalmi.
Räisälä	Мельниково	Village on northern Karelian Isthmus.
Ravansaari Island	Малый Высоцкий, Ра́вансаари	Small Island north of Uuras inthe Bay of Viipuri.
Reuhkavaara Motti	-	Location of a determined resistance by the encircled Soviets during the Kuhmo Battles.
Riihivaara hill	-	Soviet staging point during the battles of Kuhmo.
Ruhtinaanmäki hill	Рухтинанмяки	Heavily contested small settlement north of Mitroand south of Syskyjärvi Lake in Ladoga-Karelia.
Ruokojärvi Lake	Оз. Руокоярви	Lake just north of Kitilä in Ladoga-Karelia.
Ruokojärvi village	Руокоярви	Small village and lake just north of Kitiläin Ladoga-Karelia.
Rupisuo (Marsh)	-	Marshy area between Lake Ägläjärvi and River Aittojoki.
Sääksjärvi Lake	Оз. Сяксьярви	Lake adjacent to the Uomaa village.
Saarijärvi Lake	Озеро Сариярви	Small lake that lends its name to a desperately defended *motti* during the battles forLadoga-Karelia
Salla village	Салле	Salla village is aproximately 50km from the old border captured by the 122nd Division during the Winter War.
Salmi village	Салми	Ladogan Karelian village located south east of Pitkäranta town lost in Winter War.
Sanginaho (peninsula)	Сангинахо	Peninsula on the northern shores of Lake Vuokkijärvi.
Sanginlampi Lake	Озёра Сангинламмит	Small lake separated from Vuokkijärvi Lake by Sanginaho Peninsula.

ENGLISH (FINNISH)	RUSSIAN	DESCRIPTION
Saunajärvi Lake	Озеро Саунаярви	Lake in the centre of the Kuhmo EncirclementBattles. The Luelahti and Reuhkavaara *motti* werealso created on the lake's shores.
Siira (crossroads)	-	Small settlement and crossroads west of Uomaavillage.
Sortavala city	Сортавала	Large town on the northern shores of Lake Ladoga.
Summa village	Сумма / Солдатское	Village lake on the western Karelian Ishtmus. Site of some of the fiercest Soviet attacks of the war.
Summajärvi Lake	Солдатское	Lake on the western Karelian Isthmus.
Suojärvi Lake	Суоярви	Large lake area with Suojärvi village lying on it's nortern shore.
Suojärvi village	Суоя́рви	Border town captured early on by the Russians,located roughly 80km north-east of Lake Ladoga.
Suomussalmi Village	Суомуссалми	Key village on the narrowest part of Finland that was practically destroyed during the December fighting in 1939. Present day Suomussalmi centrehas been rebuilt on the southern shores of Lake Kiantajärvi at Ämmänsaari.
Suvanto/Lake Sukhodolskoye	Суходольское озеро	Wider part of the River Vuoksi turning into a long lake running through the Karelian Isthmus to Taipale River which ends on Lake Ladoga.
Syskyjärvi Lake	Оз. Сюскюярви	Lake and namesake village northeast of Kitilä, the northern most extent of the 168th Division's advance.
Syskykärvi village	Сюскюярви	Village and namesake lake north-east of Kitilä, location of the Finnish defensive lines during the battles for Kitilä area.
Taipale River	Бу́рная (since 1948)	Narrowest part of the river/lake network that bisectsthe Karelian Isthmus. Taipale River runds fromSuvanto to Lake Ladoga.
Taipale village	Соловьёво (since 1948)	Village at the mouth of the Taipale Riveron the shores of Lake Ladoga.
Taivaljärvi Lake	Озеро Толваярви	Part of the larger Tolvajärvi Lake.
Tali village	Пальцево	Village and critical crossroads northeast of Viipuri. The location of the decisive battle of the Continuation War.
Teikarsaari Island	Остров Игривый	Island on the Bay of Viipuri.
Terenttilä	-	Small settlement near the mouth of River Taipale.
Terijoki village	Терио́ки (after 1948 Зеленогорск)	Closest Finnish village to Leningrad and a famous holiday resort on the gulf of Finland. It was the first larger settlement to be occupied by the Soviets and the founding place of their own puppet governemnt for Finland.
Tolvajärvi Lake	Озеро Толваярви	Lake in northern Karelia, the Soviet offensive reached the Lakes shores early in December 1939.
Tolvajärvi village	Толвоярви	Village on the western shores of the namesake lake, first Finnish major victory of the war achieved byGroup Talvela for control of the area.
Tuppura Island	Вихревой (Туппурасаари)	Island on the Bay of Viipuri.
Turkinsaari Island	Остров Овчиный (Турецкий остров)	Island on the Bay of Viipuri.

ENGLISH (FINNISH)	RUSSIAN	DESCRIPTION
Tyynelä (Crossroads)	-	Area where the road splits towards Raate in the south and Puras in the north, just west of Kokkojärvi Lake.
Uomaa Village	Уомас	Village north of Ladoga on the easterly road from Kitilä towards Käsnärselkä and the border.
Uuras Island	Высо́цк	Large island on centre of the Bay of Viipuri.
Valamo Island	Валаам	Large island with a famous monastery on the Lake Ladoga.
Varpajärvi Lake	Озеро Танковое	Lake along the road to Siira, due east of SyskyjärviLake.
Värtsilä town	Вя́ртсиля	Important Finnish town located about 55km north of Sortovala and Lake Ladoga, lost in the warand close to present day border.
Vasikkasaari Island	Остров Телячий	Small island located in centre of River Vuoksi allowing the crossing from Äyräpää on the south bank to Vuosalmi on north much easier.
Vegarus village	Вегарус	Village on the shores on the namesake lake just north of Aittojoki village.
Vegarusjärvi Lake		Lake roughly 5km north of Aittojoki village in Northern Karelia.
Vetko (Isthmus)	-	Narrow isthmus between lakes Kälkänen and Iso-Valkoinen on the Kuhma Sector.
Viborg City	Выборг	Finland's second city, lost in the truce after the war.
Vilajoki River	Ви́лайоки (after 1948 Балтиец)	Flows south from Patrusjärvi Lake to the Bay of Viipuri.
Vilaniemi peninsula	Мыс Кубенский	Peninsula with the mouth of River Vilajoki, site of Soviet armoured assault across the frozen Bay of Viipuri.
Vitsaari Island	Остров Геройский	Large island in the centre of Vuoksi river north-west of Äyräpää area.
Vuokkijärvi Lake	Озеро Вуоккиярви	Large lake south-east of Suomussalmi.
Vuoksi River	Вуокса	Wide river flowing from the large lakes of Saimaato Lake Ladoga on the Karelian Isthmus.
Vuosalmi village	-	Village on the northern shore of Vuoksi River opposite to Äyräpää village.

COMPARATIVE OFFICER RANKS

FINNISH OFFICER RANKS (in English)	RED ARMY OFFICER RANKS (Winter War)
Commander-in-Chief	People's Commissar for Defence
Marshal of Finland	Marshal of the Soviet Union
Field Marshal	
Colonel-General	Army Commander 1st Class
General	Army Commander 2nd Class
Lieutenant-General	Corps Commander
	Division Commander
Major-General	Brigade Commander
Colonel	Colonel
Lieutenant-Colonel	
Major	Major
Captain	Captain
Senior Lieutenant	Senior Lieutenant
Lieutenant	Lieutenant
	Junior Lieutenant

COMMANDER BIOGRAPHY IMAGES

Page 10 (Angelina Rasmus, author's collection); Pages 46, 90, 91, 94, 96, 112, 128, 131, 134, 143, 147, 172, 202, 218, 235 Bottom, 238, 239, 243, 250, 257, 258 Top, 262, 267 (Sa-kuva); Page 48 (US Signal Corps); Pages 49, 73, 88, 92, 137, 176, 232, 271, 274 (Wikipedia); Pages 56, 67, 82, 99, 108, 109, 121, 129, 132, 150, 161, 177, 201, 203, 218 Top, 251, 258 Bottom (Ministry of Defence of the Russian Federation Central Archives): Pages 70, 89 (Itsenäisyyden puolustajat, Sodan taisteluja I Weilin-Göös 2005); Page 74 (Painting by Isaak Brodski); Page 110 (Author's collection); Page 173 Top, 241 (Public Domain); Page 173 Bottom (Vilho Lindén).

INDEX